Body codes used within this publication

Type of vehicle

GU00779220

B	Single-deck vehicle
C	Single-deck coach
CO	Convertible open-top vehicle
DP	Coach-seated bus
H	Double-deck vehicle
M	Minibus (16 seats of less)
O	Open-top vehicle
PO	Partial open-top vehicle

Vehicle type is then followed by seating capacity and then door position and addition equipment; in the instance of double-deck vehicles, upstairs is shown "over" lower deck.

Door position

D	Dual-door vehicle
C	Central-fitted door
F	Front (single-door) vehicle
R	Rear entrance vehicle
T	Triple-door vehicle

Additional equipment

T	Toilet
L	Wheelchair lift

For example, a vehicle shown as H45/31F is a double-deck vehicle, seating 45 upstairs and 31

Our thanks go to Kevin Cooper, for his assistance with the rail section, including supply of photographs, and to Ian Attenborough for various regular updates from across the country which have contributed towards this publication.

Unless otherwise stated, all photography in this publication is by Brian Cheyney, who also proof read this publication.

First edition 2017

This publication is up to date as at February 2017. While every effort is also made to ensure maximum accuracy, unfortunately 100% accuracy cannot be guaranteed. The authors hold no responsibility for any inconvenience caused by any errors contained within this publication.

Written by Andrew Woolhouse, owner of Woolybus,

211 Marlborough Road, Dagenham, Essex

Printed by Book Printing UK

Front cover: First West of England Alexander Enviro 400 33569 seen having left Temple Meads Station

Back cover: Great Western Railway 43 189 seen just after leaving Swindon heading for London

Contents

* - also includes Heathrow Connect operation

3

Aberdeen

A   Aberdeen - 395 King Street, Aberdeen, AB24 5RP

| 10046 | K1GRT | Mercedes-Benz O405G | | Alexander Cityranger | | | AB60T | p |

| 10154-10183 | | Volvo B7LA | | Wright Eclipse Fusion * AB54D | | | AB56D | |

10154	SV05DXA	A	10161	SV05DXJ	A	10168	SV05DXS	A
10155	SV05DXC	A	10162	SV05DXK	A	10169	SV05DXT	A
10156	SV05DXD	A	10163	SV05DXL	A	10170	SV05DXU	A
10157	SV05DXE	A	10164	SV05DXM	A	10171	SV05DXW	A
10158	SV05DXF	A	10165	SV05DXO	A	10172	SV05DXX	A
10159	SV05DXG	A	10166	SV05DXP	A	10173	SV05DXY	A
10160	SV05DXH	A	10167	SV05DXR	A	10183*	SF05KUH	A

A dying breed with the FirstGroup fleet in the shape of the articulated vehicle, fondly known as "bendybuses". Seen here in the centre of Aberdeen is 10166, a Volvo B7LA with Wright Eclipse Fusion bodywork, pictured while on route 1 to Danestone

| 20021 | WSU489 | Volvo B12B | | Jonckheere Mistral 50 | | | C53F | A |

| 20300-20374 | | Volvo B7R | | Plaxton Profile * - C53F, $ - C45FL | | | C46FTL | |

20300*	WX54ZHM	A	20367	CV55AGX	A	20374	CV55AOO	u
20301*	WX54ZHN	A	20372	CV55ANF	u			
20353$	WA05UNF	A	20373	CV55ANP	u			

| 20505 | AO02RCV | Volvo B12M | | Plaxton Paragon | | | C53F | w |

20506	AO02RCX	Volvo B12M	Plaxton Paragon	C53F	A
20507	AO02RCY	Volvo B12M	Plaxton Paragon	C53F	A
23021	YN54APF	Scania K114IB	Irizar Century	C49F	A

23305-23314		Scania K124IB	Irizar PB	C49FT	
23305	PSU628	w	23307	YN54NXZ	A
23306	PSU629	w	23314	YN54NYV	A

23330	PSU627	Scania K340EBX2	Irizar PB	C49FT	A
23401	LSK570	Scania K114IB	Irizar Century	C49FT	A
23402	LSK571	Scania K114IB	Irizar Century	C49FT	A
24101	BF65HVN	Mercedes-Benz Tourismo	Mercedes-Benz	C49FTL	A
24102	BF65HVO	Mercedes-Benz Tourismo	Mercedes-Benz	C49FTL	A

32958-32976		Dennis Trident SFD113	Plaxton President 9.9m	H39/20F	
			* - H39/24F, $ - H39/??F		
32958*	X958HLT	A	32971$	X971HLT	A	32975	X975HLT	A
32962*	X962HLT	A	32973	X973HLT	A	32976	Y223NLF	A
32970	X613HLT	A	32974	X974HLT	A			

37633-37644		Volvo B9TL	Wright Eclipse Gemini	H45/29F	
37633	SV08FXP	A	37637	SV08FXU	A	37641	SV08FXZ	A
37634	SV08FXR	A	37638	SV08FXW	A	37642	SV08FYA	A
37635	SV08FXS	A	37639	SV08FXX	A	37643	SV08FYB	A
37636	SV08FXT	A	37640	SV08FXY	A	37644	SV08FYC	A

Pictured in central Aberdeen is Wright Eclipse Gemini-bodied Volvo B9TL 37637, seen while on route 19 to Tillydrone, showing the Platinum livery and branding carried for this service

38201-38225		Dennis Trident 3 SFD159		Alexander Enviro 500			H53/29F	
38201	SN09CAU	A	38210	SN09CCA	A	38219	SN09CCX	A
38202	SN09CAV	A	38211	SN09CCD	A	38220	SN09CCY	A
38203	SN09CAX	A	38212	SN09CCE	A	38221	SN09CCZ	A
38204	SN09CBF	A	38213	SN09CCF	A	38222	SN09CDE	A
38205	SN09CBO	A	38214	SN09CCJ	A	38223	SN09CDF	A
38206	SN09CBU	A	38215	SN09CCK	A	38224	SN09CDK	A
38207	SN09CBV	A	38216	SN09CCO	A	38225	SN09CDO	A
38208	SN09CBX	A	38217	SN09CCU	A			
38209	SN09CBY	A	38218	SN09CCV	A			

56005-56009		Mercedes-Benz Vario 0814		Plaxton Cheetah			C33F	
56005	EY54BPZ	A	56007	EY54BRV	A	56009	EY54BRZ	A
56006	EY54BRF	A	56008	EY54BRX	A			

56501	FSU382	Mercedes-Benz Vario 0814	Optare Nouvelle 2	C28F	A
60197	X253USH	Scania L94UB	Wright Floline	B43F	At
62119	SRS56K	AEC Swift	Alexander W	B43D	p

62138-62181		Volvo B10BLE		Wright Renown			B44F	
62138	X617NSS	w	62152	X624NSS	A	62163	Y628RSA	A
62149	X621NSS	A	62153	X477NSS	A	62164	Y629RSA	A
62150	X622NSS	w	62154	Y626RSA	A	62165	Y701RSA	A
62151	X623NSS	A	62155	Y627RSA	A	62166	Y631RSA	A

A further dying breed, largely as a result of recent changes to accessibility legislation is the Wright Renown-bodied Volvo B10BLE and similar bodied Scania L94UBs. Seen here is one example of the former, by way of 62166, seen in central aberdeen while on route 13 to Seaton, complete with offside advert for cancer charity CLAN.

62167	Y632RSA	A	62177	Y635RSA	A	62180	Y638RSA	A
62168	Y633RSA	A	62178	Y636RSA	A	62181	Y639RSA	A
62169	Y634RSA	A	62179	Y637RSA	A			

62187	W588RFS	Volvo B10BLE	Alexander ALX300	B44F	w
62227	W609RFS	Volvo B10BLE	Alexander ALX300	B44F	w
62228	YS51JVD	Bluebird RE	Bluebird	B60F	At

63193-63218		Wright Streetlite Max		Wright Streetlite 11.5m		B41F	
63193	SN14ECZ	A	63202	SN14FDU	A	63211	SN14FEK	A
63194	SN14EDC	A	63203	SN14FDV	A	63212	SN14EDR	A
63195	SN14EDF	A	63204	SN14FDX	A	63213	SN14EDU	A
63196	SN14EDJ	A	63205	SN14FDY	A	63214	SN14EDV	A
63197	SN14EDK	A	63206	SN14FDZ	A	63215	SN14FEM	A
63198	SN14EDL	A	63207	SN14FEF	A	63216	SN14FEO	A
63199	SN14EDO	A	63208	SN14FEG	A	63217	SN14FEP	A
63200	SN14EDP	A	63209	SN14FEH	A	63218	SN14FET	A
63201	SN14FDP	A	63210	SN14FEJ	A			

Seen here is Wright Streetlite Max 63200, complete with "Sunshine Line" branding, pictured in central Aberdeen while on route 23 to Heathryfold

64994-64997		Van Hool A330 Hydrogen	Van Hool	B44F	
64994	SV14FYR	A	64996	SV14FZD	A
64995	SV14FYS	A	64997	SV14FZC	A

| 65594 | W594SNG | Scania L94UB | Wright Floline | B43F | At |

As part of a project in Aberdeen looking at hydrogen being used as an alternative fuel to diesel, ten special vehicles were ordered in the shape of Van Hool A330s, of which four were delivered to First Aberdeen. Seen here in central Aberbeen is 64997, one such vehicle, pictured while on route X40 to Dubford

67084-67090		ADL E20D SFDDLA		ADL Enviro 200MMC 11.5m			B41F	
67084	SN65ZFZ	A	67087	SN65ZGC	A	67090	SN65ZGH	A
67085	SN65ZGA	A	67088	SN65ZGE	A			
67086	SN65ZGB	A	67089	SN65ZGG	A			

67783-67805		ADL E30D SFD1C8		ADL Enviro 300 11.5m			B41F	
67783	SN13CMO	A	67791	SN13CNE	A	67799	SN13CNY	A
67784	SN13CMU	A	67792	SN13CNF	A	67800	SN13CNZ	A
67785	SN13CMV	A	67793	SN13CNJ	A	67801	SN13COA	A
67786	SN13CMX	A	67794	SN13CNK	A	67802	SN13COH	A
67787	SN13CMY	A	67795	SN13CNO	A	67803	SN13COJ	A
67788	SN13CMZ	A	67796	SN13CNU	A	67804	SN13COU	A
67789	SN13CNA	A	67797	SN13CNV	A	67805	SN13CPE	A
67790	SN13CNC	A	67798	SN13CNX	A			

68000	Q275LBA	Bluebird A3RE	Bluebird	B15F	t
68518	SV54CFY	BMC 1100FE	BMC	B60FL	A
68519	SV54CFV	BMC 1100FE	BMC	B60FL	A

69110-69357		Volvo B7RLE		Wright Eclipse Urban			B44F	
				* B43F				
69110*	SV06GRF	A	69125	SV07EHB	A	69129	SV07EHF	A
69122*	SV06GRK	A	69126	SV07EHC	A	69130	SV07EHG	A
69123*	SV06GRU	A	69127	SV07EHD	A	69131	SV07EHH	A
69124*	SV06GRX	A	69128	SV07EHE	A	69132	SV07EHJ	A

69133	SV07EHK	A	69267	SV57EYK	A	69354	SV08FHD	A
69134	SV07EHL	A	69351	SV08FHA	A	69355	SV08FHE	A
69265	SV57EYH	A	69352	SV08FHB	A	69356	SV08FHF	A
69266	SV57EYJ	A	69353	SV08FHC	A	69357	SV08FHG	A

Pictured in central Aberdeen is 67794, an ADL Enviro 300, seen while making its way to Dyce on route 18

| PA171 | CWG273 | Leyland Tiger PS1 | Alexander | C35F | p |

Previous registrations

20021	FC52AFC		56501	YX05AVV
23305	YN54NXX		62138	X617NSS, OIG1788
23306	YN54NXY		69110	SF06GZW
23330	SV58ASZ		69122	SF06HBD
23401	SV54FRZ		69123	SF06HBE
23402	SV54FTA		69124	SF06HBG

Liveries
Unless stated below, all vehicles in this fleet carry FirstGroup corporate livery;
GRT Advance: 10046
First Coaching: 20021, 20353, 20367, 20372-20374, 20505-20507, 23021, 23305-23307, 23314, 23330, 23402, 24101, 24102, 56005, 56007-56009, 56501
Allover white: 20300, 20301, 23401, 56006
Platinum: 37633-37644, 67084-67090, 69133, 69134, 69265-69267, 69351-69357
Aberdeen Corporation: 62119, 62138
Schoolbus: 62228, 68518, 68519
Aberdeen Hydrogen Bus Project: 64994-64997
First Training: 68000
W Alexander & Sons: PA171

Berkshire

Garage
SL   Slough - Stanley Cottages, Stoke Road, Slough, Berkshire, SL2 5AQ

Outstations
CH   Chertsey - Thorpe Park, Staines Lane, Chertsey, KT16 8PN (schoolbuses)
RG   Reading - Great Knollys Street, Reading, RG1 7HH (RailAir)

20611	LK07CDE	Volvo B12B		Plaxton Paragon			C49FL	RG
20612	LK07CDF	Volvo B12B		Plaxton Paragon			C49FL	RG
20613	LK07CDN	Volvo B12B		Plaxton Paragon			C49FL	RG

20806-20811		Volvo B9R		Plaxton Panther			C49FL	

20806	YX11HPO	RG	20808	YN62GYR	RG	20810	YY63WBT	RG
20807	YX11HPP	RG	20809	YN62GXS	RG	20811	YY63WBU	RG

Pictured entering Reading is Plaxton Panther 20806, showing the striking RailAir livery carried by this vehicle for a service linking Reading with Heathrow Airport

23015	YN04AJV	Scania K114IB	Irizar Century		C53F	RG
33179	LR02LYY	Dennis Trident SFD136	Plaxton President 9.9m		H39/22F	SL
33181	LR02LZA	Dennis Trident SFD136	Plaxton President 9.9m		H39/24F	u
37276	LK58EDL	Volvo B9TL	Wright Eclipse Gemini		CH39/26F	SL

37985-37999		Volvo B9TL		Wright Eclipse Gemini 2			CH39/26F	

37985	BJ11XGY	SL	37987	BJ11ECX	SL	37998	BF63HDX	SL
37986	BJ11ECY	SL	37997	BF63HDV	SL	37999	BF63HDY	SL

41403	RG51FWZ	Dennis Dart SLF SFD2B2	Marshall Capital 10.2m	B28D	SLt

Keeping the Green Line name going in London are two routes, one of which is operated by First Berkshire. 37997, a Wright Eclipse Gemini 2 on Volvo B9TL chassis, is seen here approaching Knightsbridge on route 702 heading for London Victoria

44527-44569		ADL E20D SFD7E1		ADL Enviro 200 10.8m			B39F
				* - B36F			
44527	SN62AYV	SL	44533	SN62DBV	SL	44565*	YX63LLE	SL
44528	SN62AYZ	SL	44560*	YX63LKV	SL	44566*	YX63LLF	SL
44529	SN62AZA	SL	44561*	YX63LKY	SL	44567*	YX63LLG	SL
44530	SN62AZB	SL	44562*	YX63LKZ	SL	44569	YX63LHR	SL
44531	SN62AZW	SL	44563*	YX63LLC	SL			
44532	SN62DBO	SL	44564*	YX63LLD	SL			

47405-47669		Wright Streetlite DF		Wright Streetlite 10.8m			B37F
47405	SK63KLE	SL	47408	SK63KLL	SL	47667	SN15ACO	SL
47406	SK63KLF	SL	47665	SN15ACF	SL	47668	SN15ACU	SL
47407	SK63KLJ	SL	47666	SN15ACJ	SL	47669	SN15ACV	SL

61135	YS51JVA	Bluebird A3RE		Bluebird		B60F	CH
61136	YS51JVK	Bluebird A3RE		Bluebird		B60F	CH

63313-63316		Wright Streetlite Max		Wright Streetlite 11.5m		B41F	
63313	SM65LNH	SL	63315	SM65LNK	SL		
63314	SM65LNJ	SL	63316	SM65LNN	SL		

64001-64048		Mercedes-Benz O530		Mercedes-Benz Citaro * - B40F			B38F	
64001*	OIG6941	SL	64033	LK07CCF	SL	64043	LK08FMC	SL
64002*	OIG6939	SL	64034	LK07CCJ	SL	64044	LK08FMD	SL
64019*	LK03LNF	SL	64035	LK07CCN	SL	64045	LK08FME	SL
64020*	BU04EZF	SL	64036	LK07CCO	SL	64046	LK08FMF	SL
64021*	BU04EZG	SL	64037	LK07CCU	SL	64047	LK08FMG	SL
64030	LK07CCA	SL	64038	LK07CCV	SL	64048	LK08FMJ	SL
64031	LK07CCD	SL	64039	LK07CCX	SL			
64032	LK07CCE	SL	64042	LK08FNL	SL			

Seen having just left Slough bus station is 44533, an ADL Enviro 200, pictured while on route 58 to Britwell

68001-68006		Bluebird A3RE		Bluebird			B60F	
68001	RD51FKV	CH	68003	RD51FKZ	CH	68005	YS51JVE	CH
68002	RD51FKW	CH	68004	RD51FLA	CH	68006	YS51JVH	CH

68522	RX54OGZ	BMC 1100FE		BMC			B60F	CH

69920-69934		Volvo 7900H		Volvo			B37F	
69920	BV13ZCF	u	69925	BV13ZCO	SL	69930	BJ63UHZ	SL
69921	BV13ZCJ	u	69926	BV13ZCT	u	69931	BJ63UJV	SL
69922	BV13ZCK	u	69927	BV13ZCU	u	69932	BJ63UJW	SL
69923	BV13ZCL	u	69928	BV13ZCX	SL	69933	BJ63UJX	SL
69924	BV13ZCN	u	69929	BV13ZCY	u	69934	BJ63UJZ	SL

Above: *Wright Streetlites are becoming FirstGroup's standard single deck vehicle. One such vehicle 63191 in the First Berkshire fleet, is seen in High Wycombe while on route X74 from Slough*

Below: *Pictured below is Mercedes-Benz Citaro 64048, having just left Slough bus station for the journey to High Wycombe on route X74, and showing the special livery carried for 7 Series routes.*

A rare type in the FirstGroup fleet is the Volvo 7900H hybrid, with 34 such vehicles split between Berkshire and Essex. Seen here in SLough is 69920, an example of one of these hybrid vehicles, pictured while on route 75 to Maidenhead

Previous registrations

41403	133CLT	64002	LT02NTX
64001	LT02NTV		

Liveries
Unless stated below, all vehicles in this fleet carry FirstGroup corporate livery;
RailAir: 20611-20613, 20806-20811, 23015
Original corporate livery with "Legoland" branding: 33179, 33181
Green Line: 37276, 37985-37987, 37997-37999
Allover red: 41403
Schoolbus: 61135, 61136, 68001-68006, 68522
Allover blue: 64020, 64030, 64032-64039, 64042-64048, 69920-69934

Cymru

Garages
BE   Bridgend - Unit 38, Aneurin Bevin Ave, Brynmenyn Ind Est, Brynmenyn, Bridgend, CF32 9SZ
CM   Carmarthen - Llanstephan Road, Johnstown, Carmarthen, SA31 3NW
CU   Coach Unit - Pentregethin Road, Ravenhill, Swansea, SA5 7BN
HV   Haverfordwest - Unit 1/2, Withybush Ind Est, Withybush Road, Haverfordwest, SA62 4BS
LL   Llanelli - Inkerman Street, Llanelli, SA15 1RY
MG   Maesteg - Heol Ty Gwyn Industrial Estate, Maesteg, CF34 0BQ
PT   Port Talbot - Acacia Avenue, Port Talbot, SA12 7DP
RV   Ravenhill - Pentregethin Road, Ravenhill, Swansea, SA5 7BN
TY   Tycroes - 40 Pontardulais Road, Tycroes, Ammanford, SA18 3QD

19000-19038		Volvo B7LA		Wright Streetcar			AB40D	
				* - AB49D, $ - AB42D				
19000*	S90FTR	RV	19033	S80FTR	w	19037	S60FTR	w
19029	S100FTR	w	19034$	S30FTR	RV	19038*	S70FTR	RV
19030$	S10FTR	RV	19035	S40FTR	w			
19032$	S20FTR	RV	19036	S50FTR	RV			

20323	YN57BVW	Volvo B7R	Plaxton Profile	C70FL	RV
20324	YN57BVX	Volvo B7R	Plaxton Profile	C70FL	RV
20325	YN57BVY	Volvo B7R	Plaxton Profile	C70FL	RV

Formerly used on Greyhound express coach services is 23323, an Irizar PB-bodied Scania K114EB coach, pictured having just left Swansea Bus Station while on route X10 to Cardiff. A route for which a special livery is carried

23319-23323		Scania K114EB		Irizar PB		C49FT
23319	YN55PXK	RV	23321	YN06CGU	RV	
23320	YN55PXL	RV	23323	YN06CGX	RV	

32037-32044		Volvo B7TL		Alexander ALX400		H49/29F
32037	W807EOW	w	32042	W812EOW	w	
32041	W811EOW	w	32044	W814EOW	w	

33061-33064		Dennis Trident SFD136		Plaxton President 9.9m		H39/22F
33061	LN51GKU	PT	33063	LN51GKX	PT	
33062	LN51GKV	PT	33064	LN51GKY	PT	

41200-41391		Dennis Dart SLF SFD212		Marshall Capital 10.2m * - B31F		B33F
41200	S220KLM	u	41386	X386HLR	PT	
41381*	X381HLR	PT	41391*	X391HLR	PT	

New in London as First London's DML41386 prior to transfer to Wales, is this Dennis Dart SLF with Marshall Capital bodywork, seen here in Bridgend Bus Station leaving on route 65 to Talbot Green

41489	LT02ZFA	Dennis Dart SLF SFD6B2	Marshall Capital 8.8m	B25F	PT
41491	LT02ZFC	Dennis Dart SLF SFD6B2	Marshall Capital 8.8m	B25F	MG
41718	W718ULL	Dennis Dart SLF SFD212	Marshall Capital 10.2m	B33F	RV
41719	W719ULL	Dennis Dart SLF SFD212	Marshall Capital 10.2m	B33F	PT
41727	W727ULL	Dennis Dart SLF SFD212	Marshall Capital 10.2m	B28F	PT

42600-42614		Dennis Dart SLF SFD1BA	Alexander Pointer 2 9.3m		B31F		
42600	CU54HYK	LL	42601	CU54HYL	TY	42602	CU54HYM	RV

42603	CU54HYN	RV	42607	CU54HYT	RV	42611	CU54HYY	LL
42604	CU54HYO	RV	42608	CU54HYV	RV	42612	CU54HYZ	TY
42605	CU54HYP	RV	42609	CU54HYW	RV	42613	CU54HZA	LL
42606	CU54HYR	RV	42610	CU54HYX	RV	42614	CU54HZB	RV

42674-42694   Dennis Dart SLF SFD3CA   Alexander Pointer 2 10.7m   B31F
                                                         * - B37F

42674	CU53APO	PT	42681*	CU53ARF	RV	42688	CU53AUW	RV
42675	CU53APV	PT	42682*	CU53APZ	HV	42689	CU53AVW	PT
42676	CU53APX	PT	42683*	CU53APY	RV	42690	CU53AUX	PT
42677	CU53ASO	RV	42684*	CU53AUP	RV	42691	CU53AUY	PT
42678	CU53ARZ	RV	42685	CU53AUO	RV	42692	CU53AVB	RV
42679*	CU53ARX	RV	42686	CU53AUT	RV	42693*	CU03BHV	RV
42680*	CU53ARO	RV	42687	CU53AUV	RV	42694*	CU03BHW	HV

To commemorate the centenary of United Welsh, 42684, a Dennis Dart SLF with Alexander Pointer 2 bodywork, was repainted into a vintage United Welsh livery. It is pictured here in Swansea Bus Station while operating on route 33 to Frederick Place

42715   R715BAE   Dennis Dart SLF SFD112   Plaxton Pointer 2 9.3m   B29F   PT

42861-42913   Dennis Dart SLF SFD3CA   Alexander Pointer 2 10.7m   B37F

42861	CU53AVJ	HV	42868	CU53AVP	RV	42881	SF05KXC	HV
42862	CU53AVK	HV	42869	CU53AVV	HV	42882	SF05KXD	HV
42863	CU53AVL	LL	42870	CU53AVT	LL	42883	SF05KXE	HV
42864	CU53AVM	LL	42877	SF05KWY	HV	42884	SF05KXH	HV
42865	CU53AVN	RV	42878	SF05KWZ	HV	42912	WX05RVW	LL
42866	CU53AVO	TY	42879	SF05KXA	HV	42913	WX05RVY	LL
42867	CU53AVR	LL	42880	SF05KXB	HV			

43836-43853		Dennis Dart SLF SFD6BA		Alexander Pointer 2 8.8m			B29F	
43836	SN53ESV	PT	43840	SN53ETE	LL	43852	WK06AFU	PT
43837	SN53ESU	RV	43841	SN53ETF	LL	43853	WK06AFV	PT
43838	SN53ESY	PT	43850	WK06AEE	RV			
43839	SN53ETD	LL	43851	WK06AEF	RV			

43901	SN03LGG	Dennis Dart SPD SFD4DB	Alexander Pointer 2 11.3m	B41F	RV
43902	SN03LGK	Dennis Dart SPD SFD4DB	Alexander Pointer 2 11.3m	B41F	RV
43903	SN03LGJ	Dennis Dart SPD SFD4DB	Alexander Pointer 2 11.3m	B41F	RV
44500	WK56ABZ	Dennis E200Dart SFD321	Alexander Enviro 200 10.8m	B38F	RV

44501-44506		Dennis E200Dart SFD361		Alexander Enviro 200 10.8m			B35F	
44501	CU08ACY	CM	44503	CU08ADO	RV	44505	CU08ADX	RV
44502	CU08ACZ	RV	44504	CU08ADV	RV	44506	CU08ADZ	LL

44552-44559		ADL E20D SFD8D1		ADL Enviro 200 10.2m			B33F	
44552	YX13AEV	RV	44555	YX13AEZ	RV	44558	YX13AKU	RV
44553	YX13AEW	RV	44556	YX13AFA	RV	44559	YX13AKV	RV
44554	YX13AEY	RV	44557	YX13AFE	RV			

44568	YX63LLJ	ADL E20D SFD7E1	ADL Enviro 200 10.8m	B39F	BE
44570	YX63LKU	ADL E20D SFD7E1	ADL Enviro 200 10.8m	B39F	u

44573-44581		ADL E20D SFD8D1		ADL Enviro 200 10.2m			B33F	
44573	YX13BNA	RV	44576	YX13BNE	RV	44579	YX13BNK	RV
44574	YX13BNB	RV	44577	YX13BNF	RV	44580	YX13BNL	RV
44575	YX13BND	RV	44578	YX13BNJ	RV	44581	YX13BNN	RV

44582-44636		ADL E20D SFD7E1		ADL Enviro 200 10.8m			B39F	
44582	YX63ZUD	BE	44605	YX14RUO	RV	44622	YX14RVR	RV
44583	YX63ZVA	BE	44606	YX14RUR	LL	44623	YX14RVT	RV
44584	YX63ZVB	BE	44607	YX14RUU	RV	44624	YX14RVU	RV
44585	YX63ZVC	BE	44608	YX14RUV	RV	44625	YX14RVV	RV
44586	YX63ZVD	BE	44609	YX14RUW	RV	44626	YX14RVW	RV
44587	YX63ZVE	BE	44610	YX14RUY	RV	44627	YX14RVY	RV
44588	YX63ZVF	BE	44611	YX14RVA	RV	44628	YX14RVZ	RV
44589	YX63ZVG	BE	44612	YX14RVC	RV	44629	YX14RWE	RV
44590	YX63ZVH	BE	44613	YX14RVE	RV	44630	YX14RWF	RV
44591	YX63LHK	BE	44614	YX14RVF	RV	44631	YX14RWJ	RV
44592	YX63LHL	BE	44615	YX14RVJ	RV	44632	YX14RWK	RV
44593	YX63LHM	BE	44616	YX14RVK	RV	44633	YX64VPJ	RV
44594	YX14RWN	TY	44617	YX14RVL	RV	44634	YX64VPK	RV
44595	YX14RWO	TY	44618	YX14RVM	RV	44635	YX64VPL	RV
44602	YX14RUC	BE	44619	YX14RVN	RV	44636	YX64VPM	RV
44603	YX14RUH	LL	44620	YX14RVO	RV			
44604	YX14RUJ	RV	44621	YX14RVP	RV			

47629-47685		Wright Streetlite DF		Wright Streetlite 10.8m			B37F	
47629	SN15ADO	MG	47634	SN15AEA	MG	47639	SN15AEF	PT
47630	SN15ADU	MG	47635	SN15AEB	MG	47640	SN15AEG	PT
47631	SN15ADV	MG	47636	SN15AEC	MG	47641	SN15AEJ	PT
47632	SN15ADX	MG	47637	SN15AED	MG	47642	SN15AEK	PT
47633	SN15ADZ	MG	47638	SN15AEE	PT	47659	SN65OKO	PT

Above: *Pictured here having just left Swansea Bus Station is 44627, an ADL Enviro 200, seen while operating on route 4 to Swansea University*

Below: *Seen here at Port Talbot is 47659, a Wright Streetlite DF pictured while on route 227 to Neath, showing the orange-fronted variant of the corporate livery carried by a number of vehicles in the fleet*

47660	SN65OKP	PT	47674	SL15RVP	RV	47680	SL15RVX	PT
47661	SN15ABK	RV	47675	SL15RVR	RV	47681	SL15RVY	PT
47662	SN15ABO	RV	47676	SL15RVT	PT	47682	SL15RWX	PT
47663	SN15ABU	RV	47677	SL15RVU	RV	47683	SL15XWY	PT
47664	SN15ABV	RV	47678	SL15RVV	RV	47684	SL15XWZ	PT
47673	SL15RVO	RV	47679	SL15RVW	PT	47685	SL15XXA	PT

49002-49010		Optare Versa V1080		Optare Versa 10.8m			B36F	
49002	YJ13HMD	BE	49005	YJ13HMG	BE	49008	YJ13HMU	BE
49003	YJ13HME	BE	49006	YJ13HMH	BE	49009	YJ13HMV	BE
49004	YJ13HMF	BE	49007	YJ13HMK	BE	49010	YJ13HMX	BE

49301-49309		Optare Versa V1170		Optare Versa 11.7m			B40F	
49301	YJ13HLR	PT	49304	YJ13HLW	PT	49307	YJ13HLZ	PT
49302	YJ13HLU	PT	49305	YJ13HLX	PT	49308	YJ13HMA	PT
49303	YJ13HLV	PT	49306	YJ13HLY	PT	49309	YJ13HMC	PT

53058-53063		Optare Solo M850		Optare Solo 8.5m		B26F	
53058	VX53OEV	u	53060	VX53OEO	PT		
53059	VX53OEN	u	53063	VX53OET	LL		

Not overly common in the FirstGroup fleet is the Optare Versa. Pictured here exiting Bridgend Bus Station is 49008, one such vehicle, seen while on route 63 to Porthcawl

53707	MX58KZA	Optare Solo M710SE	Optare Solo 7.1m	B21F	LL
53708	MX58KZB	Optare Solo M710SE	Optare Solo 7.1m	B21F	LL
53711	YJ60LRN	Optare Solo M780SE	Optare Solo 7.8m	B26F	HV
53802	WX05RRV	Optare Solo M850SL	Optare Solo Slimline 8.5m	B28F	PT
53804	WX05RRZ	Optare Solo M850SL	Optare Solo Slimline 8.5m	B28F	PT

| 62189 | W591RFS | Volvo B10BLE | | Alexander ALX300 | | | B44F | t |
| 62208 | W596RFS | Volvo B10BLE | | Alexander ALX300 | | | B44F | t |

63079-63095		Wright Streetlite Max		Wright Streetlite 11.5m			B41F	
63079	SN14DTX	PT	63085	SN14DUU	PT	63091	SN14DVG	PT
63080	SN14DTY	PT	63086	SN14DUV	PT	63092	SN14DVH	PT
63081	SN14DTZ	PT	63087	SN14DUY	PT	63093	SN14DVJ	PT
63082	SN14DUA	PT	63088	SN14DVB	PT	63094	SN14DVK	MG
63083	SN14DUH	PT	63089	SN14DVC	PT	63095	SN14DVL	MG
63084	SN14DUJ	PT	63090	SN14DVF	PT			

| 66350 | MV02VEA | Volvo B7L | | Wright Eclipse | | | B41F | RV |
| 66351 | MV02VEB | Volvo B7L | | Wright Eclipse | | | B41F | RV |

66716-66961		Volvo B7RLE		Wright Eclipse Urban			B43F	
66716	WX54XDA	PT	66944	WX55TZF	RV	66958	WX55TZV	PT
66717	WX54XDD	TY	66945	WX55TZG	RV	66960	WX55TZY	PT
66718	WX54XDB	TY	66953	WX55TZP	RV	66961	WX55TZZ	PT

A further specimen of the Wright Streetlite, this time in its longest "Max" form, is seen 63090, seen here in Swansea while operating on route X55 to Pontneddfechan

67091-67095		ADL E20D SFDDMA		ADL Enviro 200MMC 11.5m			B41F	
67091	YX65RHY	RV	67093	YX65RJJ	RV	67095	YX65RJU	RV
67092	YX65RHZ	RV	67094	YX65RJO	RV			

67431-67439		ADL E30D SFD1C8		ADL Enviro 300 11.8m			B42F	
67431	SL63GBF	TY	67434	SL63GBV	RV	67437	SL63GBZ	RV
67432	SL63GBO	RV	67435	SL63GBX	RV	67438	SL63GCF	TY
67433	SL63GBU	RV	67436	SL63GBY	RV	67439	SL63GCK	TY

68506	CU54CYZ	BMC 1100FE		BMC			B60F	u
68568	BV57MSU	BMC 1100FE		BMC			B55F	MGt

69231-69384		Volvo B7RLE		Wright Eclipse Urban			B43F	
				* - B44F, $ - B41F				
69231	MX56AEZ	PT	69241	MX56AFY	LL	69303*	CU08AHP	CU
69232	MX56AFA	PT	69242	MX56AFZ	TY	69304*	CU08AHV	LL
69233	MX56AFE	PT	69243	MX56AGO	LL	69305*	CU08AHX	LL
69234	MX56AFF	PT	69244	MX56AGU	LL	69380$	HY09AJX	u
69235	MX56AFJ	PT	69249*	YJ07WFR	LL	69381$	HY09AKG	u
69236	MX56AFK	PT	69250*	YJ07WFS	LL	69382$	HY09AOU	TY
69237	MX56AFN	LL	69251*	YJ07WFT	LL	69383$	HY09AZA	TY
69238	MX56AFO	RV	69252*	YJ07WFU	LL	69384$	HY09AKF	u
69239	MX56AFU	TY	69301*	CU08AHN	CU			
69240	MX56AFV	TY	69302*	CU08AHO	CU			

For new services that serve Swansea University, a batch of five 11.5m ADL Enviro 200MMCs were delivered in 2015, carrying a special version of the FirstGroup corporate livery. Seen here is 67095, pictured having just left Swansea Bus Station while on route 8 to Swansea Bay Campus

Previous registrations

19000	YK06CZN		19036	CU57AKJ
19030	CU57AJV		19038	CU57AKK
19034	CU57AJY			

Liveries
Unless stated below, all vehicles in this fleet carry FirstGroup corporate livery;
Ftr: 19000, 19030, 19032, 19033, 19037
Swansea Unibus: 19034, 19036, 19038, 66944, 66945, 66953, 67091-67095
Dark blue: 20323-20325
Route X10: 23319-23321, 23323
Carmarthen Park & Ride: 42674
Llanelli & District Centenary: 42681
United Welsh Centenary: 42684
Cymru Clipper: 42685-42688, 42692, 49301-49309, 63079-63095, 66960, 66961, 69241, 69243, 69244, 69249-69252, 69301-69305, 69380-69384
South Wales Centenary: 42693
Thomas Bros Centenary: 42694
Black front on corporate livery: 47636-47638
Orange front on corporate livery: 47659, 47660, 47679-47685
Red front on corporate livery: 47661-47664, 47673-47678
Carmarthen Dial-a-Ride: 53707, 53708
Traws Cymru: 67431, 67436, 67438, 67439
Landore Green Park & Ride: 67432, 67433
Fabian Way Park & Ride: 67434, 67435
Swansea Park & Ride: 67437
Schoolbus: 68506, 68568

Pictured here is ADL Enviro 300 67433, part of a batch of six that carry this special livery for Park & Ride services in Swansea, seen here leaving the bus station on its way back to Landore Park & Ride

Eastern Counties

Garages

GY	Great Yarmouth - Caister Road, Great Yarmouth, NR30 4DF
IP	Ipswich - Star Lane, Ipswich, IP4 1JN
KL	King's Lynn - Vancouver Avenue, King's Lynn, PE30 5RD
L	Lowestoft - Gas Works Road, Lowestoft, NR32 1UZ
N	Norwich - Roundtree Way, Norwich, NR7 9DA, and Vulcan Road, Hethersett, Norwich, NR6 6AE

20500-20515		Volvo B12M		Plaxton Paragon * - C49FLT			C53F	
20500	AO02RBX	GY	20514*	VV02EUP	IP			
20501	AO02RBY	GY	20515*	VV02EUR	N			

30886-32065		Volvo B7TL		Alexander ALX400			H49/29F	
30886	W741DWX	L	30902	W757DWX	GY	32063	W223XBD	GY
30887	W742DWX	GY	32058	W218XBD	GY	32064	W224XBD	GY
30888	W743DWX	L	32059	W219XBD	GY	32065	W425SRP	GY
30900	W774DWX	L	32061	W221XBD	IP			
30901	W756DWX	L	32062	W422SRP	GY			

32100-32214		Volvo B7TL		Plaxton President * - H39/20F, $ - H42/??F			H42/27F	
32100*	LT02ZCJ	N	32112*	LT02ZDL	N	32206	LT52WTM	GY
32101*	LT02ZCK	N	32201	LT52WTF	GY	32210	LT52WTR	GY
32105*	LT02ZCU	N	32203	LT52WTJ	N	32212	LT52WTV	GY
32106*	LT02ZCV	GY	32204	LT52WTK	GY	32213$	LT52WTW	N
32107*	LT02ZCX	N	32205	LT52WTL	GY	32214	LT52WTX	N

Previous page: *Plaxton President bodied-Volvo B7TL 32206 started life in London as their VTL1106 before cascade out to the countryside. It is seen in Norwich, Castle Meadows while on route 18 to Long Stratton*

32348	LK53LZL	Volvo B7TL	Wright Eclipse Gemini	H41/25F	GY

32479-32494		Volvo B7TL	Alexander ALX400	H49/27F	

32479	AU53HJV	IP	32489	AU53HKG	IP	32493	AU53HKL	IP
32486	AU53HKD	IP	32490	AU53HKH	IP	32494	AU53HKM	IP
32487	AU53HKE	N	32491	AU53HKJ	IP			
32488	AU53HKF	IP	32492	AU53HKK	IP			

32629	KP54KAX	Volvo B7TL	Wright Eclipse Gemini	H45/29F	GY
32653	AU05MUV	Volvo B7TL	Alexander ALX400	H49/27F	IP
32655	AU05MUY	Volvo B7TL	Alexander ALX400	H49/27F	IP
32656	AU05MVA	Volvo B7TL	Alexander ALX400	H49/27F	IP
32905	W905VLN	Dennis Trident SFD313	Plaxton President 10.5m	O43/28F	GY
33003	LK51UZS	Dennis Trident SFD339	Plaxton President 10.5m	H42/23F	u

Seen at Showbus, Duxford is 32653, an Alexander ALX400-bodied Volvo B7TL, showing the allover advert for childrens charity Save the Children which was carried by the vehicle

33055-33248		Dennis Trident SFD136	Plaxton President 9.9m	H39/23F
			* - H39/21F, $ - H39/24F, % - H39/20F	

33055*	LN51GKO	N	33149	LR02LXH	w	33155	LR02LXO	u
33060$	LN51GJU	N	33150	LR02LXJ	N	33156	LR02LXP	w
33113*	LT02NVX	N	33151	LR02LXK	GY	33157	LR02LXS	N
33126%	LT02NVO	N	33152	LR02LXL	N	33158	LR02LXT	w
33146	LR02LXB	w	33154	LR02LXN	N	33159	LR02LXU	N

33160	LR02LXV	N	33168	LR02LYG	N	33239	LT52WVH	u
33161	LR02LXW	N	33169	LR02LYJ	N	33240	LT52WVJ	u
33162	LR02LXX	N	33170	LR02LYK	N	33244	LT52WUV	N
33163	LR02LXZ	N	33233	LT52WWV	u	33245	LT52WUW	N
33164	LR02LYA	N	33234	LT52WWX	N	33246	LT52WUX	N
33165	LR02LYC	N	33236	LT52WWZ	N	33247	LT52WUY	N
33166	LR02LYD	N	33237	LT52WVF	N	33248	LT52WVA	u
33167	LR02LYF	N	33238	LT52WVG	N			

33423   SN60CAA   Dennis Trident SFD1DS   Alexander Enviro 400 10.2m   H35/27F   GY

33803-33824   ADL E40D SFD4DS   ADL Enviro 400 10.8m   H41/26F

33803	YX63LJF	KL	33811	YX63LJY	KL	33819	YX63LKJ	L
33804	YX63LJJ	KL	33812	YX63LJZ	KL	33820	YX63LKK	L
33805	YX63LJK	KL	33813	YX63LKA	KL	33821	YX63LKL	L
33806	YX63LJL	KL	33814	YX63LKC	KL	33822	YX63LKM	L
33807	YX63LJN	KL	33815	YX63LKD	KL	33823	YX63LKN	L
33808	YX63LJO	KL	33816	YX63LKE	KL	33824	YX63LKO	L
33809	YX63LJU	KL	33817	YX63LKF	KL			
33810	YX63LJV	KL	33818	YX63LKG	L			

In 2013, a batch of upgraded ADL Enviro 400s were ordered for corridor route X1, linking Peterborough with Lowestoft. Seen entering Showbus at Woburn is 33808, one such vehicle, showing the special livery carried

35193-35201   Wright Streetdeck   Wright Streetdeck   H45/28F

35193	SK16GVR	N	35196	SK16GVV	N	35199	SK16GVY	N
35194	SK16GVT	N	35197	SK16GVW	N	35200	SK16GVZ	N
35195	SK16GVU	N	35198	SK16GVX	N	35201	SK16GWA	N

36166-36202		Volvo B9TL		Wright Eclipse Gemini 2 * - H45/29F			H45/27F	
36166*	BD11CFK	N	36179*	BD11CDY	N	36192	BN12JYS	N
36167*	BD11CFM	N	36180*	BD11CDZ	N	36193	BN12JYT	N
36168*	BD11CFN	N	36181	BF12KXU	GY	36194	BN12JYU	N
36169*	BD11CFO	N	36182	BF12KXV	GY	36195	BN12JYV	N
36170*	BD11CFP	N	36183	BN12JYF	GY	36196	BN12JYW	N
36171*	BD11CFU	N	36184	BN12JYG	GY	36197	BN12WNX	N
36172*	BD11CFV	N	36185	BN12JYH	GY	36198	BN12WNY	N
36173*	BD11CFX	N	36186	BN12JYJ	GY	36199	BN12WNZ	N
36174*	BD11CFY	N	36187	BN12JYK	GY	36200	BN12WOA	N
36175*	BD11CFZ	N	36188	BN12JYL	GY	36201	BN12WOB	N
36176*	BD11CGE	N	36189	BN12JYO	N	36202	BN12WOC	N
36177*	BD11CGF	N	36190	BN12JYP	N			
36178*	BD11CDX	N	36191	BN12JYR	N			

37274-37579		Volvo B9TL		Wright Eclipse Gemini * - CH39/26F, $ - H45/29F, % - H43/26F			H45/26F	
37274*	LK58EDF	GY	37567	AU58ECF	L	37574	AU58ECY	GY
37275*	LK58EDJ	GY	37568%	AU58ECJ	L	37575%	AU58ECZ	L
37562$	FJ08FYN	GY	37569%	AU58ECN	L	37576	AU58EDC	L
37563%	AU58ECA	L	37570	AU58ECT	L	37577	AU58EDF	L
37564%	AU58ECC	L	37571	AU58ECV	L	37578	AU58EDJ	GY
37565	AU58ECD	L	37572%	AU58ECW	L	37579	AU58EDK	L
37566	AU58ECE	L	37573	AU58ECX	GY			

Showing the previous version of the X1 Excel livery is Wright Eclipse Gemini-bodied Volvo B7TL, seen in Great Yarmouth while on route X1 to Lowestoft

42908-42943		Dennis Dart SLF SFD3CA		Alexander Pointer 2 10.7m			B37F	
				* - B36F, $ - B38F				
42908	WX05RVR	L	42920	EU05AUM	GY	42938	WX05SVD	L
42911	WX05RVV	L	42921	EU05AUN	GY	42943$	WA56OAS	L
42914	WX05RVZ	L	42926*	SN05EAE	L			
42919	EU05AUL	GY	42929*	SN05EAJ	GY			

44512	DK57SXF	Dennis E200Dart SFD321	Alexander Enviro 200 10.8m	B36F	L
44513	DK57SXG	Dennis E200Dart SFD321	Alexander Enviro 200 10.8m	B36F	L

44516-44519		Dennis E200Dart SFD361		Alexander Enviro 200 10.8m		B35F
44516	YX09ACV	N	44518	YX09ACZ	N	
44517	YX09ACY	N	44519	YX09ADO	IP	

44928-45119		Dennis E200Dart SFD151		Alexander Enviro 200 9.4m			B29F	
44928	EU08FHB	IP	45117	ST58JPT	L	45119	RT09JPT	IP
45116	VT09JPT	L	45118	ST09JPT	GY			

47501-47512		Wright Streetlite DF		Wright Streetlite 10.8m			B37F	
47501	SN64CPU	GY	47505	SN64CPZ	GY	47509	SN64CRU	N
47502	SN64CPV	GY	47506	SN64CRF	GY	47510	SN64CRV	N
47503	SN64CPX	GY	47507	SN64CRJ	N	47511	SN64CRX	N
47504	SN64CPY	GY	47508	SN64CRK	N	47512	SN64CRZ	N

Seen here leaving Norwich is 63320, a Wright Streetlite DF, pictured while on route 14 heading for Wymondham Cross. This photo shows the green-fronted version of the corporate livery carried by a number of buses in Norwich (photo courtesy of Steve Maskell)

60618	R781WKW	Volvo B10BLE	Wright Renown	B41F	N

60807	S658RNA	Volvo B10BLE	Wright Renown	B41F	N
60808	S659RNA	Volvo B10BLE	Wright Renown	B41F	N
60915	YG02DLZ	Volvo B7L	Wright Eclipse	B41F	N
60916	YG02DKU	Volvo B7L	Wright Eclipse	B41F	N
61148	MV02VBU	Volvo B7L	Wright Eclipse	B41F	N

63317-63327   Wright Streetlite Max   Wright Streetlite 11.5m   B45F

63317	SK65PWX	N	63321	SK65PXB	N	63325	SK65PXF	N
63318	SK65PWY	N	63322	SK65PXC	N	63326	SK65PXG	N
63319	SK65PWZ	N	63323	SK65PXD	N	63327	SK65PXH	N
63320	SK65PXA	N	63324	SK65PXE	N			

65679   YR52VEH   Scania L94UB   Wright Solar   B43F   IP

66328-66348   Volvo B7L   Wright Eclipse   B41F

66328	MV02VBC	N	66338	MV02VCN	N	66344	MV02VCX	GY
66329	MV02VBD	N	66340	MV02VCP	N	66348	MV02VDC	N
66333	MV02VBY	N	66341	MV02VCT	GY			
66334	MV02VBZ	GY	66343	MV02VCW	N			

66850-69428   Volvo B7RLE   Wright Eclipse Urban   B43F

66850	MX05CHD	IP	66976	KX05MGZ	N	66980	KX05MHJ	N
66950	WX55TZM	IP	66977	KX05MHA	N	66981	KX05MHK	IP
66957	WX55TZU	IP	66978	KX05MHE	N	66982	KX05MHL	N
66959	WX55TZW	IP	66979	KX05MHF	IP	66983	KX05MHM	IP

Seen in Norwich is Wright Eclipse Urban-bodied Volvo B7RLE 69006, pictured on route 19 to Costessey

66984	KX05MHN	IP	69007	AU05DMO	IP	69423	AU58FFK	IP
66985	KX05MHO	IP	69008	AU05DMV	IP	69424	AU58FFL	IP
66986	KX05MHU	IP	69009	AU05DMX	IP	69425	AU58FFM	IP
66987	KX05MHV	IP	69010	AU05DMY	IP	69426	AU58FFN	IP
69005	AU05DME	IP	69011	AU05DMZ	IP	69427	AU58FFO	IP
69006	AU05DMF	IP	69422	AU58FFJ	IP	69428	AU58FFP	IP

Previous registrations

33423	J57156	45117	MX58VCN

Liveries
Unless stated below, all vehicles in this fleet carry FirstGroup corporate livery:
First Coaching: 20500, 20514
Allover white: 20501, 20515
Lowestoft Corporation: 30888
Great Yarmouth Transport: 32059
Eastern Counties: 32479
Grey front on corporate livery: 32486-32493, 32655, 32656, 44516-44519, 44928, 45119, 66850, 66950, 66957, 66979, 66981, 66983-66987, 69005-69008, 69010, 69011, 69426, 69428
Orange front on corporate livery: 33150, 33157, 33159, 33160
Route X1 Excel: 33803-33824, 37274, 37275, 37578, 37579
Old Route X1 Excel: 37564, 37565, 37567, 37569
Salmon front on corporate livery: 35193-35199
Blue front on corporate livery: 36166-36171, 36173-36179
Red front on corporate livery: 36189, 36192, 36193
First Training: 60807
Green front on corporate livery: 63317-63323
Yellow front on corporate livery: 66976, 66980, 66982
Purple front on corporate livery: 66978
Ipswich Park & Ride: 69424

Essex

Garages
BN   Basildon - Cherrydown, Basildon, SS16 5AG
CF   Chelmsford - Westway, Chelmsford, CM1 3AR
CN   Clacton - Coastline House, Telford Road, Gorse Lane Industrial Estate, Clacton, CO15 4LP
CR   Colchester - Quayside Depot, Haven Road, Colchester, CO2 8HT
HH   Hadleigh - London Road, Hadleigh, Benfleet, SS7 2QL

23019	YN54APX	Scania K114IB		Irizar Century			C49F	CF
23020	YN54APK	Scania K114IB		Irizar Century			C49F	CF

32068-32485		Volvo B7TL		Alexander ALX400		H49/27F	
32068	KP51VZS	CR	32477	AU53HJN	CR	32482	AU53HJZ	CF
32087	KP51WBZ	CR	32478	AU53HJO	CR	32483	AU53HKA	CF
32475	AU53HJJ	CR	32480	AU53HJX	CF	32484	AU53HKB	CF
32476	AU53HJK	CR	32481	AU53HJY	CF	32485	AU53HKC	CF

32628-32642		Volvo B7TL		Wright Eclipse Gemini		H45/29F	
32628	KP54KAU	CR	32640	KP54AZB	CR	32642	KP54AZD	CR
32631	KP54KBF	CR	32641	KP54AZC	CR			

32651	AU05MUO	Volvo B7TL	Alexander ALX400	H49/27F	CF
32652	AU05MUP	Volvo B7TL	Alexander ALX400	H49/27F	CF
32654	AU05MUW	Volvo B7TL	Alexander ALX400	H49/27F	CF
32856	V856HBY	Dennis Trident SFD113	Plaxton President 9.9m	H39/21F	w
32864	T864KLF	Dennis Trident SFD113	Plaxton President 9.9m	H39/21F	w

Starting life in London as First London TN1047 is First Essex 33047, a Plaxton President-bodied Dennis Trident, seen here exiting Basildon Bus Station while on route 15 to Basildon Hospital

| 33044 | LN51DVH | Dennis Trident SFD136 | Plaxton President 9.9m | H39/24F | CR |
| 33047 | LN51DVM | Dennis Trident SFD136 | Plaxton President 9.9m | H39/24F | BN |

33072-33136		Dennis Trident SFD336		Plaxton President 10.5m		H42/27F	
33072	LN51GOC	HH	33081	LN51GNU	HH	33098	LN51GOA	HH
33073	LN51GOE	HH	33086	LN51GMG	CR	33132	LT02ZBY	HH
33074	LN51GOH	HH	33087	LN51GMO	CR	33133	LT02ZBZ	HH
33077	LN51GNF	BN	33088	LN51GMU	CR	33134	LT02ZCA	HH
33078	LN51GNJ	CR	33090	LN51GMX	HH	33136	LT02ZCF	HH
33080	LN51GNP	CR	33095	LN51NRL	HH			

33178-33232		Dennis Trident SFD136		Plaxton President 9.9m		H39/24F	
33178	LR02LYX	BN	33190	LT52XAA	CR	33196	LT52XAG	CR
33184	LR02LZD	w	33191	LT52XAB	HH	33229	LT52WXG	HH
33186	LT52WVB	CR	33192	LT52XAC	BN	33232	LT52WXK	HH
33188	LT52WVD	BN	33194	LT52XAE	BN			
33189	LT52WVE	HH	33195	LT52XAF	CR			

33373-33385		Dennis Trident SFD33G		Alexander ALX400 10.5m		H42/26F	
33373	LK53EYR	HH	33383	LK53EZC	HH	33385	LK53EZE	HH
33376	LK53EYV	HH	33384	LK53EZD	HH			

| 33424 | VT59JPT | Dennis Trident SFD46M | Alexander Enviro 400 10.8m | H47/33F | BN |
| 33425 | SN59AWV | Dennis Trident SFD18S | Alexander Enviro 400 10.2m | H41/29F | BN |

Seen approaching its terminus in Southend while on route 25 is 33424, an Alexander Enviro 400-bodied Dennis Trident, acquired from the Ensign dealership in 2013

33504-33574		Dennis Trident SFD16M		Alexander Enviro 400 10.2m			H41/26F	
33504	LK08FLX	BN	33552	SN58CFY	BN	33563	SN58CGZ	BN
33507	LK08FKZ	BN	33553	SN58CFZ	BN	33567	SN58CHG	BN
33544	SN58CFK	BN	33555	SN58CGF	BN	33568	SN58CHH	BN
33545	SN58CFL	BN	33557	SN58CGK	BN	33570	SN58CHK	BN
33546	SN58CFM	BN	33558	SN58CGO	BN	33572	SN58CHO	BN
33548	SN58CFP	BN	33559	SN58CGU	BN	33573	SN58ENR	BN
33549	SN58CFU	BN	33561	SN58CGX	BN	33574	SN58ENT	BN
33551	SN58CFX	BN	33562	SN58CGY	BN			

41513-41544		Dennis Dart SLF SFD2BA		Caetano Nimbus 10.2m			B33F	
41513	LK03NGF	BN	41527	LK53FDD	BN	41542	LK53FEG	BN
41523	LK03UFA	BN	41538	LK53FDX	BN	41543	LK53FEH	BN
41524	LK03UFB	BN	41539	LK53FDY	BN	41544	LK53FEJ	CF
41525	LK03UFC	BN	41541	LK53FEF	BN			

41730	X503JLO	Dennis Dart SLF SFD212	Marshall Capital 10.2m	B31F	HH
41735	X735HLF	Dennis Dart SLF SFD212	Marshall Capital 10.2m	B31F	CN

42482-42489		Dennis Dart SLF SFD3CA		Alexander Pointer 2 10.7m			B37F	
42482	SN03WLD	HH	42485	SN03WME	HH	42488	SN53KJX	HH
42483	SN03WLK	HH	42486	SN03WMM	HH	42489	SN53KJY	HH
42484	SN03WLW	CF	42487	SN03WMX	HH			

42519	LK03NKN	Dennis Dart SLF SFD2BA	Caetano Nimbus 10.2m	B33F	BN

Seen entering Chelmsford Bus Station while on route 31X is 42932, a Dennis Dart SLF with Alexander Pointer 2 bodywork

42555-42561		Dennis Dart SLF SFD1BA		Alexander Pointer 9.3m			B31F	
42555	WX05UAM	CN	42557	WX05UAO	CN			
42556	WX05UAN	CN	42561	SN05DZX	CN			

42918-42937		Dennis Dart SLF SFD3CA		Alexander Pointer 2 10.7m			B36F	
				* - B37F				
42918*	EU05AUK	CN	42930	SN05EAM	CF	42935	SN05DZR	CF
42922*	EU05AUO	CN	42931	SN05EAO	CF	42936	SN05DZS	CF
42923*	EU05AUP	CN	42932	SN05EAP	CF	42937	SN05DZT	CN
42927	SN05EAF	CN	42933	SN05DZO	CF			
42928	SN05EAG	CN	42934	SN05DZP	CF			

43360	V360DVG	Dennis Dart SLF SFD612	Plaxton Pointer 2 8.8m	B29F	CR
43480	R680DPW	Dennis Dart SLF SFD322	Plaxton Pointer 2 10.7m	B37F	CF
43485	R685DPW	Dennis Dart SLF SFD322	Plaxton Pointer 2 10.7m	B37F	w
43488	R688DPW	Dennis Dart SLF SFD322	Plaxton Pointer 2 10.7m	B37F	CR
43801	AO02UDM	Dennis Dart SLF SFD6B2	Alexander Pointer 2 8.8m	B29F	CF
43802	AO02UDN	Dennis Dart SLF SFD6B2	Alexander Pointer 2 8.8m	B29F	CF

43845-43848		Dennis Dart SLF SFD6BA		Alexander Pointer 2 8.8m		B29F
43845	SN55CXH	CF	43847	SN55CXJ	CF	
43846	SN55CXF	CF	43848	SN55CXE	CF	

44001-44006		Dennis E200Dart SFD511		Alexander Enviro 200 10.2m			B32F	
44001	LK57EJD	HH	44003	LK57EJF	HH	44005	LK57EJJ	HH
44002	LK57EJE	HH	44004	LK57EJG	HH	44006	LK57EJL	HH

44076-44081		Dennis E200Dart SFD551		Alexander Enviro 200 10.2m			B32F	
44076	YX58HVF	HH	44078	YX58HVH	HH	44080	YX58HVK	HH
44077	YX58HVG	HH	44079	YX58HVJ	HH	44081	YX58HVL	HH

44537-44551		ADL E20D SFD7E1		ADL Enviro 200 10.8m			B39F	
44537	YX13AEF	CF	44542	YX13AHV	CF	44547	YX13AKK	CF
44538	YX13AHN	CF	44543	YX13AHZ	CF	44548	YX13AKN	CF
44539	YX13AHO	CF	44544	YX13AKF	CF	44549	YX13AKO	CF
44540	YX13AHP	CF	44545	YX13AKG	CF	44550	YX13AKP	CF
44541	YX13AHU	CF	44546	YX13AKJ	CF	44551	YX13AKY	CF

44596	EU60LFS	Dennis E200Dart SFD3E1	Alexander Enviro 200 10.8m	B33F	CN
44597	FJ58YSL	Dennis E200Dart SFD361	Alexander Enviro 200 10.8m	B36F	CN
44598	KX57BWF	Dennis E200Dart SFD321	Alexander Enviro 200 10.8m	B37F	CN
44599	YX08HJF	Dennis E200Dart SFD361	Alexander Enviro 200 10.8m	B37F	CN

44659-44662		ADL E20D SFDBLA		ADL Enviro 200MMC 10.9m		B37F
44659	YX66WBD	CF	44661	YX66WBF	CF	
44660	YX66WBE	CF	44662	YX66WBG	CF	

44900	AY08EKT	Dennis E200Dart SFD151	Alexander Enviro 200 9.4m	B29F	CF

47521-47658		Wright Streetlite DF		Wright Streetlite 10.8m			B37F	
47521	SN64CMV	HH	47524	SN64CMZ	HH	47527	SN64CNE	HH
47522	SN64CMX	HH	47525	SN64CNA	HH	47528	SN64CNF	HH
47523	SN64CMY	HH	47526	SN64CNC	HH	47529	SN64CNJ	HH

Pictured on its way towards Chelmsford town centre is 44550, one of a batch of 15 ADL Enviro 200s new in 2013, seen on route 56 to Beaulieu Park

47530	SN64CNK	HH	47648	SN15AFK	HH	47654	SN15AEU	BN
47643	SN15AEZ	HH	47649	SN15AEL	HH	47655	SN15AEV	BN
47644	SN15AFA	HH	47650	SN15AEM	BN	47656	SN15AEW	BN
47645	SN15AFE	HH	47651	SN15AEO	BN	47657	SN15AEX	BN
47646	SN15AFF	HH	47652	SN15AEP	BN	47658	SN15AEY	BN
47647	SN15AFJ	HH	47653	SN15AET	BN			

53008	W808PAF	Optare Solo M850		Optare Solo 8.5m			B27F	CF

53112-53137		Optare Solo M920		Optare Solo 9.2m			B30F	

53112	EO02NDX	CF	53125	EO02NFG	CF	53132	EO02NFP	CF
53113	EO02NDY	CF	53126	EO02NFH	CF	53133	EO02NFR	CF
53114	EO02NDZ	CF	53127	EO02NFJ	CF	53134	EO02NFT	CF
53115	EO02NEF	CF	53128	EO02NFK	CF	53135	EO02NFU	CF
53116	EO02NEJ	CF	53129	EO02NFL	CF	53136	EO02NFV	CF
53117	EO02NEN	CF	53130	EO02NFM	CF	53137	EO02NFX	CF
53121	EO02NFC	CF	53131	EO02NFN	CF			

53138	EU54BNK	Optare Solo M950	Optare Solo 9.5m	B33F	CF
53139	EU54BNJ	Optare Solo M950	Optare Solo 9.5m	B33F	CF
62139	X618NSS	Volvo B10BLE	Wright Renown	B44F	CF
62195	X689ADK	Volvo B10BLE	Wright Renown	B43F	CF
62197	X692ADK	Volvo B10BLE	Wright Renown	B43F	CF

62407-62410		Scania L94UB		Wright Solar		B44F	

62407	YS03ZKB	CR	62409	YS03ZKG	CR
62408	YS03ZKD	CR	62410	YS03ZKF	CR

Seen in Chelmsford is First Essex 53132, an Optare Solo, seen while on route 40 to Readers and Maltings

63161-63344		Wright Streetlite Max		Wright Streetlite 11.5m			B41F	
63161	SN64CHX	HH	63170	SN64CJX	HH	63336	SM65EEU	CR
63162	SN64CHY	HH	63328	SK65PXJ	CR	63337	SM65EEV	CR
63163	SN64CHZ	HH	63329	SK65PXL	CR	63338	SM65EEW	CR
63164	SN64CJE	HH	63330	SK65PXM	CR	63339	SM65EEX	CR
63165	SN64CJF	HH	63331	SK65PXN	CR	63340	SM65EEY	CR
63166	SN64CJJ	HH	63332	SK65PXO	CR	63341	SM65EEZ	CR
63167	SN64CJO	HH	63333	SK65PXP	CR	63342	SM65EFA	CR
63168	SN64CJU	HH	63334	SK65PXR	CR	63343	SM65EFB	CR
63169	SN64CJV	HH	63335	SK65PXS	CR	63344	SM65EFC	CR

65028-65032		Scania CN94UB		Scania OmniCity			B41F	
65028	YN06TDO	CF	65030	YN06TDV	CF	65032	YN06TDZ	CF
65029	YN06TDU	CF	65031	YN06TDX	CF			

65665-65692		Scania L94UB		Wright Solar *- B44F			B43F	
65665	SN51UXX	CN	65674	SN51UYH	CR	65684	YR52VEY	CR
65666	SN51UXY	CN	65675	SN51UYJ	CN	65685	YR52VFO	CR
65667	SN51UXZ	CN	65676	SN51UYK	CN	65686	YS03ZKC	CR
65668	SN51UYA	CN	65677	SN51UYL	CR	65687*	YS03ZKG	CR
65669	SN51UYB	CN	65678	YP02ABN	CR	65688	YS03ZKH	CR
65670	SN51UYC	CN	65680	YR52VEK	CR	65689	YS03ZKJ	CR
65671	SN51UYD	CN	65681	YR52VEL	CR	65690	YS03ZKK	CN
65672	SN51UYE	CR	65682	YR52VEP	CR	65691	YS03ZKL	CN
65673	SN51UYG	CR	65683	YR52VEU	CR	65692	YS03ZKM	CN

One of five Scania Omnicity integral vehicles in the First Essex fleet, 65029 is seen entering Chelmsford Bus Station while on route 71A

| 66165 | W365EOW | Volvo B10BLE | | | Wright Renown | | | B44F | CN |
| 66179 | W379EOW | Volvo B10BLE | | | Wright Renown | | | B44F | w |

66794-66987		Volvo B7RLE			Wright Eclipse Urban			B43F	
66794	MX05CBF	CF	66804	MX05CCO	CR	66815	MX05CDV	CF	
66795	MX05CBU	CR	66806	MX05CCV	BN	66816	MX05CDY	CR	
66796	MX05CBV	w	66807	MX05CCY	CR	66817	MX05CDZ	CF	
66797	MX05CBY	CF	66808	MX05CCZ	CF	66818	MX05CEA	CR	
66798	MX05CCA	CR	66809	MX05CDE	w	66819	MX05CEF	BN	
66799	MX05CCD	CF	66810	MX05CDF	CR	66821	MX05CEK	BN	
66800	MX05CCF	CR	66811	MX05CDK	CF	66822	MX05CEO	BN	
66801	MX05CCJ	CR	66812	MX05CDN	CF	66823	MX05CEU	BN	
66802	MX05CCK	CF	66813	MX05CDO	BN	66824	MX05CEV	BN	
66803	MX05CCN	CR	66814	MX05CDU	CF	66825	MX05CEY	BN	
66826	MX05CFA	BN	66829	MX05CFG	CF	66975	KX05MGY	u	
66827	MX05CFD	BN	66830	MX05CFJ	CF				
66828	MX05CFE	CR	66837	MX05CFU	CF				

67160-67171		ADL E20D SFDDLA			ADL Enviro 200MMC 11.5m			B39F	
67160	YY66OZV	BN	67164	YY66PBF	BN	67168	YY66PBX	CF	
67161	YY66OZW	BN	67165	YY66PBO	CF	67169	YY66PBZ	CF	
67162	YY66OZX	BN	67166	YY66PBU	CF	67170	YY66PCF	CF	
67163	YY66PAO	BN	67167	YY66PBV	CF	67171	YY66PCO	CF	

67189-67197		ADL E20D SFDDPC			ADL Enviro 200MMC 11.8m			B41F	
67189	SN66WKK	CF	67190	SN66WKL	CF	67191	SN66WKM	CF	

| 67192 | SN66WKO | CF | 67194 | SN66WKR | CF | 67196 | SN66WKT | CF |
| 67193 | SN66WKP | CF | 67195 | SN66WKS | CF | 67197 | SN66WKU | CF |

New in 2005 to First Manchester but since cascaded is First Essex Buses 66826, a Wright Eclipse Urban-bodied Volvo B7RLE, is seen here in Basildon while on route 8A to Laindon

67901-67904		ADL E350H SFD111		ADL Enviro 350H 11.5m			B38F	
67901	SN13CHO	CF	67903	SN13CHX	CF			
67902	SN13CHV	CF	67904	SN13CHY	CF			

68508-68551		BMC 1100FE		BMC * - B55FL			B60F	
68508	KX54AHU	CF	68520	KP54AZU	CF	68535	EU05DXR	CF
68509	KX54AHY	CF	68531	LK54FNC	CF	68551*	EU05DXS	CF
68510	KX54ANR	CF	68532	LK54FNE	CF			

69421-69533		Volvo B7RLE		Wright Eclipse Urban			B43F	
69421	AU58FFH	CF	69431	AU58FFT	CF	69434	EU58JWZ	CF
69429	AU58FFR	CR	69432	AU58FFV	CR			
69430	AU58FFS	CR	69433	AU58FFW	CR			

69515-69520		Volvo B7RLE		Wright Eclipse Urban 2			B44F	
69515	BJ11ECN	CF	69517	BJ11ECD	CF	69519	BJ11ECV	CF
69516	BJ11ECE	CF	69518	BJ11ECT	CF	69520	BJ11ECW	CF

| 69532 | PL05UBR | Volvo B7RLE | | Wright Eclipse Urban | | B44F | CF |
| 69533 | PL05UBS | Volvo B7RLE | | Wright Eclipse Urban | | B44F | CF |

Above: *Seen outside Chelmsford Station is ADL Enviro 350H hybrid 67903, pictured while on route 42 to Galleywood*

Below: *Pictured here in Chelmsford is Wright Eclipse Urban 2-bodied Volvo B7RLE 69514, seen on Park & Ride duties for which this special black livery is carried*

69901-69919		Volvo 7900H		Volvo			B40F	
69901	BV13ZBC	BN	69908	BV13ZBN	BN	69915	BV13ZBX	BN
69902	BV13ZBD	BN	69909	BV13ZBO	BN	69916	BV13ZBY	BN
69903	BV13ZBE	BN	69910	BV13ZBP	BN	69917	BV13ZBZ	BN
69904	BV13ZBF	BN	69911	BV13ZBR	BN	69918	BV13ZCA	BN
69905	BV13ZBG	BN	69912	BV13ZBT	BN	69919	BV13ZCE	BN
69906	BV13ZBJ	BN	69913	BV13ZBU	BN			
69907	BV13ZBL	BN	69914	BV13ZBW	BN			

A second type of hybrid vehicle in the First Essex fleet is the Volvo 7900H. Seen here in Chelmsford Bus Station is 69902, one such vehicle, seen while on route 100 to Lakeside

Previous registrations

44596	J52083		69516	BJ11ECF
69515	BJ11ECE		69517	BJ11ECN

Liveries
Unless stated below, all vehicles carry FirstGroup corporate livery:
First Aircoach: 20801-20805
Allover white: 23019, 23020
Westcliff Motor Company: 33191
Aberdeen Corporation: 62139
Pier to Air: 67160-67171
Chelmsford Park & Ride: 67189-67198, 69512-69520
First Hybrid: 67901-67904, 99901-69919
Schoolbus: 68508-68510, 68520, 68531, 68532, 68535, 68551

Glasgow

Garages

BL	Blantyre - 32 Glasgow Road, Blantyre, Glasgow, G72 0LA
CA	Caledonia - 100 Cathcart Road, Glasgow, G42 7BH
D	Dumbarton - Broadmeadow Industrial Estate, Birch Road, Dumbarton, G82 2RE
O	Overtown - 5 Castlehill Road, Overtown, Glasgow, ML2 0QS
SC	Scotstoun - 1073 South Street, Glasgow, G14 0AQ

20508	AO02RCZ	Volvo B12M	Plaxton Paragon	C53F	w

| 31787-31804 | | Volvo B7TL | | Wright Eclipse Gemini | | H45/29F | |

31787	YN53EFE	BL	31795	YN53EFO	BL	31800	YN53EFV	BL
31788	YN53EFF	BL	31796	YN53EFP	BL	31801	YN53EFW	BL
31789	YN53EFG	BL	31797	YN53EFR	BL	31802	YN53EFX	BL
31793	YN53EFL	BL	31798	YN53EFT	BL	31803	YN53EFZ	BL
31794	YN53EFM	BL	31799	YN53EFU	BL	31804	YN53EGC	CA

Pictured at the exit of Buchanan Bus Station is 31788, a Wright Eclipse Gemini-bodied Volvo B7TL, seen while operating on route X11

| 32300-32305 | | Volvo B7TL | | Plaxton President | | H42/28F | |

32300	LK03NGZ	SC	32302	LK03NHB	SC	32304	LK03NHD	SC
32301	LK03NHA	SC	32303	LK03NHC	SC	32305	LK03NHE	SC

| 32543-32657 | | Volvo B7TL | | Wright Eclipse Gemini | | H45/29F | |

32543	SF54OSD	CA	32546	SF54OSJ	CA	32549	SF54OSM	CA
32544	SF54OSE	CA	32547	SF54OSK	CA	32550	SF54OSN	CA
32545	SF54OSG	CA	32548	SF54OSL	CA	32551	SF54OSO	CA

32552	SF54OSP	CA	32577	SF54OTW	CA	32602	SF54TKA	CA
32553	SF54OSR	CA	32578	SF54OTX	CA	32603	SF54TKC	CA
32554	SF54OSU	CA	32579	SF54OTY	CA	32604	SF54TKD	CA
32555	SF54OSV	SC	32580	SF54OTZ	CA	32605	SF54TKE	CA
32556	SF54OSW	CA	32581	SF54OUA	CA	32606	SF54TKJ	CA
32557	SF54OSX	CA	32582	SF54OUB	CA	32607	SF54TKK	CA
32558	SF54OSY	CA	32583	SF54OUC	CA	32608	SF54TKO	CA
32559	SF54OSZ	CA	32584	SF54OUD	CA	32609	SF54TKN	BL
32560	SF54OTA	CA	32585	SF54OUE	CA	32610	SF54TKT	CA
32561	SF54OTB	CA	32586	SF54OUG	CA	32611	SF54TKU	CA
32562	SF54OTC	CA	32587	SF54OUH	CA	32612	SF54TKV	CA
32563	SF54OTD	CA	32588	SF54OUJ	CA	32613	SF54TKX	CA
32564	SF54OTE	CA	32589	SF54OUK	SC	32614	SF54TKY	CA
32565	SF54OTG	CA	32590	SF54OUL	SC	32615	SF54TKZ	CA
32566	SF54OTH	CA	32591	SF54OUM	SC	32616	SF54TLJ	CA
32567	SF54OTJ	CA	32592	SF54OUN	SC	32617	SF54TLK	CA
32568	SF54OTK	CA	32593	SF54THV	SC	32618	SF54TLN	CA
32569	SF54OTL	CA	32594	SF54THX	SC	32619	SF54TLO	BL
32570	SF54OTM	CA	32595	SF54THZ	SC	32620	SF54TLU	BL
32571	SF54OTN	CA	32596	SF54TJO	SC	32621	SF54TLX	BL
32572	SF54OTP	CA	32597	SF54TJU	SC	32622	SF54TLY	CA
32573	SF54OTR	CA	32598	SF54TJV	CA	32623	SF54TLZ	CA
32574	SF54OTT	CA	32599	SF54TJX	CA	32624	SF54TMO	CA
32575	SF54OTU	CA	32600	SF54TJY	CA	32625	SF54TMU	CA
32576	SF54OTV	CA	32601	SF54TJZ	CA	32626	SF54TMV	CA

Painted in predominantly allover white as a special vehicle used for wedding hires is First Glasgow 32570, a Volvo B7TL with Wright Eclipse Gemini bodywork, seen about to cross the Clyde at the bottom of Jamaica Street while on route 57 to South Nitshill

32657	LK55ACO	Volvo B7TL				Wright Eclipse Gemini		H41/25F	CA

32956-33000		Dennis Trident SFD113			Plaxton President 9.9m		H39/20F		

* - H39/25F, \$ - H39/24F, % - H39/21F

32840%	T840LLC	CAt	32982	Y346NLF	BL	32991*	Y991NLP	BL
32956*	X956HLT	CA	32984	Y984NLP	BL	32992	Y992NLP	BL
32960$	X612HLT	CA	32985*	Y985NLP	CA	32993	Y993NLP	w
32969	X969HLT	CA	32986*	Y986NLP	CA	32996*	Y996NLP	CA
32977	X977HLT	CA	32987*	Y987NLP	BL	32997	Y997NLP	w
32979	Y224NLF	SC	32988*	Y988NLP	BL	32998	Y998NLP	CA
32980	X614HLT	CA	32989*	Y989NLP	BL	32999*	Y933NLP	BL
32981	X981HLT	CA	32990*	Y932NLP	BL	33000*	Y934NLP	CA

33008-33035		Dennis Trident SFD339			Plaxton President 10.5m		H42/28F		

* - H42/27F, \$ - H42/22F, % - H42/23F

33008	LK51UZF	SC	33016	LK51UYT	CA	33024$	LK51UZB	CA
33009	LK51UZG	CA	33017*	LK51UYU	CA	33025$	LK51UYF	CA
33010	LK51UZH	CA	33018	LK51UYV	CA	33026$	LK51UYG	u
33011	LK51UZJ	CA	33019	LK51UYW	CA	33027$	LK51UYH	CA
33012	LK51UZL	CA	33020$	LK51UYX	CA	33028$	LK51UYJ	CA
33013	LK51UZM	CA	33021$	LK51UYY	CA	33033$	LK51UYP	CA
33014	LK51UZN	CA	33022$	LK51UYZ	CA	33034$	LK51UYR	CA
33015	LK51UYS	CA	33023$	LK51UZA	CA	33035%	LK51UYD	CA

New in London with First Capital as TNL1025, is 33025, a Dennis Trident with Plaxton President bodywork, seen leaving the terminus of route 60 in Clydebank before turning around for its next journey

33040-33054		Dennis Trident SFD136		Plaxton President 9.9m		H39/20F

33040	LN51DWE	CA	33053	LN51GKK	CA
33046	LN51DVL	CA	33054	LN51GKL	CA

33089-33097		Dennis Trident SFD336		Plaxton President 10.5m * - H42/28F			H42/26F	
33089*	LN51GMV	CA	33093	LN51NRJ	u	33097	LN51GNZ	SC
33091	LN51GMY	CA	33094	LN51NRK	CA			
33092	LN51GMZ	CA	33096	LN51GNY	CA			

33114-33122		Dennis Trident SFD136		Plaxton President 9.9m			H39/24F	
33114	LT02NVW	CA	33117	LT02NVZ	CA	33120	LT02NWC	CA
33115	LT02NVV	CA	33118	LT02NWA	CA	33121	LT02NWD	CA
33116	LT02NVU	CA	33119	LT02NWB	CA	33122	LT02NVL	BL

33138	LT02ZFK	Dennis Trident SFD336		Plaxton President 10.5m			H42/26F	u

33343-33386		Dennis Trident SFD33G		Alexander ALX400 10.5m * - H42/26F			H42/20F	
33343	LK53EZV	CA	33354*	LK53FDA	CA	33365*	LK53EYF	CA
33344*	LK53EZW	CA	33355*	LK53EXT	CA	33366*	LK53EYG	CA
33345	LK53EZX	CA	33356*	LK53EXU	CA	33367	LK53EYH	CA
33346*	LK53EZZ	CA	33357*	LK53EXV	CA	33368*	LK53EYJ	CA
33347	LK53FCF	CA	33358	LK53EXW	CA	33369	LK53EYL	CA
33348*	LK53FCG	CA	33359	LK53EXX	CA	33370	LK53EYM	CA
33349	LK53FCJ	CA	33360*	LK53EXZ	CA	33371*	LK53EYO	CA
33350	LK53FCL	CA	33361	LK53EYA	CA	33372	LK53EYP	CA
33351*	LK53FCX	CA	33362*	LK53EYB	CA	33374	LK53EYT	CA
33352	LK53FCY	CA	33363	LK53EYC	CA	33375*	LK53EYU	CA
33353	LK53FCZ	CA	33364*	LK53EYD	CA	33386	LK53EZF	CA

Pictured in Jamaica Street, Glasgow is 33355, an Alexander ALX400-bodied Dennis Trident which started life with First London as TAL1355, seen while on route 60A to Easterhouse

33901-33923		ADL E40D SFD4DS		ADL Enviro 400 10.8m			H47/30F	
33901	SN11FOJ	SC	33909	SN11FPC	CA	33917	SN61BEO	CA
33902	SN11FOK	SC	33910	SN11FPD	CA	33918	SN61BEU	CA
33903	SN11FOM	SC	33911	SN61BDU	CA	33919	SN61BEY	CA
33904	SN11FOP	CA	33912	SN61BDV	CA	33920	SN61BFA	CA
33905	SN11FOT	CA	33913	SN61BDX	CA	33921	SN61BFE	CA
33906	SN11FOU	CA	33914	SN61BDY	CA	33922	SN61BFF	CA
33907	SN11FOV	CA	33915	SN61BDZ	CA	33923	SN61BFJ	CA
33908	SN11FPA	CA	33916	SN61BEJ	CA			

33976-33999		ADL E40D SFDB32		ADL Enviro 400MMC 10.8m			H45/29F	
33976	SN65OFR	CA	33984	SN65OFZ	CA	33992	SN65OGH	CA
33977	SN65OFS	CA	33985	SN65OGA	CA	33993	SN65OGJ	u
33978	SN65OFT	CA	33986	SN65OGB	CA	33994	SN65OGK	CA
33979	SN65OFU	CA	33987	SN65OGC	CA	33995	SN65OGL	CA
33980	SN65OFV	CA	33988	SN65OGD	CA	33996	SN65OGM	CA
33981	SN65OFW	CA	33989	SN65OGE	CA	33997	SN65OGO	CA
33982	SN65OFX	CA	33990	SN65OGF	CA	33998	SN65OGP	CA
33983	SN65OFY	CA	33991	SN65OGG	CA	33999	SN65OGR	CA

37147-37185		Volvo B7TL		Wright Eclipse Gemini			H45/29F	
37147	YN06URA	CA	37167	SF07FCV	BL	37177	SF07FDK	CA
37148	YN06URB	CA	37168	SF07FCX	BL	37178	SF07FDL	CA
37149	YN06URC	CA	37169	SF07FCY	BL	37179	SF07FDM	CA
37150	YN06URD	CA	37170	SF07FCZ	BL	37180	SF07FDN	BL
37151	YN06URE	CA	37171	SF07FDA	BL	37181	SF07FDO	BL
37152	YN06URF	CA	37172	SF07FDC	CA	37182	SF07FDP	BL
37153	YN06URG	CA	37173	SF07FDD	CA	37183	SF07FDU	BL
37154	YN06URH	CA	37174	SF07FDE	CA	37184	SF07FDV	BL
37155	YN06URJ	CA	37175	SF07FDG	CA	37185	SF07FDX	BL
37166	SF07FCP	BL	37176	SF07FDJ	CA			

37186-37751		Volvo B9TL		Wright Eclipse Gemini			H45/29F	
37186	SF07FDY	CA	37207	SF57MKD	CA	37238	YN08LCT	BL
37187	SF07FDZ	CA	37208	SF57MKG	CA	37239	YN08LCU	BL
37188	SF07FCC	CA	37209	SF57MKJ	CA	37240	YN08LCV	BL
37189	SF07FCD	CA	37210	SF57MKK	SC	37241	YN08LCW	BL
37190	SF07FCE	CA	37211	SF57MKL	SC	37242	YN08LCY	BL
37191	SF07FCG	CA	37212	SF57MKM	SC	37243	YN08LCZ	BL
37192	SF07FCJ	CA	37213	SF57MKN	SC	37244	YN08LDA	BL
37193	SF07FEG	CA	37214	SF57MKO	D	37245	YN08LDC	BL
37194	SF07FEH	CA	37215	SF57MKP	SC	37277	FJ08FYK	u
37195	SF07FEJ	CA	37216	SF57MKU	SC	37278	YN08LDD	BL
37196	SF07FEK	CA	37217	SF57MKV	SC	37530	SF08SMU	CA
37197	SF07FEM	CA	37218	SF57MKX	D	37531	SF08SMV	CA
37198	SF07FEO	CA	37219	SF57MKZ	D	37532	SF08SMX	CA
37199	SF07FCL	CA	37220	SF57MLE	D	37533	SF08SNJ	CA
37200	SF07FEP	CA	37221	SF57MLJ	D	37534	SF08SNK	CA
37201	SF07FCM	CA	37222	SF57MLK	D	37535	SF08SNN	CA
37202	SF07FCO	CA	37223	SF57MLL	D	37536	SF08SNU	CA
37203	SF07FET	CA	37224	SF57MLN	D	37537	SF08SNV	CA
37204	SF07FEU	CA	37225	SF57MLO	D	37538	SF08SNX	CA
37205	SF57MKA	CA	37226	SF57MLU	D	37539	SF08SNY	CA
37206	SF57MKC	CA	37227	SF57MLV	D	37540	SF08SNZ	CA

37541	SF58ATY	CA	37739	SF09LDK	CA	37746	SF09LDY	CA
37542	SF58ATZ	CA	37740	SF09LDL	CA	37747	SF09LDZ	CA
37543	SF58AUA	CA	37741	SF09LDN	CA	37748	SF09LEJ	CA
37544	SF58AUC	CA	37742	SF09LDO	CA	37749	SF09LEU	CA
37736	SF09LDO	CA	37743	SF09LDU	CA	37750	SF09LFA	CA
37737	SF09LDE	CA	37744	SF09LDV	CA	37751	SF09LFB	CA
37738	SF09LDJ	CA	37745	SF09LDX	CA

39101-39110		ADL E40H SFD4BU		ADL Enviro 400 10.8m			H45/30F
39101	SN61BFK	SC	39105	SN61BFP	SC	39109	SN61BFY	SC
39102	SN61BFL	SC	39106	SN61BFU	SC	39110	SN61BFZ	SC
39103	SN61BFM	SC	39107	SN61BFV	SC
39104	SN61BFO	SC	39108	SN61BFX	SC

Seen in central Glasgow is ADL Enviro 400 hybrid 39105, showing the special hybrid livery carried along with route branding for route 6, upon which it is pictured while heading for East Kilbride

| 40965 | SJ03DNY | Optare Solo M920 | | Optare Solo 9.2m | | B30F | SC |
| 40966 | SJ03DOA | Optare Solo M920 | | Optare Solo 9.2m | | B30F | SC |

41408-41422		Dennis Dart SLF SFD2B2		Marshall Capital 10.2m		B33F
41408	RG51FXE	SC	41415	LN51DWY	SC	41422	LN51DXF	SC
41410	RG51FXH	SC	41416	LN51DWZ	O
41414	LK51JYO	SC	41417	LN51DXA	SC

41446	LN51DUJ	Dennis Dart SLF SFD1B2	Marshall Capital 9.3m	B29F	SC
41447	LN51DUU	Dennis Dart SLF SFD1B2	Marshall Capital 9.3m	B29F	O
41448	LN51DUV	Dennis Dart SLF SFD1B2	Marshall Capital 9.3m	B29F	SC
41775	X511HLR	Dennis Dart SLF SFD112	Marshall Capital 9.3m	B27F	SC

| 41777 | X512HLR | Dennis Dart SLF SFD112 | Marshall Capital 9.3m | B27F | w |
| 41779 | X779HLR | Dennis Dart SLF SFD112 | Marshall Capital 9.3m | B27F | O |

A further vehicle which started life in London with First Capital as their DM775 is 41775, a Dennis Dart SLF with Marshall Capital bodywork, seen here laying over in Clydebank before taking up route M60 to Drumchapel

42885-42888		Dennis Dart SLF SFD3CA	Alexander Pointer 2 10.7m		B37F	
42885	SF05KXJ	O	42887	SF05KXL	O	
42886	SF05KXK	O	42888	SF05KXM	O	

44651-44658		ADL E20D SFDCLA	Alexander Enviro 200MMC 10.8m B37F			
44651	SN65OHR	BL	44654	SN65OHU	BL	44657	SN65OHX	BL
44652	SN65OHS	BL	44655	SN65OHV	BL	44658	SN65OHY	BL
44653	SN65OHT	BL	44656	SN65OHW	BL			

47618-47628		Wright Streetlite DF	Wright Streetlite 10.8m		B37F	
47618	SN14DZA	CA	47622	SN14DZE	CA	47626	SN14DZJ	CA
47619	SN14DZB	CA	47623	SN14DZF	CA	47627	SN14DZK	CA
47620	SN14DZC	CA	47624	SN14DZG	CA	47628	SN14DZL	CA
47621	SN14DZD	CA	47625	SN14DZH	CA			

48045	N345CJA	Volvo B6-50	Alexander Dash 9.9m	B13F	BLa

| 50461-53103 | | Optare Solo M850 | Optare Solo 8.5m | | B27F | |
			* - B26F			
50461	SJ03DPE	SC	50464	SJ03DPU	SC	53102*	EO02FLB	SC
50463	SJ03DPN	BL	50465	SJ03DPV	BL	53103*	EO02FLC	BL

Carrying a special allover blue livery for a special ScotRail link is 50463, an Optare Solo, seen passing Buchanan Bus Station while heading for Glasgow Central Station. This vehicle has since been repainted into corporate livery

53201	YJ54BSV	Optare Solo M950	Optare Solo 9.5m	B30F	SC
53202	SF05KUJ	Optare Solo M950	Optare Solo 9.5m	B30F	SC
53203	SF05KUK	Optare Solo M950	Optare Solo 9.5m	B30F	SC
53204	TU04TRU	Optare Solo M880	Optare Solo 8.8m	B29F	SC
53710	YJ09OUS	Optare Solo M780SE	Optare Solo 7.8m	B28F	BL

53751-53754		Optare Solo SR M780SE	Optare Solo 7.8m	B22F	
53751	YJ15AOW	O	53753	YJ15AOY	BL
53752	YJ15AOX	O	53754	YJ15AOZ	BL

53755	YJ66AOB	Optare Solo SR M790SE	Optare Solo 7.9m	B22F	BL
54302	YX10AXP	Volkswagen Transporter	Bluebird Tucana	B14F	BL
54304	YX10AYL	Volkswagen Transporter	Bluebird Tucana	B14F	BL

54401-54407		Fiat Ducato	Bluebird Orion	B16F			
54401	YX12CHK	O	54404	YX12CJF	CA	54407	YX12CJU CA
54402	YX12CHL	CA	54405	YX12CJJ	CA		
54403	YX12CHU	CA	54406	YX12CJO	CA		

60464	G609NWA	Volvo B10M-55	Alexander PS	B34F	wt
60466	G613NWA	Volvo B10M-55	Alexander PS	B51F	CAt
61028	T427GUG	Scania L94UB	Wright Floline	B42F	wt

Having spent a large part of its life on the streets of Sheffield, First Glasgow 60466, an Alexander PS-bodied Volvo B10M-55 now finds itself as a driver trainer, seen in central Glasgow while on training duties

61217-61232		Scania L94UB			Wright Solar			B43F	
61217	YM52UVO	u		61223	YM52UVW	CA	61231	YM52UWJ	u
61218	YM52UVP	u		61228	YM52UWF	u	61232	YM52UWK	u

61306	SJ51DJZ	Volvo B7L	Wright Eclipse	B41F	SC
61478	P106MFS	Scania L113CRL	Wright Axcess-ultralow	B47F	CAt

61587-61596		Volvo B7L			Wright Eclipse			B41F	
61587	SA02BZD	SC		61590	SA02BZG	SC	61593	SA02BZK	SC
61588	SA02BZE	SC		61591	SA02BZH	SC	61595	SA02BZM	SC
61589	SA02BZF	SC		61592	SA02BZJ	SC	61596	SA02BZN	CA

61597-61614		Volvo B10BLE			Wright Renown			B44F	
61597	SF51YAA	BL		61603	SF51YAK	O	61609	SF51YAY	D
61598	SF51YAD	BL		61604	SF51YAO	D	61610	SF51YBA	O
61599	SF51YAE	BL		61605	SF51YAU	D	61611	SF51YBB	D
61600	SF51YAG	BL		61606	SF51YAV	D	61612	SF51YBC	D
61601	SF51YAH	BL		61607	SF51YAW	D	61613	SF51YBD	D
61602	SF51YAJ	O		61608	SF51YAX	D	61614	SF51YBE	D

61615	SF51YBG	Volvo B7L	Wright Eclipse	B41F	CA

61616-61626		Volvo B10BLE			Wright Renown			B44F	
61616	SF51YBH	D		61620	SF51YBM	O	61624	SF51YBR	O
61617	SF51YBJ	D		61621	SF51YBN	O	61625	SF51YBS	BL
61618	SF51YBK	O		61622	SF51YBO	O	61626	SF51YBT	O
61619	SF51YBL	O		61623	SF51YBP	O			

61627-61651		Volvo B7L		Wright Eclipse			B41F	
61627	SH51MHY	CA	61637	SJ51DHE	CA	61646	SJ51DHV	CA
61628	SH51MHZ	CA	61640	SJ51DHK	CA	61647	SJ51DHX	CA
61629	SH51MJE	CA	61641	SJ51DHL	CA	61648	SJ51DHZ	CA
61630	SH51MJF	CA	61642	SJ51DHM	CA	61649	SJ51DJD	CA
61632	SH51MKG	CA	61643	SJ51DHN	CA	61650	SJ51DJE	CA
61634	SH51MKK	CA	61644	SJ51DHO	CA	61651	SJ51DJF	CA
61635	SH51MKL	CA	61645	SJ51DHP	CA			

61652	SJ51DJK	Volvo B10BLE	Wright Renown	B44F	O
61653	SJ51DJO	Volvo B10BLE	Wright Renown	B44F	O
61654	SJ51DJU	Volvo B10BLE	Wright Renown	B44F	O

61656-61664		Volvo B7L		Wright Eclipse			B41F	
61656	SJ51DJX	CA	61659	SJ51DKD	CA	61663	SJ51DKL	CA
61657	SJ51DJY	CA	61660	SJ51DKE	CA	61664	SJ51DKN	CA
61658	SJ51DKA	CA	61661	SJ51DKF	CA			

61669-61695		Scania L94UB		Wright Floline			B43F	
				* - B20F, $ - B18F				
61669	V118FSF	CAt	61677$	X426UMS	CAt	61695	X448UMS	SCt
61676*	X425UMS	BLt	61682*	X433UMS	BLt			

61705-61710		Volvo B10BLE		Wright Renown			B44F	
61705	Y301RTD	O	61707	Y303RTD	O	61709	Y307RTD	O
61706	Y302RTD	O	61708	Y304RTD	O	61710	Y949RTD	O

63224-63240		Wright Streetlite Max		Wright Streetlite 11.5m			B41F	
63224	SN14DYB	BL	63230	SN14DYJ	BL	63236	SN14DYU	BL
63225	SN14DYC	BL	63231	SN14DYM	BL	63237	SN14DYV	BL
63226	SN14DYD	BL	63232	SN14DYO	BL	63238	SN14DYW	BL
63227	SN14DYF	BL	63233	SN14DYP	BL	63239	SN14DYX	BL
63228	SN14DYG	BL	63234	SN14DYS	BL	63240	SN14DYY	BL
63229	SN14DYH	BL	63235	SN14DYT	BL			

65693-65758		Scania L94UB		Wright Solar			B43F	
65693	SN53KHH	CA	65700	SN04CKY	u	65756	SK02ZYH	CA
65696	SN53KHL	CA	65703	SN04CNK	u	65757	SN03CLX	CA
65697	SN53KHM	CA	65755	SK02ZYG	CA	65758	SN03CLY	CA

66281	Y181BGB	Volvo B10BLE	Wright Renown	B44F	O
66282	Y182BGB	Volvo B10BLE	Wright Renown	B44F	O
66349	MV02VDZ	Volvo B7L	Wright Eclipse	B41F	CA

66735-66991		Volvo B7RLE		Wright Eclipse Urban			B43F	
				* - B40F				
66735	WX54XCW	BL	66947	WX55TZJ	SC	66955	WX55TZS	O
66736	WX54XCY	BL	66948	WX55TZK	BL	66988	SF56GYP	BL
66737	WX54XCZ	BL	66949	WX55TZL	SC	66989	SF56GYR	SC
66770*	YJ05VVN	BL	66951	WX55TZN	BL	66990	SF56GYS	SC
66771*	YJ05VVO	BL	66952	WX55TZO	BL	66991	SF56GYT	BL
66946	WX55TZH	BL	66954	WX55TZR	O			

Above: *About to cross the Clyde on Crown street is 63231, a Wright Streetlite Max, pictured while on route 267 to Hamilton Bus Station*

Below: *At the same location is 65755, a Wright Solar-bodied Scania L94UB, while on route 7A to Cambuslang*

67041-67083		ADL E20D SFDDLA		ADL Enviro 200MMC 11.5m			B41F	
67041	SN65OGT	BL	67056	SN65ZDU	O	67071	SN65ZFK	CA
67042	SN65OGU	BL	67057	SN65ZDV	O	67072	SN65ZFL	CA
67043	SN65OGV	BL	67058	SN65ZDW	O	67073	SN65ZFM	CA
67044	SN65OGW	BL	67059	SN65ZDX	O	67074	SN65ZFO	CA
67045	SN65OGX	BL	67060	SN65ZDY	O	67075	SN65ZFP	CA
67046	SN65OGY	BL	67061	SN65ZDZ	O	67076	SN65ZFR	CA
67047	SN65OGZ	O	67062	SN65ZFA	O	67077	SN65ZFS	CA
67048	SN65OHA	O	67063	SN65ZFB	O	67078	SN65ZFT	CA
67049	SN65ZDL	O	67064	SN65ZFC	O	67079	SN65ZFU	CA
67050	SN65ZDM	O	67065	SN65ZFD	CA	67080	SN65ZFV	CA
67051	SN65ZDO	O	67066	SN65ZFE	CA	67081	SN65ZFW	CA
67052	SN65ZDP	O	67067	SN65ZFF	CA	67082	SN65ZFX	CA
67053	SN65ZDR	O	67068	SN65ZFG	CA	67083	SN65ZFY	CA
67054	SN65ZDS	O	67069	SN65ZFH	CA			
67055	SN65ZDT	O	67070	SN65ZFJ	CA			

67096-67105		ADL E20D SFDDWC		ADL Enviro 200MMC 11.8m			B32F	
67096	SN16OSC	CA	67100	SN16OSG	CA	67104	SN16OSM	CA
67097	SN16OSD	CA	67101	SN16OSJ	CA	67105	SN16OSO	CA
67098	SN16OSE	CA	67102	SN16OSK	CA			
67099	SN16OSF	CA	67103	SN16OSL	CA			

Pictured in central Glasgow is 67733, an ADL Enviro 300, seen while operating on route 1A to Balloch, a route for which special route branding is carried

67711-67894		ADL E30D SFD1C8		ADL Enviro 300 11.5m			B41F	
67711	SN62ABU	D	67713	SN62ABX	D	67715	SN62ACX	D
67712	SN62ABV	D	67714	SN62ABZ	D	67716	SN62ACZ	D

67717	SN62ADU	D	67744	SN62AMV	SC	67823	SN13ECC	SC
67718	SN62ADV	D	67749	SN62AOF	SC	67824	SN13ECD	SC
67719	SN62AEA	D	67750	SN62AOG	SC	67825	SN13ECF	SC
67720	SN62AEF	SC	67766	SN13CGF	SC	67826	SN13ECJ	SC
67721	SN62AEK	SC	67767	SN13CGG	SC	67827	SN13ECT	SC
67722	SN62AET	D	67768	SN13CGK	SC	67828	SN13ECV	SC
67723	SN62AEU	D	67769	SN13CGO	SC	67829	SN13ECW	SC
67724	SN62AEY	D	67770	SN13CGU	SC	67830	SN13ECX	SC
67725	SN62AFE	D	67771	SN13CGV	CA	67831	SN13ECY	SC
67726	SN62AFJ	D	67772	SN13CGX	CA	67832	SN13ECZ	SC
67727	SN62AFK	D	67806	SN13EAY	SC	67833	SN13EDC	BL
67728	SN62AFU	D	67807	SN13EBA	SC	67834	SN13EDF	BL
67729	SN62AFY	D	67808	SN13EBC	SC	67835	SN13EDJ	BL
67730	SN62AFZ	D	67809	SN13EBD	SC	67836	SN13EDK	BL
67731	SN62AGV	D	67810	SN13EBF	SC	67837	SN13EDL	BL
67732	SN62AGY	D	67811	SN13EBG	SC	67838	SN13EDO	BL
67733	SN62AHD	D	67812	SN13EBJ	SC	67839	SN13EDP	BL
67734	SN62AHF	D	67813	SN13EBK	SC	67840	SN13EDR	BL
67735	SN62AHL	D	67814	SN13EBL	SC	67841	SN13EDU	BL
67736	SN62AHV	D	67815	SN13EBM	SC	67842	SN13EDV	BL
67737	SN62AHX	D	67816	SN13EBO	SC	67843	SN13EDX	BL
67738	SN62AJU	D	67817	SN13EBP	SC	67844	SN13EEF	BL
67739	SN62AJV	D	67818	SN13EBU	SC	67845	SN13EEG	BL
67740	SN62AKG	D	67819	SN13EBV	SC	67846	SN13EEH	BL
67741	SN62AKJ	SC	67820	SN13EBX	SC	67847	SN13EEJ	BL
67742	SN62AKO	SC	67821	SN13EBZ	SC	67848	SN13EEM	BL
67743	SN62AKP	SC	67822	SN13ECA	SC	67849	SN13EEO	BL

Pictured in central Glasgow is 67803, an ADL Enviro 300, seen while operating on route 6 to East Kilbride, complete with "simpliCITY" branding above the windows

67850	SN13EEP	BL	67865	SN13EFG	SC	67880	SN63MZD	SC
67851	SN13EES	BL	67866	SN13EFH	SC	67881	SN63MZE	SC
67852	SN13EET	BL	67867	SN13EFJ	SC	67882	SN63MZF	SC
67853	SN13EEU	BL	67868	SN13EFK	SC	67883	SN63MZG	SC
67854	SN13EEV	BL	67869	SN13EFL	SC	67884	SK63ATY	SC
67855	SN13EEW	BL	67870	SN63MYP	SC	67885	SK63ATZ	SC
67856	SN13EEX	BL	67871	SN63MYR	SC	67886	SK63AUA	SC
67857	SN13EEY	BL	67872	SN63MYS	SC	67887	SK63AUC	SC
67858	SN13EEZ	BL	67873	SN63MYT	SC	67888	SK63AUE	SC
67859	SN13EFA	BL	67874	SN63MYU	SC	67889	SK63AUF	SC
67860	SN13EFB	BL	67875	SN63MYV	SC	67890	SK63AUG	SC
67861	SN13EFC	BL	67876	SN63MYW	SC	67891	SK63AUJ	SC
67862	SN13EFD	BL	67877	SN63MYX	SC	67892	SK63AUL	SC
67863	SN13EFE	BL	67878	SN63MYY	SC	67893	SK63AUM	SC
67864	SN13EFF	SC	67879	SN63MYZ	SC	67894	SK63AUN	SC

69014-69298		Volvo B7RLE		Wright Eclipse Urban * B38F			B43F	
69014	SF55UAG	O	69074	SF06GXX	SC	69106	SF06GZR	SC
69015	SF55UAH	O	69075	SF06GXY	SC	69107	SF06GZS	SC
69016	SF55UAJ	O	69076	SF06GXZ	O	69108	SF06GZT	SC
69019	SF55UAM	O	69077	SF06GYA	O	69109	SF06GZV	SC
69021	SF55UAO	O	69078	SF06GYJ	SC	69111	SF06GZX	SC
69027	SF55UAV	CA	69079	SF06GYK	SC	69112	SF06GZY	SC
69034	SF55UBU	O	69080	SF06GYN	SC	69113	SF06GZZ	SC
69035	SF55UBV	O	69081	SF06GYO	SC	69114	SF06HAA	SC
69036	SF55UBW	O	69082	SF06GYP	SC	69115	SF06HAE	SC
69037	SF55UBX	O	69083	SF06GYR	SC	69116	SF06HAO	SC
69038	SF06GXJ	O	69084	SF06GYS	SC	69117	SF06HAU	SC
69039	SF06GXG	SC	69085	SF06GYT	SC	69118	SF06HAX	SC
69040	SF06GKX	CA	69086	SF06GYU	SC	69119	SF06HBA	SC
69041	SF06GXL	O	69087	SF06GYV	u	69120	SF06HBB	SC
69042	SF55UBB	CA	69088	SF06GYW	SC	69121	SF06HBC	SC
69057	SF06GXM	CA	69089	SF06GYX	SC	69181	MX06YXN	CA
69058	SF06GXN	CA	69090	SF06GYY	SC	69182	MX06YXO	CA
69059	SF06GXH	CA	69091	SF06GYZ	SC	69183	MX06YXP	CA
69060	SF06GXO	CA	69092	SF06GZA	SC	69184	MX06YXR	CA
69061	SF06GXP	CA	69093	SF06GZB	CA	69187	MX56ACZ	CA
69062	SF06GXR	CA	69094	SF06GZC	SC	69188	MX56ADO	CA
69063	SF06GXS	CA	69095	SF06GZD	SC	69189	MX56ADU	CA
69064	SF06GXT	CA	69096	SF06GZE	SC	69190	MX56ADV	CA
69065	SF06GXU	CA	69097	SF06GZG	SC	69191	MX56ADZ	CA
69066	SF06GYB	CA	69098	SF06GZH	SC	69192	MX56AEA	CA
69067	SF06GYC	CA	69099	SF06GZJ	SC	69193	MX56AEC	CA
69068	SF06GYD	CA	69100	SF06GZK	SC	69194	MX56AEB	CA
69069	SF06GYE	CA	69101	SF06GZL	SC	69295*	SF04HXW	BL
69070	SF06GYG	CA	69102	SF06GZM	SC	69296*	SF04HXX	BL
69071	SF06GYH	CA	69103	SF06GZN	SC	69297*	SF04ZPE	BL
69072	SF06GXV	SC	69104	SF06GZO	SC	69298*	SF04ZPG	BL
69073	SF06GXW	SC	69105	SF06GZP	SC			

Seen in Jamaica Street is 69098, a Wright Eclipse Urban-bodied Volvo B7RLE, pictured while on route 9 to Paisley

Previous registrations

41408	809DYE	41410	811DYE

Liveries

Unless stated below, all vehicles in this fleet carry FirstGroup corporate livery:

First Coaching: 20508

Allover white: 32555, 32570, 61028, 61478, 61669, 61676, 61677, 61682

First Hybrid (silver with pink skirt): 33901, 33903-33905, 33908-33910, 33913-33919, 33921-33923, 39101-39110

SPT MyBus- 53710, 53751-53755, 54302, 54304, 54307, 54401-54407

First Training: 60464, 60466, 61217, 61223

Glasgow Airport Express: 67096-67105

Hampshire & Dorset

Garages

ER	Southampton - Empress Road, Southampton SO14 0JW
HA	Hilsea - London Road, Portsmouth, PO2 9RP
HD	Hoeford - Gosport Road, Fareham, PO16 0ST
WH	Weymouth - Edward Street, Weymouth, DT4 7DP

20417	P177NAK	Volvo B10M-62	Plaxton Premiere 350	C53F	HDt
20418	P176NAK	Volvo B10M-62	Plaxton Premiere 350	C53F	HDt
20457	R813HWS	Volvo B10M-62	Plaxton Expressliner 2	C46FT	HDt
20550	CU04AYP	Volvo B12B	Plaxton Paragon	C49FT	u
20551	CU04AYS	Volvo B12B	Plaxton Paragon	C49FT	ER

32031-32046		Volvo B7TL	Alexander ALX400		H49/29F
			* - PO49/29F		

32031	W801EOW	WH	32035	W805EOW	WH	32043	W813EOW	WH
32032	W802EOW	WH	32036*	W806EOW	WH	32045	W815EOW	WH
32033	W803COW	WH	32038	W808EOW	ER	32046	W816EOW	WH
32034	W804EOW	WH	32039	W809EOW	WH			

Seen in Southampton is 32038 in the First Hampshire fleet, an Alexander ALX400-bodied Volvo B7TL, pictured while on a special service heading for Weston

32701-32708		Dennis Trident SFD313		East Lancs Lolyne 10.5m			H49/30F	
32701	V701FFB	HD	32704	W704PHT	ER	32707	W707PHT	HD
32702	W702PHT	HD	32705	W705PHT	ER	32708	W708PHT	HD
32703	W703PHT	HD	32706	W706PHT	ER			

32763-32768		Dennis Trident SFD338		E Lancs Myllenium Lolyne 10.5m			H49/30F	
32763	WJ55CSF	HD	32765	WJ55CSU	HD	32767	WJ55CTE	HD
32764	WJ55CSO	HD	32766	WJ55CSV	WH	32768	WJ55CTF	HD

32801-32887		Dennis Trident SFD113		Plaxton President 9.9m			H39/21F	
32801	T801LLC	HD	32810	T810LLC	ER	32850	T850LLC	WH
32804	T804LLC	WH	32847	T847LLC	ER	32855	V855HBY	HD
32809	T809LLC	ER	32849	T849LLC	HD	32887	V887HBY	WH

33001	LK51UZO	Dennis Trident SFD339	Plaxton President 10.5m	H43/28F	HD
33002	LK51UZP	Dennis Trident SFD339	Plaxton President 10.5m	H43/28F	HD

33056-33183		Dennis Trident SFD136		Plaxton President 9.9m			H39/24F	
				* - H39/21F, $ - H39/23F, % - H39/22F				
33056*	LN51GKP	ER	33143	LR02LWY	HD	33153$	LR02LXM	u
33057*	LN51GJJ	ER	33144	LR02LWZ	HD	33180	LR02LYZ	u
33058*	LN51GJK	ER	33145$	LR02LXA	ER	33182	LR02LZB	u
33141$	LR02LWW	u	33147	LR02LXC	ER	33183%	LR02LZC	u
33142$	LR02LWX	HD	33148	LR02LXG	ER			

33895	SN14TPZ	ADL E40D SFD4DS	ADL Enviro 400 10.8m	H45/29F	HD
33896	SN14TRV	ADL E40D SFD4DS	ADL Enviro 400 10.8m	H45/29F	HD
33897	SN14TRX	ADL E40D SFD4DS	ADL Enviro 400 10.8m	H45/29F	HD
34079	P579EFL	Volvo Olympian	NC Palatine 1	H49/33F	ER
34258	N528LHG	Volvo Olympian	NC Palatine 1	PO48/27D	WH

Due to building work at The Hard bus station in Portsmouth a diversion requiring a sharp left turn opposite the old bus station was in operation. Performing this manoeuvre is ADL Enviro 400 33796, showing the special Portsmouth Park & Ride livery carried by this vehicle

36001-36006		Scania N94UD		East Lancs Omnidekka			H43/26F	
36001	YN04GNV	WH	36003	YN04GNY	WH	36005	YN04GLV	WH
36002	YN04GNX	WH	36004	YN04GNZ	WH	36006	YN05HGA	WH

37161-37165		Volvo B7TL		Wright Eclipse Gemini			H45/29F	
37161	HY07FTA	HD	37163	HY07FSZ	ER	37165	HY07FSX	ER
37162	HY07FSV	ER	37164	HY07FSU	ER			

37580-37586		Volvo B9TL		Wright Eclipse Gemini			H45/29F	
37580	HX08DHL	WH	37583	HX08DHE	WH	37586	HX08DHJ	WH
37581	HX08DHF	WH	37584	HX08DHG	WH			
37582	HX08DHK	WH	37585	HX08DHY	WH			

Leaving Exeter Bus Station is Wright Eclipse Gemini-bodied Volvo B7TL 37580 with branding for the Jurassic Coast service. It is about to operate a short working on route X53 to Seaton

39920	L650SEU	Volvo Olympian	NC Palatine 2	O47/29F	w
42728	T728REU	Dennis Dart SLF SFD322	Plaxton Pointer 2 10.7m	B37F	HD
42953	WX06OMK	Dennis Dart SLF SFD3CA	Alexander Pointer 2 10.7m	B37F	WH

44507-44510		Dennis E200Dart SFD361		Alexander Enviro 200 10.8m		B35F	
44507	YX58HWF	HA	44509	YX58HWH	HA		
44508	YX58HWG	HA	44510	YX58HWJ	HA		

44916-44921		Dennis E200Dart SFD151		Alexander Enviro 200 9.4m		B28F	
44916	YX09AHC	HA	44918	YX09AHE	HA	44920	YX09AHG	HA
44917	YX09AHD	HA	44919	YX09AHF	HA	44921	YX09ADU	HA

47409-47695		Wright Streetlite DF		Wright Streetlite 10.8m			B37F	
47409	SK63KLM	WH	47574	SN14EBJ	HA	47601	SN14FFE	ER
47410	SK63KLO	WH	47575	SN14EBK	HA	47602	SN14FFG	ER
47411	SK63KLP	HA	47576	SN14EBL	HA	47603	SN14FFH	ER
47412	SK63KLS	HA	47577	SN14EBM	HA	47604	SN14FFJ	ER
47413	SK63KLU	HD	47578	SN14EBO	HA	47605	SN14FFK	ER
47414	SK63KLV	HD	47579	SN14EBP	HA	47606	SN14FFL	ER
47415	SK63KLX	HA	47580	SN14EBU	HA	47607	SN14FFM	ER
47416	SK63KLZ	HD	47581	SN14EBV	HD	47608	SN14FFO	ER
47417	SK63KMA	HA	47582	SN14EBX	HD	47609	SN14FFP	ER
47418	SK63KME	HA	47583	SN14EBZ	HD	47610	SN14FFR	ER
47419	SK63KMF	ER	47584	SN14ECA	HD	47611	SN14FFS	ER
47420	SK63KMG	ER	47585	SN14ECC	HD	47612	SN14FFT	ER
47421	SK63KMJ	ER	47586	SN14ECD	HD	47670	SN15ACX	ER
47422	SK63KMM	ER	47587	SN14ECE	HD	47671	SN15ACY	ER
47423	SK63KMO	ER	47588	SN14ECF	HD	47672	SN15ACZ	ER
47424	SK63KMU	ER	47589	SN14ECJ	HD	47686	SL15RVZ	ER
47425	SK63KMV	ER	47590	SN14ECT	HD	47687	SL15RWE	ER
47426	SK63KMX	ER	47591	SN14ECV	HA	47688	SL15RWF	ER
47427	SK63KMY	ER	47592	SN14ECW	HD	47689	SL15RWJ	ER
47428	SK63KMZ	ER	47593	SN14ECX	HD	47690	SL15RWK	ER
47429	SK63KNA	ER	47594	SN14ECY	HD	47691	SL15RWN	ER
47430	SK63KNB	ER	47595	SN14FEU	ER	47692	SL15RWO	ER
47431	SK63KNC	HA	47596	SN14FEV	ER	47693	SL15RWU	ER
47432	SK63KND	HA	47597	SN14FEX	ER	47694	SL15RWV	ER
47433	SK63KNE	HA	47598	SN14FFA	ER	47695	SL15RWW	ER
47434	SK63KNF	HA	47599	SN14FFC	ER			
47573	SN14EBG	HA	47600	SN14FFD	ER			

Previous page: *Seen in Southampton city centre is 47602, a Wright Streetlite DF allocated to Southampton, pictured at the terminus of route 2. This vehicle carries the City Red Southampton local livery*

53065	YJ58CEV	Optare Solo M950	Optare Solo 9.5m	B28F	HA
53140	YJ05XOP	Optare Solo M850	Optare Solo 8.5m	B26F	HA
53151	YN03ZVW	Optare Solo M920	Optare Solo 9.2m	B26F	HD
53206	T77TRU	Optare Solo M950	Optare Solo 9.5m	B33F	HA

53601-53615	Optare Solo SR M970	Optare Solo SR 9.7m	B35F

53601	YJ14BKA	HD	53606	YJ14BKK	HD	53611	YJ14BVB	WH
53602	YJ14BKD	HD	53607	YJ14BKL	HD	53612	YJ14BVC	WH
53603	YJ14BKE	HD	53608	YJ14BKN	HD	53613	YJ14BVD	WH
53604	YJ14BKF	HD	53609	YJ14BKO	HD	53614	YJ14BVE	WH
53605	YJ14BKG	HD	53610	YJ14BVA	WH	53615	YJ14BVF	WH

Pictured in the outskirts of Weymouth is Optare Solo SR 53611 in the First Hampshire fleet, seen here while on route 8 to Chickerell

60164	S651RNA	Scania L94UB	Wright Floline	B40F	u
60337	N542WWR	Volvo B10B-58	Wright Endurance	DP50F	HDt
62200	X695ADK	Volvo B10BLE	Wright Renown	B43F	HD

62209-62225	Volvo B10BLE	Alexander ALX300	B44F

62209	W597RFS	HD	62219	W601RFS	u
62210	W598RFS	HD	62225	W607RFS	u

63042-63312	Wright Streetlite Max	Wright Streetlite 11.5m	B41F

63042	SK63KHT	HA	63044	SK63KHV	HA	63046	SK63KHX	HA
63043	SK63KHU	HA	63045	SK63KHW	HA	63047	SK63KHY	HA

63048	SK63KHZ	HA	63065	SK63KKF	HA	63296	SN65OKW	HD
63049	SK63KJA	HA	63066	SK63KKG	HA	63297	SN65OKX	HD
63050	SK63KJE	HA	63067	SK63KKH	HA	63298	SN65OKZ	HD
63051	SK63KJF	HA	63109	SM13NCU	HA	63299	SN65OLA	HD
63052	SK63KJJ	HA	63110	SM13NCV	HA	63300	SN65OLB	HD
63053	SK63KJN	HA	63181	SN14DWZ	WH	63301	SN65OLC	HD
63054	SK63KJO	HA	63182	SN14DXA	WH	63302	SN65OLE	HD
63055	SK63KJU	HA	63183	SN14DXB	WH	63303	SN65OLG	HD
63056	SK63KJV	HA	63184	SN14DXC	WH	63304	SN65OLH	HD
63057	SK63KJX	HA	63185	SN14DXD	WH	63305	SN65OLJ	HD
63058	SK63KJY	HA	63186	SN14DXE	WH	63306	SN65OLK	HD
63059	SK63KJZ	HA	63187	SN14DXF	WH	63307	SN65OLM	HD
63060	SK63KKA	HA	63188	SN14DXG	WH	63308	SN65OLO	HD
63061	SK63KKB	HA	63189	SN14DXH	WH	63309	SN65OLP	HD
63062	SK63KKC	HA	63190	SN14EBC	HA	63310	SN65OLR	HD
63063	SK63KKD	HA	63191	SN14EBD	HA	63311	SN65OLT	HD
63064	SK63KKE	HA	63192	SN14EBF	HA	63312	SN65OLU	HD

Just leaving Fareham Bus Station is Wright Streetlite Max 63302, seen while heading for Southampton on route X5. This picture also shows the special Solent Ranger livery carried by this vehicle

64005-64018		Mercedes-Benz O530		Mercedes-Benz Citaro			B40F	
64005	OIG6949	ER	64014	OIG6944	ER	64017	OIG6947	ER
64012	OIG6942	ER	64015	OIG6945	ER	64018	OIG6948	ER
64013	OIG6943	ER	64016	OIG6946	ER			

65006-65025		Scania CN94UB		Scania OmniCity			B41F	
65006	YN54NZA	HD	65009	YN54NZE	HD	65012	YN54NZH	HD
65007	YN54NZC	HD	65010	YN54NZF	HD	65013	YN54NZJ	HD
65008	YN54NZD	HD	65011	YN54NZG	HD	65014	YN54NZK	HD

65015	YN54NZM	HD	65019	YN54NZT	HD	65023	YN54NZX	HD
65016	YN54NZO	HD	65020	YN54NZU	HD	65024	YN54NZY	HD
65017	YN54NZP	HD	65021	YN54NZV	HD	65025	YN54NZZ	HD
65018	YN54NZR	HD	65022	YN54NZW	HD			

Seen in Southampton City Centre on route 12 is First Hampshire 64017, a Mercedes-Benz Citaro which started life in Berkshire with First BeeLine

66122-66197		Volvo B10BLE		Wright Renown * - B44F			B41F	
66122	S122UOT	w	66154	S354NPO	w	66181*	W381EOW	w
66152	S352NPO	w	66164*	W364EOW	w	66197	S797RWG	w
66153	S353NPO	w	66176*	W376EOW	t			

67172-67188		ADL E20D SFDDLA		ADL Enviro 200MMC 11.3m			B39F	
67172	YX66WBJ	HD	67178	YX66WBT	HD	67184	YX66WCA	HD
67173	YX66WBL	HD	67179	YX66WBU	HD	67185	YX66WCC	HD
67174	YX66WBM	HD	67180	YX66WBV	HD	67186	YX66WCD	HD
67175	YX66WBN	HD	67181	YX66WBW	HD	67187	YX66WCE	HD
67176	YX66WBO	HD	67182	YX66WBY	HD	67188	YX66WCG	HD
67177	YX66WBP	HD	67183	YX66WBZ	HD			

68301	BX55NZV	Autosan Eagle A1012T		Autosan			B67FL	ER
68302	BX06NZT	Autosan Eagle A1012T		Autosan			B67FL	ER

68511-68565		BMC 1100FE		BMC * - B60F, % - B47FL			B55FL	
68511*	RX54AOV	ER	68536*	LK54FNF	ER	68553	HX05BUJ	ER
68512*	RX54AOY	u	68537*	LK54FNH	ER	68554	LK05FCE	ER
68533*	LK54FNJ	HD	68550	HX05BUO	ER	68557*	MX55NWD	ER

| 68562% | HX55AOH | t | 68564 | SF55TXA | HD |
| 68563% | HX55AOK | HDt | 68565 | SF55TXB | ER |

69245-69401		Volvo B7RLE		Wright Eclipse Urban * - B44F			B41F	
69245*	YJ07WFM	ER	69388	HY09AOT	ER	69395	HY09AZF	ER
69246*	YJ07WFN	ER	69389	HY09AUO	ER	69396	HY09AZO	ER
69247*	YJ07WFO	ER	69390	HY09AOS	ER	69397	HY09AZL	ER
69248*	YJ07WFP	ER	69391	HY09AUV	ER	69398	HY09AUX	ER
69385	HY09AJV	ER	69392	HY09AOR	ER	69399	HY09AZN	ER
69386	HY09AZB	ER	69393	HY09AZD	ER	69400	HY09AZJ	ER
69387	HY09AUW	ER	69394	HY09AZC	ER	69401	HY09AZG	HA

Seen in Fareham Bus Station is 69551, a Wright Eclipse Urban 2-bodied Volvo B7RLE, showing the special Eclipse livery carried for a rapid bus link service between Gosport and Fareham. This batch of vehicles has recently been replaced on this service by a new batch of Enviro 200MMCs

69444-69555		Volvo B7RLE		Wright Eclipse Urban 2 * B43F			B42F	
69444*	WX59BYW	u	69544	BF12KWD	WH	69551	BF12KWN	HD
69445*	WX59BYY	u	69545	BF12KWC	WH	69552	BF12KWP	HD
69537	BF63HDN	HA	69546	BF12KWL	WH	69553	BF12KWM	HD
69538	BF63HDU	HD	69547	BF12KWH	HD	69554	BF12KWS	HD
69539	BF63HDO	HD	69548	BF12KWJ	HD	69555	BF12KWR	HD
69542	BF12KWE	WH	69549	BF12KWK	HD			
69543	BF12KWG	WH	69550	BF12KWO	HD			

Previous registrations

64005	LT02NUB	64015	LT52WXN
64012	LT52WXA	64016	LT52WXO
64013	LT52WXB	64017	LT52WXP
64014	LT52WXL	64018	LK03LNE

Liveries

Unless stated below, all vehicles in this fleet carry FirstGroup corporate livery;
Allover white: 20417, 20418, 20457, 20551
Jurassic Coaster: 32036, 36001-36004, 37580-37584
Atlantic Connection: 32766, 32767
Portsmouth Park & Ride: 33895-33897, 37161
City Red: 47419-47430, 47595-47612, 47672, 47686-47695, 69386-69399, 69401
The Star: 63042-63067
Solent Ranger: 63296-63310
Eclipse: 67172-67188, 69542-69555
Schoolbus: 68301, 68302, 68511, 68512, 68533, 68536, 68537, 68550, 68553, 68554, 68557, 68562-68565

Pictured here in Weymouth is First Hampshire 39920, an open-top converted Northern Counties Palatine 2-bodied Volvo Olympian which was new in Bristol, seen while on sightseeing route 501 to Portland Bill. This vehicle has since left the fleet.

Leicester

32643-32646		Volvo B7TL			Wright Eclipse Gemini		H45/29F
32643	KP54AZF	LE		32645	KP54AZJ	LE	
32644	KP54AZG	LE		32646	KP54AZL	LE	

Pictured here at Woburn for the 2015 Showbus rally is First Leicester 32646, a Wright Eclipse Gemini-bodied Volvo B7TL, showing the commemorating Leicester City Transport livery carried

35151-35192		Wright Streetdeck			Wright Streetdeck		H45/28F
35151	SN65OKC	LE	35173	SK16GUF	LE	35183	SK16GVD	LE
35152	SN65OKD	LE	35174	SK16GUG	LE	35184	SK16GVE	LE
35153	SN65OKE	LE	35175	SK16GUH	LE	35185	SK16GVF	LE
35154	SN65OKF	LE	35176	SK16GUJ	LE	35186	SK16GVG	LE
35155	SN65OKG	LE	35177	SK16GUO	LE	35187	SK16GVJ	LE
35168	SK16GTZ	LE	35178	SK16GUU	LE	35188	SK16GVL	LE
35169	SK16GUA	LE	35179	SK16GUW	LE	35189	SK16GVM	LE
35170	SK16GUC	LE	35180	SK16GUX	LE	35190	SK16GVN	LE
35171	SK16GUD	LE	35181	SK16GVA	LE	35191	SK16GVO	LE
35172	SK16GUE	LE	35182	SK16GVC	LE	35192	SK16GVP	LE

55106	MX62AXH	Wright Streetlite WF	Wright Streetlite	B37F	LE
55107	MX62ANR	Wright Streetlite WF	Wright Streetlite	B37F	LE
60374	J461OVU	Volvo B10M-55	NC Paladin	B49F	LEt
60460	G605NWA	Volvo B10M-55	Alexander PS	B51F	LEt

Pictured here in Newport is Wright Streetdeck 35192 in the First Leicester, seen while on loan to First West of England for rail replacement duties for Great Western Railway (photo courtesy of Steve Maskell)

63102-63357		Wright Streetlite Max			Wright Streetlite 11.5m * - B44F			B41F	
63102	SM13NCC	LE	63346	SM65WMP	LE	63353	SM65WMZ	LE
63103	SM13NCD	LE	63347	SM65WMT	LE	63354	SM65WNA	LE
63104	SM13NCE	LE	63348	SM65WMU	LE	63355	SM65WNB	LE
63105	SM13NCF	LE	63349	SM65WMV	LE	63356	SM65LNO	LE
63180*	DRZ9713	LE	63350	SM65WMW	LE	63357	SM65LNP	LE
63250	SN15ABF	LE	63351	SM65WMX	LE			
63345	SM65WMO	LE	63352	SM65WMY	LE			

66307-66323		Volvo B7L			Wright Eclipse			B41F	
66307	KV02VVJ	LE	66313	KV02VVP	LE	66319	KV02VVX	u
66308	KV02VVK	u	66314	KV02VVR	LE	66320	KV02VVY	LE
66309	KV02VVL	LE	66315	KV02VVS	LE	66321	KV02VVZ	LE
66310	KV02VVM	LE	66316	KV02VVT	LE	66322	KV02VWA	LE
66311	KV02VVN	LE	66317	KV02VVU	u	66323	KV02VWB	LE
66312	KV02VVO	LE	66318	KV02VVW	LE			

66805-66975		Volvo B7RLE			Wright Eclipse Urban * - B40F			B43F	
66805	MX05CCU	LE	66847	MX05CGY	LE	66971*	KX05MJY	LE
66820	MX05CEJ	LE	66965*	KX05MJF	LE	66972	KX05AOC	LE
66838	MX05CFV	LE	66966*	KX05MJJ	LE	66973	KX05AOD	LE
66839	MX05CFY	LE	66967*	KX05MJK	LE	66974	KX05AOE	LE
66840	MX05CGE	LE	66968*	KX05MJO	LE	66975	KX05MGY	LE
66841	MX05CGF	LE	66969*	KX05MJU	LE			
66842	MX05CGG	LE	66970*	KX05MJV	LE			

Above: *Seen in the centre of Leicester while on route 12 heading for Ryder Road is Wright Eclipse-bodied Volvo B7L 66318*

Below: *Also seen at Woburn for the 2015 Showbus rally is 66970, pictured showing the fuchsia-fronted variation of FirstGroup corporate livery which is being adopted for buses in Leicester*

69435-69460		Volvo B7RLE		Wright Eclipse Urban 2 * - B43F			B44F	

69435*	WX59BYM	LE	69451	WX59BZE	LE	69455	WX59BZJ	LE
69436*	WX59BYN	LE	69452	WX59BZF	LE	69456	WX59BZK	LE
69449	WX59BZC	LE	69453	WX59BZG	LE	69459	WX59BZN	LE
69450	WX59BZD	LE	69454	WX59BZH	LE	69460	WX59BZO	LE

Liveries
Unless stated below, all vehicles in this fleet carry FirstGroup corporate livery;
Leicester City Transport: 32646, 66965
Fuchsia front on corporate livery: 35168-35192, 63180, 63345-63357, 66307-66313, 66316-66318, 66805, 66820, 66838-66841, 66970
Allover white: 55106, 55107
First Training: 60374, 60460

Showing the second commemorative livery, celebrating 90 years of Leicester City Transport is Wright Eclipse Urban-bodied Volvo B7RLE 66965, seen here at Showbus 2014 rally

Manchester

Garages
AS   Ashton – Rothesay Garage, Globe Lane Industrial Estate, Broadway, Dukinfield, SK16 4UU
BN   Bolton - Weston Street, Bolton, BL3 2AW
BY   Bury - 55 Rochdale Road, Bury, BL9 0QZ
MA   Manchester - Boyle Street, Cheetham Hill, Manchester, M8 8UT
OM   Oldham - Wallshaw Street, Oldham, Lancashire, OL1 3TR
RU   Rusholme - 261 Wilmslow Road, Rusholme, Manchester, M14 5LJ

| 10017 | X401CSG | Scania L94UA | | Wright Fusion | | AB56D | BY |

12001-12018		Scania N94UA		Scania OmniCity		AB58D	
12001	YN05GYA	BY	12007	YN05GYE	BY	12013	YN05GYU	BY
12002	YN05GYB	BY	12008	YN05GYF	BY	12014	YN05GYP	BY
12003	YN05GYH	BY	12009	YN05GYG	BY	12015	YN05GYR	BY
12004	YN05GYJ	BY	12010	YN05GYK	BY	12016	YN05GYS	BY
12005	YN05GYC	BY	12011	YN05GYO	BY	12017	YN05GYT	BY
12006	YN05GYD	BY	12012	YN05GYV	BY	12018	YN05GYW	BY

Seen in Piccadilly Gardens is 12008, a rare breed in the FirstGroup empire by way of a Scania CN94UA OmniCity artic, pictured while on route 135 to Bury

| 30894-30965 | | Volvo B7TL | | Alexander ALX400 | | H49/29F | |
				* - H49/27F			
30894*	X749VUA	OM	30944	YJ51RPY	OM	30954	YJ51RDO	OM
30912*	X767VUA	OM	30945	YJ51RPZ	BY	30955	YJ51RCU	OM
30915*	X779VUA	OM	30946	YJ51RRO	OM	30956	YJ51RCV	OM
30935*	X356VWT	OM	30947	YJ51RRU	BY	30957	YJ51RCX	OM
30936*	X357VWT	BY	30948	YJ51RRV	BY	30958	YJ51RCZ	OM

30959	YJ51RCO	OM	30962	YJ51RDX	OM	30965	YJ51RAX	OM
30960	YJ51RDU	OM	30963	YJ51RDY	OM			
30961	YJ51RDV	OM	30964	YJ51RAU	OM			

Pictured arriving in Ashton is 30915, a Volvo B7TL with Alexander ALX400 bodywork, seen while on route 333, soon after the vehicle transferred from West Yorkshire

32867	V867HBY	Dennis Trident SFD113	Plaxton President 9.9m	H39/21F	u
32869	V869HBY	Dennis Trident SFD113	Plaxton President 9.9m	H39/21F	RU

32899-32926		Dennis Trident SFD313		Plaxton President 10.5m			H43/26F	
32899	V899HLH	RU	32912	W912VLN	RU	32916	W916VLN	RU
32908	W908VLN	BY	32913	W913VLN	BY	32926	W926VLN	BY
32911	W896VLN	u	32915	W915VLN	RU			

32959	X959HLT	Dennis Trident SFD113	Plaxton President 9.9m	H39/24F	RU
32972	X972HLT	Dennis Trident SFD113	Plaxton President 9.9m	H39/20F	RU

33656-33857		ADL E40D SFD4DS		ADL Enviro 400 10.8m			H45/30F	
33656	SN12ADU	OM	33675	SN12AEW	OM	33686	SN12AFV	OM
33657	SN12ADV	BN	33676	SN12AEX	OM	33687	SN12AFX	OM
33663	SN12AEE	u	33677	SN12AEY	BN	33688	SN12AFY	OM
33668	SN12AEL	OM	33678	SN12AEZ	OM	33689	SN12AFZ	OM
33669	SN12AEM	OM	33679	SN12AFA	OM	33690	SN12AGO	OM
33670	SN12AEO	OM	33680	SN12AFE	OM	33691	SN12AGU	BN
33671	SN12AEP	OM	33681	SN12AFF	OM	33692	SN12AGV	OM
33672	SN12AET	OM	33682	SN12AFJ	OM	33693	SN12AGX	BN
33673	SN12AEU	BN	33683	SN12AFK	OM	33694	SN12AGY	OM
33674	SN12AEV	OM	33684	SN12AFO	OM	33695	SN12AGZ	BN

33696	SN12AHA	BN	33722	SN12AKP	BN	33748	SN12AOH	OM
33697	SN12AHC	BN	33723	SN12AKU	OM	33749	SN12AOJ	OM
33698	SN12AHD	OM	33724	SN12AKV	BN	33751	SN12AOL	OM
33699	SN12AHE	BN	33725	SN12AKX	BN	33752	SN12AOM	RU
33700	SN12AHF	BN	33726	SN12AKY	BN	33753	SN12AOO	BN
33701	SN12AHG	OM	33727	SN12AKZ	BN	33755	SN12AOR	OM
33702	SN12AHJ	OM	33728	SN12ALO	BN	33831	SN14CTV	RU
33703	SN12AHK	OM	33729	SN12ALU	BN	33832	SN14CTX	RU
33704	SN12AHL	BN	33730	SN12AMK	BN	33833	SN14CTY	RU
33705	SN12AHO	BN	33731	SN12AMO	BN	33834	SN14TRZ	RU
33706	SN12AHP	OM	33732	SN12AMU	BN	33835	SN14TSO	RU
33707	SN12AHU	BN	33733	SN12AMV	BN	33836	SN14TSU	RU
33708	SN12AHV	OM	33734	SN12AMX	BN	33837	SN14TSV	RU
33709	SN12AHX	BN	33735	SN12ANF	BN	33838	SN14TSX	RU
33710	SN12AHY	BN	33736	SN12ANP	OM	33839	SN14TSY	RU
33711	SN12AHZ	BN	33737	SN12ANR	BN	33840	SN14TSZ	RU
33712	SN12AJO	BN	33738	SN12ANU	OM	33841	SN14TTE	RU
33713	SN12AJU	BN	33739	SN12ANV	BN	33842	SN14TTF	RU
33714	SN12AJV	BN	33740	SN12ANX	BN	33843	SN14TTJ	RU
33715	SN12AJX	BN	33741	SN12AOA	OM	33844	SN14TTK	RU
33716	SN12AJY	BN	33742	SN12AOB	BN	33845	SN14TTO	RU
33717	SN12AKF	BN	33743	SN12AOC	BN	33846	SN14TTU	RU
33718	SN12AKG	BN	33744	SN12AOD	OM	33847	SN14TTV	RU
33719	SN12AKJ	BN	33745	SN12AOE	OM	33848	SN14TTX	RU
33720	SN12AKK	BN	33746	SN12AOF	OM	33849	SN14TTY	RU
33721	SN12AKO	BN	33747	SN12AOG	OM	33850	SN14TTZ	RU

Seen in Piccadilly Gardens is 33693, an ADL Enviro 400 which started life in London as part of an operation for the 2012 Olympics, seen while preparing to take up service

33851	SN14TUA	RU	33854	SN14TUO	RU	33857	SN14TUW	RU
33852	SN14TUH	RU	33855	SN14TUP	RU			
33853	SN14TUJ	RU	33856	SN14TUV	RU			

36279	BD12TDU	Volvo B9TL	Wright Eclipse Gemini 2	H45/27F	BN
36280	BD12TCJ	Volvo B9TL	Wright Eclipse Gemini 2	H45/27F	BN

37279-37561		Volvo B9TL	Wright Eclipse Gemini	H45/29F
			* - DPH45/29F	

37279	MX07BPY	MA	37397	MX58DXH	BN	37443	MX58DZS	BY
37280	MX07BPZ	MA	37398	MX58DXJ	BY	37444	MX58DZT	OM
37281	MX07BRF	MA	37399	MX58DXK	BY	37445	MX58DZU	BY
37282	MX07BRV	MA	37400	MX58DXL	BY	37446	MX58DZV	OM
37283	MX07BRZ	MA	37401	MX58DXM	BY	37447	MX58DZW	BY
37284	MX07BSO	MA	37402	MX58DXO	BN	37448	MX58DZY	OM
37285	MX07BSU	MA	37403	MX58DXP	BY	37449	MX58DZZ	OM
37286	MX07BSV	MA	37404	MX58DXR	BY	37450	MX58EAA	OM
37287	MX07BSY	MA	37405	MX58DXS	BN	37451	MX58EAC	OM
37288	MX07BSZ	MA	37406	MX58DXT	BY	37452	MX58EAF	MA
37289	MX07BTE	MA	37407	MX58DXU	BN	37453	MX58EAG	OM
37290	MX07BTF	MA	37408	MX58DXV	BN	37454	MX58EAJ	OM
37297	MX07BUE	BY	37409	MX58DXW	BY	37455	MX58EAK	OM
37301	MX57HDZ	MA	37410	MX58DXZ	BY	37456	MX58EAM	BN
37303*	MX07BUU	MA	37411	MX58DYA	MA	37457	MX58EAO	OM
37304*	MX07BUV	MA	37412	MX58DYC	OM	37458	MX58EAP	OM
37367*	MX58DVU	MA	37413	MX58DYD	MA	37459	MX58EAY	OM
37368*	MX58DVV	MA	37414	MX58DYF	MA	37460	MX58EBA	OM
37369*	MX58DVW	MA	37415	MX58DYG	BN	37461	MX58EBC	OM
37370*	MX58DVY	MA	37416	MX58DYH	BN	37462	MX58EBD	AS
37371*	MX58DVZ	MA	37417	MX58DYJ	BY	37463	MX58EBF	AS
37372*	MX58DWA	MA	37418	MX58DYM	BY	37464	MX58EBG	AS
37373*	MX58DWC	MA	37419	MX58DYN	BY	37465	MX58EBK	AS
37374*	MX58DWD	MA	37420	MX58DYO	BY	37466	MX58EBL	AS
37375*	MX58DWE	MA	37421	MX58DYP	BY	37467	MX58EBM	OM
37376*	MX58DWF	MA	37422	MX58DYS	BY	37468	MX58EBN	OM
37377*	MX58DWG	MA	37423	MX58DYT	BY	37469	MX09GXY	OM
37378*	MX58DWJ	MA	37424	MX58DYU	BY	37470	MX09GXZ	OM
37379*	MX58DWK	MA	37425	MX58DYV	BY	37471	MX09GYG	BY
37380*	MX58DWL	MA	37426	MX58DYW	BY	37545	MX09GYE	OM
37381	MX58DWM	MA	37427	MX58DYY	BY	37546	MX09GYJ	OM
37382	MX58DWN	MA	37428	MX58DZA	BY	37547	MX09GYK	BN
37383	MX58DWO	OM	37429	MX58DZB	BY	37548	MX09GYC	OM
37384	MX58DWP	MA	37430	MX58DZC	BN	37549	MX09GYA	OM
37385	MX58DWU	MA	37431	MX58DZD	BY	37550	MX09GYD	OM
37386	MX58DWV	MA	37432	MX58DZE	OM	37551	MX09HUK	BY
37387	MX58DWW	BY	37433	MX58DZF	BY	37552	MX09GYB	OM
37388	MX58DWY	BY	37434	MX58DZG	BN	37553	MX09GYF	OM
37389	MX58DWZ	MA	37435	MX58DZH	BN	37554	MX09GYH	BY
37390	MX58DXA	MA	37436	MX58DZJ	BY	37555	MX09LMK	OM
37391	MX58DXB	BY	37437	MX58DZK	OM	37556	MX09LML	OM
37392	MX58DXC	BY	37438	MX58DZL	BY	37557	MX09HUO	OM
37393	MX58DXD	BN	37439	MX58DZN	BY	37558	MX09HUU	OM
37394	MX58DXE	MA	37440	MX58DZO	MA	37559	MX09HUP	OM
37395	MX58DXF	MA	37441	MX58DZP	BY	37560	MX09LMF	OM
37396	MX58DXG	MA	37442	MX58DZR	MA	37561	MX09LMJ	OM

Arriving in Bolton is First Manchester 37393, a Wright Eclipse Gemini-bodied Volvo B7TL, pictured while on route 47

39207-39220		Volvo B5LH			Wright Eclipse Gemini 2			DPH41/23F	
39207	BN61MWE	MA	39212	BN61MWL	MA	39217	BN61MWV	MA
39208	BN61MWF	MA	39213	BN61MWM	MA	39218	BN61MWW	MA
39209	BN61MWG	MA	39214	BN61MWO	MA	39219	BN61MWX	MA
39210	BN61MWJ	MA	39215	BN61MWP	MA	39220	BN61MWY	MA
39211	BN61MWK	MA	39216	BN61MWU	MA			

39237-39261		Volvo B5LH			Wright Gemini 3			DPH37/26F	
39237	BL65YZD	BN	39246	BL65YZJ	u	39255	BW65DCX	BN
39238	BL65YZF	BN	39247	BL65OXT	BN	39256	BL65OXV	BN
39239	BL65OXU	BN	39248	BL65YZK	BN	39257	BT66MRU	u
39240	BL65YZG	BN	39249	BL65OYZ	BN	39258	BT66MRO	u
39241	BL65YZH	BN	39250	BW65DBX	BN	39259	BT66MRV	u
39242	BW65DBZ	BN	39251	BW65DCE	BN	39260	BT66MRW	u
39243	BW65DCO	BN	39252	BW65DCF	BN	39261	BT66MRX	u
39244	BW65DBY	BN	39253	BW65DCU	BN			
39245	BL65YZE	BN	39254	BW65DCV	BN			

40318	Y901KND	Optare Solo M920		Optare Solo 9.2m			B28F	w

40323-40336		Optare Solo M850		Optare Solo 8.5m			B26F	
40323	MA51AET	w	40329	ML02OFY	AS	40333	ML02OGC	AS
40326	MA51AEW	w	40330	ML02OFZ	AS	40334	ML02OGD	MA
40327	ML02OFW	AS	40331	ML02OGA	MA	40335	ML02OGE	AS
40328	ML02OFX	u	40332	ML02OGB	MA	40336	ML02OGF	OM

41433	LN51DWW	Dennis Dart SLF SFD1B2	Marshall Capital 9.3m	B24D	t
41780	X513HLR	Dennis Dart SLF SFD112	Marshall Capital 9.3m	B27F	w
41788	X788HLR	Dennis Dart SLF SFD112	Marshall Capital 9.3m	B27F	w

A large number of vehicles within the FirstGroup empire started their life in London. Seen here is 41780, a Marshall Capital-bodied Dennis Dart SLF new to First Capital as DM780, about to turn into Ashton bus station while on route 393

42940-42945		Dennis Dart SLF SFD3CA		Alexander Pointer 2 10.7m		B37F	
42940	MX56HXZ	AS	42944	WA56OAU	AS		
42941	WA56OAO	AS	42945	WA56OAV	AS		

47466-47481		Wright Streetlite DF		Wright Streetlite 10.8m		B37F	
47466	SN14DZM	AS	47472	SN14EAF	AS	47478	SN14EAW	AS
47467	SN14DZO	AS	47473	SN14EAG	AS	47479	SN14EAX	AS
47468	SN14DZP	AS	47474	SN14EAJ	AS	47480	SN14EAY	AS
47469	SN14EAA	AS	47475	SN14EAM	AS	47481	SN14EBA	AS
47470	SN14EAC	AS	47476	SN14EAO	AS			
47471	SN14EAE	AS	47477	SN14EAP	AS			

49101-49112		Optare Versa V970		Optare Versa 9.7m		B28F	
49101	YJ60KCU	MA	49107	YJ60KDK	MA	49110	YJ60KDU	MA
49102	YJ60KCV	MA	49108	YJ60KDN	MA	49111	YJ60KDV	MA
49106	YJ60KDF	MA	49109	YJ60KDO	MA	49112	YJ60KDX	MA

49202-49228		Optare Versa V1200		Optare Versa 12m		B57F	
49202	YJ12MYF	OM	49205	YJ12MYK	OM	49209	YJ12MYO	OM
49203	YJ12MYG	OM	49206	YJ12MYL	OM	49210	YJ12MYP	OM

49211	YJ12MYR	BN	49215	YJ12MYV	OM	49222	YJ12MZF	OM
49212	YJ12MYS	OM	49216	YJ12MYW	OM	49227	YJ12GXZ	BN
49213	YJ12MYT	MA	49220	YJ12MZD	MA	49228	YJ12GXV	BN

49230-49233		Optare Versa V1210		Optare Versa 12.1m		B57F		
49230	YJ14BPO	OM	49232	YJ14BPF	MA			
49231	YJ14BPK	BN	49233	YJ64DYX	BN			

49921	YJ14BJX	Optare Versa V1040EV	Optare Versa EV 10.4m	B29F	MA
49922	YJ14BJZ	Optare Versa V1040EV	Optare Versa EV 10.4m	B29F	MA
49923	YJ14BJY	Optare Versa V1040EV	Optare Versa EV 10.4m	B29F	MA

53143-53150		Optare Solo M950		Optare Solo 9.5m		B30F		
53143	MX54GZA	OM	53146	MX54GZD	OM	53149	MX54GZG	OM
53144	MX54GZB	OM	53147	MX54GZE	OM	53150	MX54GZH	OM
53145	MX54GZC	OM	53148	MX54GZF	OM			

Arriving in Ashton is First Manchester 53150, an Optare Solo, seen while on route 38

59001-59008		Optare Solo SR M820		Optare Solo 8.2m		B23F		
59001	YJ60KCA	MA	59004	YJ60KCF	MA	59007	YJ60KCN	MA
59002	YJ60KCC	MA	59005	YJ60KCG	MA	59008	YJ60KCO	MA
59003	YJ60KCE	MA	59006	YJ60KCK	MA			

60181	V129DND	Scania L94UB	Wright Floline	B42F	t
60188	V136DND	Scania L94UB	Wright Floline	B41F	OMt

60233-60283			Mercedes-Benz O530			Mercedes-Benz Citaro * - B38F, $ - B41F		B39F	
60233	W311JND	BY	60253	W331RJA	BY	60270	W348RJA	w
60235	W313JND	w	60254	W332RJA	w	60271	W349RJA	BY
60237	W315JND	u	60255	W363RJA	w	60272	W362RJA	w
60238	W334JND	BY	60256	W334RJA	w	60273	W351RJA	OM
60239	W317JND	u	60257	W335RJA	w	60274	W352RJA	BY
60241	W319JND	w	60258	W336RJA	BY	60275	W353RJA	w
60242	W337JND	BY	60259	W337RJA	w	60276	W354RJA	w
60243	W341JND	w	60260	W338RJA	w	60277	W366RJA	OM
60245	W339JND	w	60261	W339RJA	w	60278	W356RJA	w
60247	W378JNE	OM	60262	W361RJA	BY	60279	W357RJA	w
60249*	W327JND	BY	60264	W342RJA	w	60280	W358RJA	w
60250	W379JNE	u	60267	W365RJA	BY	60282$	W364RJA	w
60251	W329JND	w	60268	W346RJA	w	60283	W179BVP	OM
60252	W331JND	BY	60269	W347RJA	BY			

Pictured is Mercedes-Benz Citaro 60283, arriving in Bolton while on route 524

60301	M506PNA	Volvo B10B-58			Wright Endurance		DP50F	t
60322	N527WVR	Volvo B10B-58			Wright Endurance		DP42F	OMt

60376-62183		Volvo B10BLE			Wright Renown * - B39F, $ - B43F		B41F	
60376	R621CVR	BNt	60657	T839MAK	MAt	61240	R340GHS	MAt
60640	T822MAK	BYt	60660	T842MAK	MAt	62183$	X684ADK	t
60651	T833MAK	BNt	60663*	T845MAK	BNt			

62221	W603RFS	Volvo B10BLE			Alexander ALX300		B44F	t

76

62231-62241		Volvo B10BLE		Wright Renown			B44F	
62231	Y941CSF	BN	62236	Y944CSF	BN			
62233	Y942CSF	BN	62241	Y951CSF	BN			

63106-63156		Wright Streetlite Max		Wright Streetlite 11.5m			B41F	
63106	SM13NCJ	OM	63116	SK63KGG	RU	63151	SN14DXR	RU
63107	SM13NCN	OM	63117	SK63KGJ	OM	63152	SN14DXS	RU
63108	SM13NCO	OM	63118	SK63KGN	OM	63153	SN14DXT	OM
63111	SK63KFY	OM	63146	SN14DXK	RU	63154	SN14DXU	OM
63112	SK63KFZ	OM	63147	SN14DXL	RU	63155	SN14DXV	OM
63113	SK63KGA	OM	63148	SN14DXM	RU	63156	SN14DXJ	RU
63114	SK63KGE	OM	63149	SN14DXO	RU			
63115	SK63KGF	OM	63150	SN14DXP	RU			

The Wright Streetlite in both DF and Max form are becoming the standard full-size single decker for FirstGroup. One such vehicle, 63152, is seen in Manchester Piccadilly while on route 41 to West Didsbury, complete with "Cross Connect" branding carried by this batch of vehicles

64029	BX02CMK	Mercedes-Benz O530	Mercedes-Benz Citaro	B39F	BY
66193	S793RWG	Volvo B10BLE	Wright Renown	B41F	BNt

66831-66933		Volvo B7RLE		Wright Eclipse Urban			B43F	
66831	MX05CFK	MA	66846	MX05CGV	BY	66858	MX05CHO	OM
66832	MX05CFL	MA	66848	MX05CGZ	BY	66859	MX05CHV	OM
66833	MX05CFM	MA	66853	MX05CHH	MA	66860	MX05CHY	BY
66834	MX05CFN	MA	66854	MX05CHJ	MA	66861	MX05CHZ	BY
66835	MX05CFO	MA	66855	MX05CHK	MA	66862	MX05CJE	OM
66836	MX05CFP	MA	66856	MX05CHL	MA	66863	MX05CJF	BY
66844	MX05CGO	MA	66857	MX05CHN	OM	66864	MX05CJJ	BY

66865	MX05CJO	BY	66891	MX55UAA	MA	66905	MX55FFS	BN
66866	MX05CJU	MA	66892	MX55LDJ	BY	66906	MX55FFT	BY
66867	MX05CJV	OM	66893	MX55LDK	OM	66907	MX55FFU	BN
66868	MX05CJY	OM	66894	MX55FFD	BY	66908	MX55FFV	MA
66869	MX05CJZ	OM	66895	MX55FFE	BN	66909	MX55FFW	BY
66870	MX05CKA	BN	66896	MX55FFG	OM	66910	MX55FFY	MA
66871	MX05CKC	OM	66897	MX55FFH	MA	66911	MX55FFZ	MA
66872	MX05CKD	BY	66898	MX55FFJ	MA	66912	MX55FGA	MA
66873	MX05CKE	BY	66899	MX55FFK	BN	66913	MX55FGC	MA
66874	MX05CKF	MA	66900	MX55FFL	BY	66914	MX55FGE	BY
66875	MX55NWE	MA	66901	MX55FFM	BN	66915	MX55FGF	BY
66876	MX05CKJ	OM	66902	MX55FFO	MA	66916	MX55FGG	BY
66880	MX05CKO	BY	66903	MX55FFP	BN	66917	MX55FGJ	BY
66890	MX55NWH	OM	66904	MX55FFR	BN	66918	MX55FGK	BY

Seen in Piccadilly Gardens approaching its terminus is 66890, a Wright Eclipse Urban-bodied Volvo B7RLE, while on route 181

66919	MX55FGM	BY	66923	MX55FGU	MA	66930	MX55FHE	BY
66920	MX55FGN	MA	66928	MX55FHC	MA	66931	MX55FHF	OM
66922	MX55FGP	MA	66929	MX55FHD	MA	66933	MX55FHH	MA

67401-67430		ADL E30D SFD1C8		ADL Enviro 300 11.8m			B41F	
67401	SN13CJV	BN	67408	SN13CKE	BN	67415	SN13CKP	OM
67402	SN13CJX	BN	67409	SN13CKF	BN	67416	SN13CKU	OM
67403	SN13CJY	BN	67410	SN13CKG	BN	67417	SN13CKV	OM
67404	SN13CJZ	BN	67411	SN13CKJ	BN	67418	SN13CKX	OM
67405	SN13CKA	BN	67412	SN13CKK	BN	67419	SN13CKY	OM
67406	SN13CKC	BN	67413	SN13CKL	OM	67420	SN13CLF	OM
67407	SN13CKD	BN	67414	SN13CKO	OM	67421	SN13CLJ	OM

67422	SN13CLO	OM	67425	SN13CLX	OM	67428	SN13CME	OM
67423	SN13CLU	OM	67426	SN13CLY	OM	67429	SN13CMF	OM
67424	SN13CLV	OM	67427	SN13CLZ	OM	67430	SN13CMK	OM

Seen in Piccadilly Gardens is 67430, an ADL Enviro 300 with First Manchester, while operating on route 81 to Moston

| 69135-69420 | | Volvo B7RLE | | Wright Eclipse Urban | | | B43F | |
| | | | | * - B44F | | | | |

69135	MV06CZS	BY	69157	MX06VNN	BY	69178	MX06YXK	BY
69136	MV06CZG	BY	69158	MX06VNO	BY	69179	MX06YXL	MA
69137	MV06CZT	BY	69159	MX06VNP	BN	69180	MX06YXM	MA
69138	MV06CXB	BY	69160	MX06VNR	BN	69185	MX56ACV	MA
69139	MX06VOP	BN	69161	MX06VNS	BN	69186	MX56ACY	BY
69141	MX06VOU	BN	69162	MX06VNT	BN	69195	MX06VPR	MA
69142	MX06VOV	BN	69163	MX06VNU	BN	69196	MX06VPT	MA
69143	MX06VOY	BY	69164	MX06VNV	BN	69197	MX06VPU	MA
69144	MX06VPA	BN	69165	MX06VMW	BY	69198	MX06VPV	MA
69145	MX06VNW	BN	69166	MX06VMZ	BY	69199	MX06VPW	MA
69146	MX06VNY	BN	69167	MX06VNB	BY	69200	MX06VPY	MA
69147	MX06VNZ	BN	69168	MX06VNC	BN	69201	MX06VPZ	BN
69148	MX06VOA	BN	69169	MX06VND	BN	69202	MX06VRC	OM
69149	MX06VOB	BY	69170	MX06VNE	BN	69203	MX06VPC	OM
69150	MX06VOC	BN	69171	MX06VNF	BN	69204	MX06VPD	OM
69151	MX06VOD	BN	69172	MV06CZJ	BN	69205	MX06VPE	MA
69152	MX06VOF	BN	69173	MV06DWZ	BN	69325*	YJ09FWV	MA
69153	MX06VOG	BY	69174	MX06VNK	BN	69326*	YJ09FWW	MA
69154	MX06VOH	BN	69175	MX06VPO	BN	69327*	YJ09FWX	MA
69155	MX06VNL	BN	69176	MX06VPP	MA	69328*	YJ09FWY	MA
69156	MX06VNM	BN	69177	MX06YXJ	OM	69420*	YJ09FXH	MA

Within the Manchester Piccadilly Bus Station is 69192, a Wright Eclipse Urban-bodied Volvo B7RLE, seen here while preparing to leave on route 37 to Bolton

69521-69531		Volvo B7RLE			Wright Eclipse Urban 2			B41F
69521	BD11CEN	BN	69525	BD11CFA	BN	69529	BD11CFJ	BN
69522	BD11CEU	BN	69526	BD11CEY	BN	69530	BD11CFF	BN
69523	BD11CEO	BN	69527	BD11CEX	BN	69531	BD11CFE	BN
69524	BD11CEV	BN	69528	BD11CFG	BN			

Previous registrations

62183	X684ADK, OIG1790		69137	06D52166
64029	BX02CMK, 02D52345		69138	06D52161
69135	06D52159		69172	06D67687
69136	06D52155		69173	06D67362

Liveries
Unless stated below, all vehicles in this fleet carry FirstGroup corporate livery;
Cross Connect branding: 33840-33849, 63153-63155
First Hybrid (silver with pink skirt): 39207-39211, 39214, 39216, 39217, 39219, 39220
Vantage: 39237-39261
MetroShuttle: 49101, 49102, 49106-49112, 49921-49923, 59001-59008
Schoolbus: 49202, 49203, 49205, 49206, 49209-49213, 49215, 49220, 49222, 49230-49233
Silver and green: 49227, 49228
First Training: 60181, 60188, 60301, 60322, 60376, 60640, 60651, 60657, 60660, 60663, 61240, 62221, 66193
Ramsbottom Corporation: 69166

Midland Red West

Garage

WR   Worcester - Padmore Street, Worcester, WR1 2PA

20201	T701JLD	Volvo B12T		Plaxton Excalibur		C51F	WR
20202	T702JLD	Volvo B12T		Plaxton Excalibur		C51F	WR
32066	KP51VZO	Volvo B7TL		Alexander ALX400		H49/27F	WR
32067	KP51VZR	Volvo B7TL		Alexander ALX400		H49/27F	WR
33039	LN51DWD	Dennis Trident SFD136		Plaxton President 9.9m		H39/24F	w
33043	LN51DVG	Dennis Trident SFD136		Plaxton President 9.9m		H39/21F	WR

33401-33405		Dennis Trident SFD338	Alexander ALX400 10.5m		H47/27F

33401	VX54MTV	WR		33403	VX54MTZ	WR	33405	VX54MUB	WR
33402	VX54MTY	WR		33404	VX54MUA	WR			

35156-33159		Wright Streetdeck	Wright Streetdeck		H45/28F

35156	SN65OKH	WR	35158	SN65OKK	WR
35157	SN65OKJ	WR	35159	SN65OKL	WR

Unloading before entering Worcester Bus Station is 35156, a Wright Streetdeck, carrying the special fuchsia fronted version of the livery carried by numerous vehicles in Worcester, this vehicle is branded for route 44

44511	DK57SPZ	Dennis E200Dart SFD321	Alexander Enviro 200 10.8m	B37F	WR
44514	MX07OZD	Dennis E200Dart SFD321	Alexander Enviro 200 10.8m	B37F	WR
44515	MX10DXU	Dennis E200Dart SFD3B1	Alexander Enviro 200 10.8m	B36F	WR

47513-47520		Wright Streetlite DF		Wright Streetlite 10.8m			B37F	
47513	SN64CFM	WR	47516	SN64CFU	WR	47519	SN64CFY	WR
47514	SN64CFO	WR	47517	SN64CFV	WR	47520	SN64CFZ	WR
47515	SN64CFP	WR	47518	SN64CFX	WR			

Leaving the Crowngate Bus Station in Worcester is 47519, a Wright Streetlite DF on route 35 to Blackpole

53044-53061		Optare Solo M850		Optare Solo 8.5m			B26F	
53044	VU03YJW	WR	53049	VU03YKC	WR	53061	VX53OEP	WR
53047	VU03YJZ	WR	53050	VU03YKD	WR	53064	VX53OEU	WR
53048	VU03YKB	WR	53051	VU03YKE	WR			

60311	M516PNA	Volvo B10B-58		Wright Endurance			DP50F	WRt
60340	N545WVR	Volvo B10B-58		Wright Endurance			DP50F	WRt
62702	G102HNP	Leyland Lynx Mk1		Leyland Lynx			B49F	t

63358-63366		Wright Streetlite Max		Wright Streetlite 11.5m			B41F	
63358	SM65LNR	WR	63361	SM65WME	WR	63364	SM65WMJ	WR
63359	SM65WMC	WR	63362	SM65WMF	WR	63365	SM65WMK	WR
63360	SM65WMD	WR	63363	SM65WMG	WR	63366	SM65WML	WR

66691-66699		Volvo B7RLE		Plaxton Centro			B45F	
66691	CN07HVG	WR	66694	CN07HVJ	WR	66697	CN57EFF	WR
66692	CN07HVH	WR	66695	CN57EFB	WR	66698	CN07HVL	WR
66693	CN07HVK	WR	66696	CN57EFE	WR	66699	CN07HVM	WR

Another rarity amongst the FirstGroup fleet is the Plaxton Centro body. Seen here is one such example, on Volvo B7RLE by way of 66695 leaving the Bus Station out of service

67647-67664			Dennis Enviro 300 SFD113 Alexander Enviro 300 11.8m				B44F	
67647	VX54MTF	WR	67653	VX05LVT	WR	67659	VX05LWC	WR
67648	VX54MTJ	WR	67654	VX05LVU	WR	67660	VX05LWD	WR
67649	VX54MTK	WR	67655	VX05LVV	WR	67661	VX05LWE	WR
67650	VX54MTO	WR	67656	VX05LVW	WR	67662	VX05LWF	WR
67651	VX54MTU	WR	67657	VX05LVY	WR	67663	VX05LWG	WR
67652	VX05LVS	WR	67658	VX05LVZ	WR	67664	VX05LWH	WR

67665	FN08AZZ	Dennis Enviro 300 SFD121 Alexander Enviro 300 11.8m	B44F	WR
67699	PT09JPT	Dennis Enviro 300 SFD161 Alexander Enviro 300 11.8m	B45F	WR
68507	KX54AHP	BMC 1100FE	BMC	B60F	WR
68559	LK55ABV	BMC 1100FE	BMC	B55FL	WR

Liveries
Unless stated below, all vehicles carry FirstGroup corporate livery:
First Coaching: 20201, 20202
1930s Midland Red: 33404
Fuchsia-fronted corporate livery: 35156-35159, 53044, 53049, 63358-63366, 66692, 66693, 67647, 67650, 67651, 67657, 67659, 67663
1970s Midland Red: 67664
Schoolbus: 68507, 68559

Potteries

Garage
AG   Adderley Green - Dividy Road, Stoke on Trent, Stafford, ST3 5YY

32056	W216XBD	Volvo B7TL			Alexander ALX400		H49/29F	w
32057	W217XBD	Volvo B7TL			Alexander ALX400		H49/29F	w
32081	KP51WBL	Volvo B7TL			Alexander ALX400		H49/27F	AG

32627-37160		Volvo B7TL			Wright Eclipse Gemini		H45/29F	

32627	KP54KAO	AG	32639	KP54AZA	AG	37156	AU07DXS	AG
32630	KP54KBE	AG	32647	KP54AZN	AG	37157	AU07DXT	AG
32632	KP54KBJ	AG	32648	KP54KBK	AG	37158	AU07DXV	AG
32633	KP54LAE	AG	32649	KP54KBN	AG	37159	AU07DXW	AG
32634	KP54LAO	AG	32650	KP54KBO	AG	37160	AU07DXX	AG
32635	KX05MGV	AG	37146	YN06UPZ	AG			

Seen at Showbus, Donnington Park, is First Potteries 37146, a Wright Eclipse Gemini-bodied Volvo B7TL, seen here in the commemorative PMT Express livery carried by vehicles in the fleet during the 1980s

41493-41540		Dennis Dart SLF SFD2BA		Caetano Nimbus 10.2m			B33F

41493	LK03LLX	AG	41499	LK03LNV	AG	41520	LK03UEX	AG
41494	LK03LLZ	AG	41500	LK03LNW	AG	41521	LK03UEY	AG
41495	LK03LME	AG	41501	LK03LNX	AG	41522	LK03UEZ	AG
41496	LK03LMF	AG	41502	LK03NLD	AG	41540	LK53FDZ	AG
41497	LK03LNU	AG	41512	LK03NGE	AG			
41498	LK03NLN	AG	41514	LK03NGG	AG			

42552	WX05UAJ	Dennis Dart SLF SFD1BA	Alexander Pointer 2 9.3m	B31F	AG

Pictured here in Stoke is First Potteries 42553, an Alexander Pointer 2-bodied Dennis Dart SLF, seen while
on route 21A to London Road in Stoke (photo courtesy of Steve Maskell)

42553	WX05UAK	Dennis Dart SLF SFD1BA	Alexander Pointer 2 9.3m	B31F	AG
42554	WX05UAL	Dennis Dart SLF SFD1BA	Alexander Pointer 2 9.3m	B31F	AG
42892	VX54MUU	Dennis Dart SLF SFD3CA	Alexander Pointer 2 10.7m	B37F	AG
42893	VX54MUV	Dennis Dart SLF SFD3CA	Alexander Pointer 2 10.7m	B37F	AG
42894	VX05JWW	Dennis Dart SLF SFD3CA	Alexander Pointer 2 10.7m	B37F	AG
43875	MX56HYO	Dennis Dart SLF SFD6BA	Alexander Pointer 2 8.8m	B29F	AG
43876	MX56HYP	Dennis Dart SLF SFD6BA	Alexander Pointer 2 8.8m	B25F	AG
43877	EU06KDK	Dennis Dart SLF SFD6BA	Caetano Nimbus 8.8m	B28F	AG
53041	VU02PKY	Optare Solo M850	Optare Solo 8.5m	B22F	AG
53062	VX53OER	Optare Solo M850	Optare Solo 8.5m	B26F	u

53122-53155		Optare Solo M920	Optare Solo 9.2m	B30F	
			* - B31F		

53122	EO02NFD	AG	53124	EO02NFF	AG
53123	EO02NFE	AG	53155*	CN06BXH	AG

53207	CN07KZK	Optare Solo M950SL	Optare Solo 9.5m	B29F	AG
53208	CN07KZL	Optare Solo M950SL	Optare Solo 9.5m	B29F	AG
53209	CN07KZM	Optare Solo M950SL	Optare Solo 9.5m	B31F	AG
53405	VX57CYO	Optare Solo M880SL	Optare Solo 8.8m	B28F	u
53828	MX56NLJ	Optare Solo M850SL	Optare Solo 8.5m	B28F	u
53829	MX56NLK	Optare Solo M850SL	Optare Solo 8.5m	B28F	u
53830	CN06BXF	Optare Solo M850SL	Optare Solo 8.5m	B31F	AG
60001	G72RND	Leyland Tiger	Alexander N	B55F	t
60316	N521WVR	Volvo B10B-58	Wright Endurance	DP50F	t
60317	N522WVR	Volvo B10B-58	Wright Endurance	DP50F	t

63096-63179		Wright Streetlite Max		Wright Streetlite 11.5m			B41F	
63096	SM13NBN	AG	63101	SM13NCA	AG	63175	SN64CGO	AG
63097	SM13NBO	AG	63171	SN64CGE	AG	63176	SN64CGU	AG
63098	SM13NBX	AG	63172	SN64CGF	AG	63177	SN64CGV	AG
63099	SM13NBY	AG	63173	SN64CGG	AG	63178	SN64CGX	AG
63100	SM13NBZ	AG	63174	SN64CGK	AG	63179	SN64CGY	AG

65001-65042		Scania CN94UB		Scania OmniCity			B41F	
				* - B42F				
65001*	YN04YJC	AG	65027*	YN05HCL	AG	65038	YN06WML	AG
65002*	YN04YJD	AG	65033	YN06WME	AG	65039	YN06WMM	AG
65003*	YN04YJE	AG	65034	YN06WMF	AG	65040	YN06WMO	AG
65004*	YN04YJF	AG	65035	YN06WMG	AG	65041	YN06WMP	AG
65005*	YN04YJG	AG	65036	YN06WMJ	AG	65042	YN06WMT	AG
65026*	YN54OCK	AG	65037	YN06WMK	AG			

65705-65733		Scania L94UB		Wright Solar			B43F	
65705	YN04GME	AG	65728	YN05HCP	AG	65731	YN05HCX	AG
65706	YN04GMF	AG	65729	YN05HCU	AG	65732	YN05HCY	AG
65727	YN05HCO	AG	65730	YN05HCV	AG	65733	YN05HCZ	AG

66302-66306		Volvo B7L		Wright Eclipse			B41F	
66302	KV02VVD	AG	66304	KV02VVF	AG	66306	KV02VVH	AG
66303	KV02VVE	AG	66305	KV02VVG	AG			

66843-66964		Volvo B7RLE		Wright Eclipse Urban			B43F	
				* - B40F				
66843	MX05CGK	AG	66851	MX05CHF	AG	66963*	KX05MHZ	AG
66845	MX05CGU	AG	66852	MX05CHG	AG	66964*	KX05MJE	AG
66849	MX05CHC	AG	66962*	KX05MHY	AG			

67151-67158		ADL E20D SFDDLA		ADL Enviro 200MMC 11.5m			B41F	
67151	YX66WFJ	AG	67154	YX66WFM	AG	67157	YX66WFP	AG
67152	YX66WFK	AG	67155	YX66WFN	AG	67158	YX66WFR	AG
67153	YX66WFL	AG	67156	YX66WFO	AG			

67601-67642		Dennis Enviro 300 SFD113		Alexander Enviro 300 11.8m			B44F	
67601	VX53VJV	AG	67633	VX54MPF	AG	67639	VX54MRO	AG
67602	VX53VJZ	AG	67634	VX54MPO	AG	67640	VX54MRU	AG
67603	VX53VKA	AG	67635	VX54MPU	AG	67641	VX54MRV	AG
67604	VX53VKB	AG	67636	VX54MPV	AG	67642	VX54MRY	AG
67631	VX54MOV	AG	67637	VX54MPY	AG	67643	VX54MSO	AG
67632	VX54MPE	AG	67638	VX54MPZ	AG			

Leaving the old Hanley Bus Station is 66843, a Wright Eclipse Urban-bodied Volvo B7RLE, pictured while on route 25 to Keele University. This vehicle carried a red and yellow livery similar to the pre-FirstGroup corporate PMT livery, and has since been repainted into red-fronted corporate livery

Previous registrations
53828   J108028   53829   J108027

Liveries
Unless stated below, all vehicles in this fleet carry FirstGroup corporate livery:
Fuchsia-fronted corporate livery: 32630, 32632, 32635, 32639, 32648, 32649, 42552-42554, 53041, 53155, 65033-65040, 65051, 65042, 67151-67158
Red-fronted corporate livery: 65705, 65727, 65728, 65730-65733, 66302-66306, 66843, 66845, 66849, 66962-66964
Heritage PMT: 32634
Silver PMT: 37146
Red and yellow: 60171, 65026
First Training: 60316, 60317

Scotland East

Garages
B   Balfron - 1 Dunmore Street, Balfron, Glasgow, G63 0TU
BN   Bannockburn - Cowie Road, Bannockburn, Stirling, FK7 8JW
G   Galashiels - Stirling Street, Galashiels, TD1 1BY
L   Larbert - 200 Stirling Road, Larbert, FK5 3NJ
LN   Livingston - Deans Road, Deans, Livingston, EH54 8JY

20321-20371		Volvo B7R			Plaxton Profile			C46FTL	

* - C70FL, $ - C45FL, % - C65FL, + - C49FTL, & - C53F

20302&	WX54ZHO	G	20352$	WA05UNE	L	20365+	CV55AHA	L
20307&	WX05OZF	L	20354	CU05LGJ	L	20366	CV55AFF	L
20321*	YN57BVU	BN	20355	CU05LGK	L	20368+	CV55AGZ	L
20322*	YN57BVV	BN	20360	CV55ACX	L	20369	CV55AMU	L
20326*	YN57BVZ	G	20361	CV55ACY	L	20370	CV55AGY	G
20327*	YN57BWU	G	20362%	CV55AFA	BN	20371	CV55AMX	G
20351$	WA05UNG	L	20364	CV55AFE	u			

Pictured leaving Falkirk Bus Station is Plaxton Profile-bodied Volvo B7R 20360, on route 1A to Hallglen

30940-31562		Volvo B7TL			Alexander ALX400			H49/29F	

* - H49/27F

30940	Y795XNW	BN	31146*	YU52VYY	BN	31562	X136NSS	w
30941	Y796XNW	BN	31147*	YU52VYZ	BN			
31143*	YU52VYV	BN	31561	X104NSS	w			

31792	YN53EFK		Volvo B7TL			Wright Eclipse Gemini			H45/29F	L

32221-32299		Volvo B7TL		Plaxton President			H42/22F	
32221	LT52WUE	LN	32228	LT52XAM	L	32297	LK03NGV	L
32225	LT52WUK	L	32294	LK03NGJ	L	32298	LK03NGX	L
32226	LT52WUL	L	32295	LK03NGN	L	32299	LK03NGY	L
32227	LT52XAL	L	32296	LK03NGU	L			

Loading in Livingston town centre is 32227, a Plaxton President-bodied Volvo B7TL which started life in London as First London VTL1227

32669-32683		Volvo B7TL		Wright Eclipse Gemini			H45/29F	
32669	SN55HDZ	L	32674	SN55HFB	L	32679	SN55HFG	L
32670	SN55HEJ	L	32675	SN55HFC	L	32680	SN55HFH	L
32671	SN55HEU	L	32676	SN55HFD	G	32681	SN55HFJ	L
32672	SN55HEV	G	32677	SN55HFE	L	32682	SN55HFK	L
32673	SN55HFA	L	32678	SN55HFF	L	32683	SN55HFL	u

32919	W919VLN	Dennis Trident SFD313	Plaxton President 10.5m	H43/27F	w
32921	W921VLN	Dennis Trident SFD313	Plaxton President 10.5m	H43/27F	L
32924	W924VLN	Dennis Trident SFD313	Plaxton President 10.5m	H43/26F	L
32951	W951ULL	Dennis Trident SFD313	Alexander ALX400 10.5m	H45/27F	w
32968	X968HLT	Dennis Trident SFD113	Plaxton President 9.9m	H39/20D	w
32995	Y995NLP	Dennis Trident SFD113	Plaxton President 9.9m	H39/25F	L
33029	LK51UYL	Dennis Trident SFD339	Plaxton President 10.5m	H42/22F	L
33030	LK51UYM	Dennis Trident SFD339	Plaxton President 10.5m	H42/22F	u
33037	LN51DWA	Dennis Trident SFD136	Plaxton President 9.9m	H39/22F	u
33050	LN51GKF	Dennis Trident SFD136	Plaxton President 9.9m	H39/22F	u
33059	LN51GJO	Dennis Trident SFD136	Plaxton President 9.9m	H39/??F	L

33131-33139		Dennis Trident SFD336		Plaxton President 10.5m			H42/26F	
33131	LT02ZBX	L	33137	LT02ZFJ	u			
33135	LT02ZCE	L	33139	LT02ZFL	u			

33431-33449		ADL E40D SFDB32		ADL Enviro 400MMC 10.5m			H45/29F	
33431	SN66WGA	LN	33438	SN66WGK	LN	33445	SN66WGX	LN
33432	SN66WGC	LN	33439	SN66WGM	LN	33446	SN66WGY	LN
33433	SN66WGD	LN	33440	SN66WGO	LN	33447	SN66WGZ	LN
33434	SN66WGE	LN	33441	SN66WGP	LN	33448	SN66WHA	LN
33435	SN66WGF	LN	33442	SN66WGU	LN	33449	SN66WHB	LN
33436	SN66WGG	LN	33443	SN66WGV	LN			
33437	SN66WGJ	LN	33444	SN66WGW	LN			

36007-36030		Scania N94UD		East Lancs Omnidekka			H47/33F	
36007	SN05HWW	B	36015	SN05HWO	B	36023	SN05HWD	BN
36008	SN05HWX	B	36016	SN05HWM	B	36024	SN05HWR	B
36009	SN05HWY	B	36017	SN05HWJ	BN	36025	SN05HWS	B
36010	SN05HWZ	B	36018	SN05HWG	BN	36026	SN05HWU	B
36011	SN05HXA	B	36019	SN05HWH	BN	36027	SN05HWV	BN
36012	SN05HXB	BN	36020	SN05HWF	B	36028	SN05HWT	BN
36013	SN05HWL	BN	36021	SN05HWP	B	36029	SN55KKE	B
36014	SN05HWK	BN	36022	SN05HWE	B	36030	SN55KKF	BN

37133-37273		Volvo B9TL		Wright Eclipse Gemini			H45/29F	
37133	SN57HDH	G	37140	SN57HCZ	G	37267	SN57JAO	LN
37134	SN57HDJ	G	37141	SN57HDA	G	37268	SN57JAU	LN
37135	SN57HCP	G	37142	SN57HDC	G	37269	SN57JBE	LN
37136	SN57HCU	G	37143	SN57HDD	LN	37270	SN57JBO	LN
37137	SN57HCV	LN	37144	SN57HDE	LN	37271	SN57JBU	LN
37138	SN57HCX	G	37145	SN57HDF	LN	37272	SN57JBV	LN
37139	SN57HCY	G	37266	SN57HDG	LN	37273	SN57JBX	LN

39301-39305		ADL E40H SFD911		ADL Enviro 400MMC 10.8m			H47/31F	
39301	SN15ELC	BN	39303	SN65CVK	BN	39305	SN65CVM	BN
39302	SN65CVJ	BN	39304	SN65CVL	BN			

47531-47617		Wright Streetlite DF		Wright Streetlite 10.8m			B37F	
47531	SN64CJY	L	47534	SN64CKC	L	47615	SN64CKV	L
47532	SN64CJZ	L	47613	SN64CKD	L	47616	SN64CKX	L
47533	SN64CKA	L	47614	SN64CKU	L	47617	SN64CKY	L

50232-50468		Optare Solo M850		Optare Solo 8.5m			B26F	
				* - B27F				
50232	Y251HHL	L	50234	Y253HHL	B	50468*	SJ03DPZ	L
50233	Y252HHL	L	50460*	SJ03DOH	B			

53702	LK05DXP	Optare Solo M780		Optare Solo 7.8m			B21F	L
53705	LK05DXT	Optare Solo M780		Optare Solo 7.8m			B21F	L
53706	LK05DXU	Optare Solo M780		Optare Solo 7.8m			B21F	L
60198	Y344XBN	Scania L94UB		Wright Floline			B43F	Lt
60199	X256USH	Scania L94UB		Wright Floline			B43F	Lt
60204	X272USH	Scania L94UB		Wright Floline			B43F	LNt

Above: *Seen here carrying a special tartan-based variation of corporate livery is 37138, a Wright Eclipse Gemini-bodied Volvo B7TL, pictured in Galashiels while on route 7 to Langlee.*

Below: *Seen in Falkirk is Wright Streetlite DF 47617 in the First Scotland East fleet, seen here while on route 3 to Falkirk Wheel, a route for which this special Craig Sibbald Express livery is carried*

61220-61233		Scania L94UB			Wright Solar			B43F	
61220	YM52UVS	w	61225	YM52UWA	BN	61233	YM52UWN	L
61222	YM52UVU	L	61229	YM52UWG	L			
61224	YM52UVZ	BN	61230	YM52UWH	G			

62190	W592RFS	Volvo B10BLE	Alexander ALX300	B44F	La
62212	W682RNA	Volvo B10BLE	Wright Renown	B43F	LNt
62356	SN51MSU	Scania L94UB	Wright Solar	B43F	w
62357	SN51MSY	Scania L94UB	Wright Solar	B43F	w

63157-63276		Wright Streetlite Max			Wright Streetlite 11.5m			B41F	
63157	SN64CKE	LN	63247	SN64CPF	LN	63263	SN65OJM	L
63158	SN64CKF	LN	63248	SN64CPK	LN	63264	SN65OJO	L
63159	SN64CKG	LN	63249	SN64CPO	LN	63265	SN65OJP	L
63160	SN64CKJ	LN	63251	SN65OKR	LN	63266	SN65OJR	L
63219	SN14DXW	LN	63252	SN65OKS	LN	63267	SN65OJS	L
63220	SN14DXX	LN	63253	SN65OKT	LN	63268	SN65OJT	L
63221	SN14DXY	LN	63254	SN65OKU	LN	63269	SN65OJU	L
63222	SN14DXZ	LN	63255	SN65OKV	LN	63270	SN65OJV	L
63223	SN14DYA	L	63256	SN65OJE	L	63271	SN65OJW	L
63241	SN64CKK	LN	63257	SN65OJF	L	63272	SN65OJX	L
63242	SN64CKL	LN	63258	SN65OJG	L	63273	SN65OJY	L
63243	SN64CKO	LN	63259	SN65OJH	L	63274	SN65OJZ	L
63244	SN64CKP	LN	63260	SN65OJJ	L	63275	SN65OKA	L
63245	SN64COU	LN	63261	SN65OJK	L	63276	SN65OKB	L
63246	SN64CPE	LN	63262	SN65OJL	L			

Seen in Livingston while on route 22A to Queensferry is First Scotland East 64011, a Mercedes-Benz Citaro which started life in London as First Capital EC2011

64003-64011		Mercedes-Benz O530		Mercedes-Benz Citaro			B36D	
64003	LT02NTY	LN	64007	LT02NUE	LN	64011	LT02NVY	LN
64004	LT02NUA	u	64010	LT02NUJ	LN			

65694-65754		Scania L94UB		Wright Solar * - B43F			B44F	
65694*	SN53KHJ	BN	65714	SN54KDX	B	65744	SN55JVJ	G
65695*	SN53KHK	BN	65715	SN54KDZ	L	65745	SN55JVK	G
65698*	SN53KHO	L	65716	SN54KEJ	L	65746	SN55JVL	G
65699*	SN53KHP	L	65717	SN54KEK	L	65747	SN55JVM	G
65701*	SN04CKX	BN	65718	SN54KEU	L	65748	SN55JVO	G
65702*	SN04CLF	BN	65719	SN54KFA	BN	65749	SN55JVP	G
65708	SN54KDF	B	65720	SN54KFC	BN	65750	SN55JVA	G
65709	SN54KDJ	BN	65721	SN54KFD	BN	65751	SN55JVC	BN
65710	SN54KDK	BN	65722	SN54KFE	BN	65752	SN55JVD	L
65711	SN54KDO	BN	65723	SN54KFF	BN	65753	SN55JVE	BN
65712	SN54KDU	BN	65742	SN55JVG	G	65754	SN06AHK	L
65713	SN54KDV	BN	65743	SN55JVH	G			

About to leave Buchanan Bus Station for Stirling is 65715, a Wright Solar-bodied Scania L94UB

67745-67782		ADL E30D SFD1C8		ADL Enviro 300 11.5m			B41F	
67745	SN62ANR	BN	67753	SN62APO	BN	67759	SN62ATZ	BN
67746	SN62ANU	G	67754	SN62APZ	BN	67760	SN62AUC	G
67747	SN62AOA	BN	67755	SN62ASO	BN	67761	SN62AUH	BN
67748	SN62AOC	BN	67756	SN62ASU	BN	67762	SN62AUJ	BN
67751	SN62AOZ	BN	67757	SN62ASX	BN	67763	SN62AUK	G
67752	SN62APF	G	67758	SN62ASZ	BN	67764	SN62AUU	BN

67765	SN62AUW	BN	67776	SN62AXU	G	67780	SN62AYA	G
67773	SN62AXH	G	67777	SN62AXW	G	67781	SN62AYB	G
67774	SN62AXK	G	67778	SN62AXY	G	67782	SN62AYJ	G
67775	SN62AXO	G	67779	SN62AXZ	G			

68504-68566		BMC 1100FE		BMC * - B60F			B55FL	
68504*	CU54CYX	u	68558	LK55ABU	L	68566	SF55TXC	L
68514*	CU54DCF	u	68560	LK55ABX	u			
68556	MX55NWC	u	68561	HX55AOJ	G			

This BMC 1100FE, 68561, which forms part of the schoolbus fleet, was acting as a crew ferry vehicle when seen in Falkirk.

69254-69410		Volvo B7RLE		Wright Eclipse Urban * - B43F			B44F	
69254*	SK07JVN	L	69281	SN57JBZ	L	69293	SN57HZY	L
69255*	SK07JVO	L	69282	SN57JCJ	L	69294	SN57HZZ	L
69256*	SK07JVP	L	69283	SN57JCO	L	69402	SN09EZW	L
69257	SK57ADO	L	69284	SN57JCU	L	69403	SN09EZX	L
69258	SK57ADU	L	69285	SN57JCV	L	69404	SN09FAU	L
69259	SK57ADV	L	69286	SN57JCX	L	69405	SN09FBA	L
69260	SK57ADX	L	69287	SN57JCY	L	69406	SN09FBB	L
69261	SK57ADZ	L	69288	SN57JCZ	L	69407	SN09FBC	L
69262	SK57AEA	L	69289	SN57JDF	L	69408	SN09FBD	L
69263	SK57AEB	L	69290	SN57JDJ	L	69409	SN09FBE	L
69264	SK57AEC	L	69291	SN57JDK	L	69410	SN09FBF	L
69280	SN57MSU	L	69292	SN57HZX	L			

Passing through Linlithgow on its way to Falkirk is 69292, a Wright Eclipse Urban-bodied Volvo B7RLE, showing the blue and gold express variation of corporate livery carried by the vehicle

Liveries
Unless stated below, all vehicles in the fleet carry FirstGroup corporate livery:
Allover white: 20302, 20307, 20354, 20355, 20360, 20362, 20368
First Coaching: 20321, 20322, 20351, 20352, 20361, 20363-20366, 20369-20371
Schoolbus: 20326, 20327, 68504, 68514, 68556, 68558, 68560, 68561, 68566
Bluebird: 32678, 32679, 33431-33449, 36007, 37137, 37272, 47531-47534, 47613-47617, 63157-63160, 63221, 63223, 63241-63244, 63246-63249, 63251-63276, 69256, 69258-69262, 69264, 69280-69282, 69284, 69290, 69292-69294, 69410
Tartan-based corporate livery: 37133-37136, 37138, 37139
Unilink: 39301-39305, 65694, 65722, 65723
First Training: 60204

South West

BR   Bridgewater - Boards Road, Bridgewater, TA6 4BB
CE   Camborne - Union Street, Camborne, TR14 8HF
TA   Taunton - Tower Street, Taunton, TA1 4AF
YE   Yeovil - Bus Garage, Reckleford, Yeovil, BA21 4EH

| 11036-11087 | | Mercedes-Benz O530G | | Mercedes-Benz Citaro | | AB27T | |
| | | | | * - AB49T | | | |

11036	AN02EDN	CE	11038	CN02EDN	CE	11087*	BX54UDU	CE
11037	BN02EDN	CE	11085*	BX54UDE	CE			

19010	YK06AUA	Volvo B7LA		Wright Streetcar		AB42D	u
20357	CV55ABK	Volvo B7R		Plaxton Profile		C46FTL	CE
20358	CV55ACO	Volvo B7R		Plaxton Profile		C46FTL	CE
20363	CV55ACZ	Volvo B7R		Plaxton Profile		C45FL	CE
20502	AO02RBZ	Volvo B12M		Plaxton Paragon		C53F	CE
20504	AO02RCU	Volvo B12M		Plaxton Paragon		C53F	CE

| 20556-20561 | | Volvo B12B | | Plaxton Panther | | C48FT | |
| | | | | * - C53F, $ - C50FT | | | |

20556*	TT04TRU	CE	20558	TT55TRU	CE
20557$	TT05TRU	CE	20561	TT07TRU	CE

| 20801-20805 | | Volvo B12M | | Plaxton Panther | | C44FT | |

20801	YN08OWO	u	20803	YN08OWR	CE	20805	YN08OWV	CE
20802	YN08OWP	CE	20804	YN08OWU	CE			

21126	YIL8826	Dennis Javelin SFD721		UVG		C70F	CE
21165	N763PAE	Dennis Javelin		WS Vanguard 2		C57F	CE

| 23008-23014 | | Scania K114IB | | Irizar Century | | C53F | |

23008	YV03UBA	w	23011	YV03UBD	CE	23014	MIG9614	CE
23009	YV03UBB	TN	23012	YV03UBE	TN			
23010	YV03UBC	TN	23013	YN04AJU	CE			

| 23208 | WM04NZU | Volvo B12B | | Plaxton Panther | | C49FT | CE |

| 23313-23325 | | Scania K114EB | | Irizar PB | | C49FT | |

23313	481FPO	CE	23317	HVJ716	u	23324	552UKT	CE
23315	TFO319	TN	23318	NER621	CE	23325	VJT738	CE
23316	530OHU	u	23322	OWB243	TN			

| 30871-30882 | | Volvo B7TL | | Alexander ALX400 | | H49/28F | |
| | | | | * - H49/29F, $ - H48/27F | | | |

30871	W726DWX	CE	30875*	W771DWX	CE	30879	W734DWX	CE
30872	W727DWX	CE	30876*	W731DWX	CE	30880	W735DWX	CE
30873*	W728DWX	CE	30877	W732DWX	CE	30882*	W737DWX	u
30874$	W729DWX	CE	30878	W733DWX	CE			

| 31820-31846 | | Volvo Olympian | | NC Palatine 1 | | | H47/27D | |
| | | | | * - DPH47/31F | | | | |

| 31820 | P920RYO | w | 31826 | P926RYO | w | | | |
| 31821 | P921RYO | w | 31846* | R346LGH | w | | | |

| 32027-32097 | | Volvo B7TL | | Alexander ALX400 | | | H49/29F | |
| | | | | * - O43/25F, $ - H49/27F | | | | |

| 32027* | V124LGC | w | 32055 | W215XBD | w | | | |
| 32053 | W213XBD | w | 32097$ | KP51WCY | CE | | | |

| 32102-32211 | | Volvo B7TL | | Plaxton President | | | H42/27F | |
| | | | | * - H39/20F | | | | |

32102*	LT02ZCL	CE	32200	LT52WTE	u	32208	LT52WTO	CE
32103*	LT02ZCN	CE	32202	LT52WTG	u	32209	LT52WTP	CE
32104*	LT02ZCO	CE	32207	LT52WTN	CE	32211	LT52WTU	u

32713	W713RHT	Dennis Trident SFD323	East Lancs Lolyne 10.5m	H49/30F	CE
32716	W716RHT	Dennis Trident SFD323	East Lancs Lolyne 10.5m	H49/30F	w
32755	WK52SYE	Dennis Trident SFD349	East Lancs Lolyne 10.5m	H49/30F	CE

| 32756-32762 | | Dennis Trident SFD338 | E Lancs Myllenium Lolyne 10.5m | H49/29F | |
| | | | * - H49/30F | | |

32756	WA54OLO	CE	32759	WA54OLN	CE	32762*	WJ55CRZ	CE
32757	WA54OLP	CE	32760	WA54OLR	CE			
32758	WA54OLT	CE	32761*	WJ55CRX	CE			

Seen in Bridgewater is First South West 32874, a Plaxton President-bodied Dennis Trident which started life in London with First Capital as TN874, pictured heading for Kings Drive

32808-32883			Dennis Trident SFD113			Plaxton President 9.9m * - H39/24F			H39/21F

32808*	T808LLC	CE	32853	HIG1512	CE	32874	HIG1524	CE
32818	OIG1788	BR	32858	HIG1528	TN	32876	HIG1527	CE
32819*	T819LLC	CE	32859	OIG1794	CE	32878	HIG1531	u
32843	MIG3842	w	32861	HIG1540	u	32879	HIG1533	CE
32844	MIG3844	u	32866	MIG3859	w	32880	HIG1538	u
32846*	T846LLC	CE	32872	HIG1521	CE	32883	OIG1797	CE
32851	HIG1519	CE	32873	HIG1523	CE			

32930	MIG4760	Dennis Trident SFD313	Plaxton President 10.5m	H43/24D	CE
32935	W935ULL	Dennis Trident SFD313	Alexander ALX400 10.5m	H45/27F	w
32936	W936ULL	Dennis Trident SFD313	Alexander ALX400 10.5m	H45/24F	w
32947	W947ULL	Dennis Trident SFD313	Alexander ALX400 10.5m	H45/27F	w
32954	MIG9615	Dennis Trident SFD113	Plaxton President 9.9m	H39/24F	BR
32955	X611HLT	Dennis Trident SFD113	Plaxton President 9.9m	H39/20F	CE
32961	MIG4761	Dennis Trident SFD113	Plaxton President 9.9m	H39/24F	BR
33004	LK51UZT	Dennis Trident SFD339	Plaxton President 10.5m	H42/23F	u
33007	LK51UZE	Dennis Trident SFD339	Plaxton President 10.5m	H42/23F	u
33066	LN51GLF	Dennis Trident SFD136	Plaxton President 9.9m	H39/20Г	CE
33067	LN51GLJ	Dennis Trident SFD136	Plaxton President 9.9m	H39/20F	u
33068	LN51GLK	Dennis Trident SFD136	Plaxton President 9.9m	H39/20F	w
33084	LN51GME	Dennis Trident SFD336	Plaxton President 10.5m	H42/22F	u
33099	LN51GLZ	Dennis Trident SFD336	Plaxton President 10.5m	H42/22F	u
33111	PJ02PZP	Dennis Trident SFD134	Plaxton President 9.9m	H41/23D	CE
33112	PJ02PZY	Dennis Trident SFD134	Plaxton President 9.9m	H41/23D	CE

Seen in Taunton Bus Station is 33379 leaving on route 22A to Tonedale It is an Alexander ALX400-bodied Dennis Trident originally new to First CentreWest as TAL1379

33171-33242		Dennis Trident SFD136		Plaxton President 9.9m * - H39/23F		H39/24F	
33171*	LR02LYO	CE	33175	LR02LYU	CE	33235*	LT52WWY CE
33173	LR02LYS	CE	33176	LR02LYV	CE	33242*	LT52WWL u
33174	LR02LYT	CE	33177	LR02LYW	CE		

33377-33382		Dennis Trident SFD33G		Alexander ALX400 10.5m		H42/34F	
33377	XFF283	TN	33379	WSV409	TN	33381	OIG1791 TN
33378	UHW661	TN	33380	OIG1790	TN	33382	OIG1792 TN

33420	WA08MVE	Dennis Trident SFD46M	Alexander Enviro 400 10.8m	H42/26F	CE
33421	WA08MVF	Dennis Trident SFD46M	Alexander Enviro 400 10.8m	H42/26F	CE
33422	WA08MVG	Dennis Trident SFD46M	Alexander Enviro 400 10.8m	H42/26F	CE

33450-33479		ADL E40D SFDB32		ADL Enviro 400MMC 10.5m * - H43/29F		H42/28F	
33450	WK66CCA	CE	33460	WK66CCY	u	33470*	WK66BYU CE
33451	WK66CCD	CE	33461	WK66CCZ	u	33471*	WK66BYV CE
33452	WK66CCE	CE	33462	WK66CDE	u	33472*	WK66BYW CE
33453	WK66CCF	CE	33463	WK66CDF	u	33473*	WK66BYX CE
33454	WK66CCJ	CE	33464	WK66CDN	u	33474*	WK66BYY CE
33455	WK66CCN	u	33465	WK66CDO	u	33475*	WK66BYZ CE
33456	WK66CCO	u	33466	WK66CDU	u	33476*	WK66BZA CE
33457	WK66CCU	u	33467	WK66CDV	u	33477*	WK66BZB CE
33458	WK66CCV	u	33468	WK66CDX	u	33478*	WK66BZC CE
33459	WK66CCX	u	33469	WK66CDY	u	33479*	WK66BZD CE

34041	P241UCW	Volvo Olympian	NC Palatine 2	H43/27F	CE
34049	P249UCW	Volvo Olympian	NC Palatine 2	H43/27F	w
34052	P252UCW	Volvo Olympian	NC Palatine 2	H43/27F	CE
34091	T891KLF	Volvo Olympian	NC Palatine 1	H47/31F	w

34137-34191		Volvo Olympian		NC Palatine 2 * - O47/29F, $ - H47/29F		H43/29F	
34137*	L637SEU	w	34173	S673AAE	w	34185	S685AAE CE
34138$	L638SEU	CE	34182	S682AAE	CE	34189	S689AAE w
34172	S672AAE	w	34183	S683AAE	CE	34191	S691AAE CE

34198	N121UHP	Volvo Olympian	Alexander Royale	CH43/28F	w
34311	L311PWR	Volvo Olympian	NC Palatine 1	H47/29F	CE
36300	BF63HDC	Volvo B5TL	Wright Eclipse Gemini 3	H45/28F	TN
38004	D704GHY	Volvo Citybus B10M-50	Alexander RV	O47/35F	w
38005	D705GHY	Volvo Citybus B10M-50	Alexander RV	O47/35F	w
38006	D706GHY	Volvo Citybus B10M-50	Alexander RV	O47/35F	TN

40033-40037		Dennis Dart SLF SFD222		Plaxton Pointer 2 10.1m		B32F	
40033	S343SUX	w	40035	S375SUX	w		
40034	S374SUX	w	40037	S377SUX	w		

40321	Y904KND	Optare Solo M920	Optare Solo 9.2m	B28F	u
40322	Y905KND	Optare Solo M920	Optare Solo 9.2m	B28F	CE

40570-40594		Volvo B6BLE		Wright Crusader 2			B38F	
40570	MIG9616	TN	40585	YJ51RJV	TN	40592	YG02DHP	BR
40581	YJ51RHY	u	40586	OIG1796	TN	40593	YG02DHY	TN
40582	YJ51RHZ	w	40588	YJ51RGO	BR	40594	YG02DLK	BR
40583	YJ51RJO	w	40590	YJ51RGV	BR			
40584	HIG8790	w	40591	YJ51RGX	BR			

41132	P132NLW	Dennis Dart SLF SFD112	Marshall Capital 9.3m	B31F	w
41383	X383HLR	Dennis Dart SLF SFD212	Marshall Capital 10.2m	B33F	w
41490	LT02ZFB	Dennis Dart SLF SFD6B2	Marshall Capital 8.8m	B25F	CE
42117	R617YCR	Dennis Dart SLF SFD322	Plaxton Pointer 2 10.7m	B37F	TN
42235	T35JCV	Dennis Dart SLF SFD212	Plaxton Pointer 2 10.1m	B34FB	w
42252	P452SCV	Dennis Dart SLF SFD212	Plaxton Pointer 10m	B34F	CEt
42358	EY05FYP	Dennis Dart SLF SFD5BA	Caetano Nimbus 11.3m	B43F	CE
42430	P430ORL	Dennis Dart SLF SFD212	Plaxton Pointer 10.1m	B35F	w

42469-42477		Dennis Dart SLF SFD322		Alexander ALX200 10.7m			B37F	
42469	T469JCV	w	42472	T472YTT	w	42475	X475SCY	w
42470	T470JCV	w	42473	T473YTT	w	42476	X476SCY	w
42471	T471JCV	w	42474	X474SCY	w	42477	X477SCY	w

42511-42526		Dennis Dart SLF SFD322		Plaxton Pointer 2 10.7m		B37F	
42511	R411WPX	w	42522	R422WPX	w		
42521	R421WPX	w	42526	R426WPX	w		

42558-42563		Dennis Dart SLF SFD1BA		Alexander Pointer 2 9.3m			B31F	
42558	SN05DZU	CE	42560	SN05DZW	CE	42563	SN05DZZ	u
42559	SN05DZV	CE	42562	SN05DZY	u			

42623	S723KNV	Dennis Dart SLF SFD322	Plaxton Pointer 2 10.7m	B39F	w
42719	R719RAD	Dennis Dart SLF SFD152	Plaxton Pointer 2 9.3m	B29F	w

42720-42802		Dennis Dart SLF SFD322		Plaxton Pointer 2 10.7m * - B36F			B37F	
42720	S720AFB	w	42752*	S652SNG	w	42801	Y1EDN	CE
42724	S724AFB	w	42758*	S658SNG	w	42802	Y2EDN	CE

42830-42835		Dennis Dart SLF SFD322		East Lancs Spryte 10.7m		B37F	
42830	T830RYC	TN	42833	V833DYD	TN		
42832	V832DYD	w	42835	V835DYD	TN		

42842	T367NUA	Dennis Dart SLF SFD322	Alexander ALX200 10.7m	B37F	w

42860-42954		Dennis Dart SLF SFD3CA		Alexander Pointer 2 10.7m * - B36F, $ - B38F			B37F	
42860	TT03TRU	CE	42875	SN53KKE	CE	42949	WX06OMF	YL
42871	SN53KKA	u	42876	SN53KJZ	CE	42950	WX06OMG	YL
42872	SN53KKB	CE	42924*	SN05EAA	CE	42951	WX06OMH	YL
42873	SN53KKC	CE	42942$	WA56OAP	CE	42952	WX06OMJ	YL
42874	SN53KKD	CE	42946$	WA56FTV	CE	42954	WX06OML	YL

Above: *Pictured here in Penzance is First South West 42872, a Dennis Dart SLF with Alexander Pointer 2 bodywork, seen while on route 17 to St Ives*

Below: *Seen here in Taunton in two-tone green Buses of Somerset livery is 43821, a Dennis Dart SLF with Plaxton Pointer 2 bodywork, pictured while on route 3 to Bishop's Hull.*

43809	S549SCV	Dennis Dart SLF SFD612	Plaxton Pointer 2 8.8m	B29F	w
43810	KU52RXJ	Dennis Dart SLF SFD6BA	Alexander Pointer 2 8.8m	B29F	CE
43811	MIG5685	Dennis Dart SLF SFD6BA	Alexander Pointer 2 8.8m	B29F	TN
43821	MIG3863	Dennis Dart SLF SFD612	Plaxton Pointer 2 8.8m	B29F	BR
43822	MIG3864	Dennis Dart SLF SFD612	Plaxton Pointer 2 8.8m	B29F	BR
43823	MIG3865	Dennis Dart SLF SFD612	Plaxton Pointer 2 8.8m	B29F	TN

| 43854-43874 | | Dennis Dart SLF SFD6BA | Caetano Slimbus 8.8m | B29F | |

43854	EG52FFZ	CE	43862	EG52FGK	CE	43869	EG52FFL	CE
43855	EG52FGC	CE	43863	EG52FFK	CE	43870	EG52FFT	u
43856	EG52FGD	CE	43864	EG52FGA	CE	43871	EG52FFU	u
43857	EG52FGE	CE	43865	EG52FGU	CE	43872	EG52FFV	u
43859	EG52FHD	TN	43866	EG52FGV	CE	43873	EG52FFJ	u
43860	EG52FGF	TN	43867	EG52FHC	CE	43874	EG52FFY	u
43861	EG52FGJ	CE	43868	EG52FGX	CE			

43904	SK52OJF	Dennis Dart SPD SFD4D8	Alexander Pointer 2 11.3m	B42F	CE
43905	SK52OKD	Dennis Dart SPD SFD4D8	Alexander Pointer 2 11.3m	B42F	CE
43906	SK52OKH	Dennis Dart SPD SFD4D8	Alexander Pointer 2 11.3m	B42F	CE
44534	SN62DCX	ADL E20D SFD7E1	ADL Enviro 200 10.8m	B39F	TN
44535	SN62DCY	ADL E20D SFD7E1	ADL Enviro 200 10.8m	B39F	TN
44536	SN62DCZ	ADL E20D SFD7E1	ADL Enviro 200 10.8m	B39F	TN
44601	MX14FUT	ADL E20D SFD8E1	ADL Enviro 200 10.2m	B39F	TN

Seen here leaving Taunton Bus Station is First South West 45112, a short wheelbase Alexander Enviro 200, pictured while on route 6 to Juniper Road, and showing the Buses of Somerset livery carried

44922	YX09ADV	Dennis E200Dart SFD151	Alexander Enviro 200 9.4m	B28F	TN
44923	YX09ADZ	Dennis E200Dart SFD151	Alexander Enviro 200 9.4m	B28F	TN
44924	YX09AHK	Dennis E200Dart SFD151	Alexander Enviro 200 9.4m	B28F	TN

44925-44934		ADL E20D SFD1D1		ADL Enviro 200 9.4m			B28F	
44925	YX11HNW	u	44927	YX11HNZ	u	44933	YW14FHU	TN
44926	YX11HNY	u	44932	MX62AVV	TN	44934	MX61BAV	TN

45111-45115		Dennis E200Dart SFD151		Alexander Enviro 200 9.4m			B28F	
45111	YX58FRJ	TN	45113	YX58FRL	TN	45115	YX58FRP	TN
45112	YX58FRK	TN	45114	YX58FRN	TN			

47535-47572		Wright Streetlite DF		Wright Streetlite 10.8m * - B42F			B41F	
47535	MX63XAM	TN	47538	MX63XAP	TN	47542	MX13BBF	TN
47536	MX63XAN	TN	47540	MX62ARU	BR	47543*	MX13BBJ	TN
47537	MX63XAO	TN	47541	MX13BAV	TN	47572	MX13BCU	u

48229-48273		Volvo B6BLE		Wright Crusader 2 * - B38F			B36F	
48229	W829PFB	w	48265	W605PAF	w	48271*	OIG1798	BR
48232	W832PFB	w	48266	W606PAF	w	48272*	WK02TYH	BR
48233	W833PFB	w	48267	W607PAF	w	48273*	YG02DLV	BR
48234	W834PFB	w	48269	W609PAF	w			
48262	W602PAF	w	48270*	WK02TYD	BR			

50236-53046		Optare Solo M850		Optare Solo 8.5m * - B26F, $ - B20F, % - B22F			B27F	
50236*	Y256HHL	u	50467$	SJ03DPY	YL	53014	W814PAF	CE
50277	W308DWX	BR	53001	V801KAF	w	53040%	VU02PKX	CE
50284	W315DWX	w	53009	W809PAF	w	53045*	VU03YJX	CE
50285	W336DWX	w	53011	W811PAF	w	53046*	VU03YJY	TN
50291	W322DWX	TN	53012	W812PAF	CE			
50466$	SJ03DPX	YL	53013	W813PAF	CE			

53052-53057		Optare Solo M920		Optare Solo 9.2m			B28F	
53052	LK53MBX	YL	53055	LK53MDF	YL	53057	LK53PNO	YL
53054	LK53MDE	YL	53056	LK53MDJ	YL			

53107-53111		Optare Solo M850		Optare Solo 8.5m			B26F	
53107	EO02FLG	w	53109	EO02FLJ	YL	53111	EO02FKZ	YL
53108	EO02FLH	CE	53110	EO02FLK	YL			

53118-53154		Optare Solo M920		Optare Solo 9.2m * - B29F			B30F	
53118	EO02NEU	TN	53120	EO02NFA	TN			
53119	EO02NEY	TN	53154*	HIG8433	CE			

53205-53404		Optare Solo M880		Optare Solo 8.8m			B29F	
53205	HIG8434	CE	53403	TL54TVL	CE			
53402	T20TVL	CE	53404	TT54TVL	CE			

53503	YJ06YSK	Optare Solo M710SE	Optare Solo 7.1m	B23F	CE
53504	YJ56AOT	Optare Solo M710SE	Optare Solo 7.1m	B23F	CE
53505	YJ56AOU	Optare Solo M710SE	Optare Solo 7.1m	B23F	CE
53701	LK05DYO	Optare Solo M780	Optare Solo 7.8m	B21F	CE

53704	LK05DXS	Optare Solo M780	Optare Solo 7.8m	B21F	CE
53709	MX59AVP	Optare Solo M780SL	Optare Solo 7.8m	B27F	CE
53801	YN04KWR	Optare Solo M780	Optare Solo 7.8m	B24F	CE
53803	WX05RRY	Optare Solo M850SL	Optare Solo 8.5m	B28F	CE
53805	WX05RSO	Optare Solo M850SL	Optare Solo 8.5m	B28F	TN
53826	YK05CDN	Optare Solo M780	Optare Solo 7.8m	B24F	CE
53827	YK05CDO	Optare Solo M920	Optare Solo 9.2m	B29F	u
54602	OIG1799	Ford Transit	Ford	M16	BR

Seen here in Penzance is First South West 53826, an Optare Solo, pictured here while running out of service

55101-55108		Wright Streetlite WF		Wright Streetlite 9.5m * - B37F		B33F	
55101	MX61BCF	TN	55103	MX12JXV	TN	55105*	MX62AXN	TN
55102*	MX12DZA	TN	55104	MX61BBZ	TN	55108*	MX12DYM	TN

56000-56004		Mercedes-Benz Vario 0814		Plaxton Cheetah * - C25F, $ - C29F		C33F	
56000*	W416RCU	CE	56002$	YN53VBU	u	56004	EY54BPX	u
56001	YN53VBT	u	56003	YN53VBV	u			

| 57000 | MX06AEB | Enterprise Bus EB01 | Plaxton Primo | B28F | TN |

62191-62245		Volvo B10BLE		Wright Renown * - B43F, $ - B41F		B44F	
62191*	X685ADK	TN	62214$	S673SVU	w	62242	Y939CSF	u
62192*	X686ADK	TN	62238	Y947CSF	TN	62245	OIG1795	TN

| 64049 | WK08ESV | Mercedes-Benz O530 | Mercedes-Benz Citaro | B39F | CE |
| 64050 | WK10AZU | Mercedes-Benz O530 | Mercedes-Benz Citaro | B39F | CE |

| 64051-64057 | | Mercedes-Benz O295 | Mercedes-Benz Citaro | B38F | |

64051	WK15DLZ	CE	64054	WK15DMO	CE	64057	WK15DMX	CE
64052	WK15DME	CE	64055	WK15DMU	CE			
64053	WK15DMF	CE	64056	WK15DMV	CE			

| 65579 | T579JNG | Scania L94UB | Wright Floline | DP40F | w |

| 65759-65764 | | Scania L94UB | Wright Solar | B43F | |

| 65759 | YN05GXF | CE | 65761 | YN06NXP | CE | 65763 | YN05GXM | CE |
| 65760 | YN05GXR | CE | 65762 | YN06NXW | CE | 65764 | YN05GXO | CE |

| 66745 | YJ54XVW | Volvo B7RLE | Wright Eclipse Urban | B40F | BR |
| 67600 | 260ERY | Dennis Enviro 300 SFD213 | Alexander Enviro 300 12.5m | B48F | TN |

| 67701-67710 | | Dennis Enviro 300 SFD1C8 | Alexander Enviro 300 11.8m | B37F | |

67701	SN60EAA	TN	67705	SN60EAG	TN	67709	SN60EAP	TN
67702	SN60EAC	TN	67706	SN60EAJ	TN	67710	SN60EAW	TN
67703	SN60EAE	TN	67707	SN60EAM	TN			
67704	SN60EAF	TN	67708	SN60EAO	TN			

| 68503-68571 | | BMC 1100FE | BMC | B60F | |
| | | | * - B55FL, $ - B55F | | |

68503	BX54VUN	CE	68534	LK54FNL	CE	68569$	BV57MSX	CE
68505	CU54CYY	CE	68552*	EU05DXT	CE	68570$	BV57MSY	t
68513	CU54DCE	CE	68555	EU55NWS	TN	68571*	BG57ZGJ	CE
68521	KP54AZV	TN	68567$	BV57MSO	CE			

| 69012-69230 | | Volvo B7RLE | Wright Eclipse Urban | B43F | |

69012	SF55UAD	TN	69212	MX06VPN	YE	69225	MX56AEP	TN
69013	SF55UAE	TN	69218	MX56AEG	TN	69226	MX56AET	TN
69017	SF55UAK	w	69219	MX56AEJ	TN	69227	MX56AEU	TN
69018	SF55UAL	TN	69220	MX56AEK	TN	69228	MX56AEV	TN
69206	MV06DYU	CE	69221	MX56AEL	TN	69229	MX56AEW	CE
69207	MX06VPG	CE	69222	MX56AEM	TN	69230	MX56AEY	CE
69208	MX06VPJ	CE	69223	MX56AEN	TN			
69209	MX06VPK	TN	69224	MX56AEO	TN			

Previous registrations

11036	04D62404, SN04XYA	23318	YN55PXJ
11037	04D62405, SN04XYY	23322	YN06CGV
11038	04D62423, SN04XXZ	23324	YN06CGY
21126	R884HEJ	23325	YN06CGZ
21165	ER86AA, N303OHX, ER86AA	31846	R346LGH, WLT346
23014	YN04AJX	32818	T818LLC
23313	YN54NYU	32843	T843LLC
23315	YN55PXF	32844	T844LLC
23316	YN55PXG	32851	T851LLC
23317	YN55PXH	32853	T853LLC

Seen here in Truro Bus Station is First South West 69225, a Wright Eclipse Urban-bodied Volvo B7RLE, pictured while on route 18 to Camborne

32858	V858HBY		40037	HY9322
32859	V859HBY		40570	YJ51PZZ
32861	V861HBY		40581	YJ51RHY, XFF283
32866	T866KLF		40582	YJ51RHZ, UHW661
32872	V872HBY		40583	YJ51RJO, 260ERY
32873	T873KLF		40584	YJ51RJU
32874	V874HBY		40585	YJ51RJV
32876	T876KLF		40586	YJ51RJX
32878	T878KLF		42358	J79350
32879	T879KLF		42752	HV5822
32880	T880KLF		42758	HV5346
32883	T883KLF		42832	T832RYC
32930	W899VLN		42833	T833RYC
32935	W935ULL, MIG6219		43811	WK52WTV
32936	W936ULL, MIG6096		43821	X201HAE
32947	W947ULL, MIG8433		43822	X202HAE
32954	X954HLT		43823	X203HAE
32961	X961HLT		43854	J101729
33377	LK53EYW		43855	J101728
33378	LK53EYX		43856	J101724
33379	LK53EYY		43857	J101721
33380	LK53EYZ		43859	J101732
33381	LK53EZA		43860	J101720
33382	LK53EZB		43861	J101719
40033	HV7438		43862	J101723
40034	HV6798		43863	J101718
40035	HZ220		43864	J101727

43865	J101725		48271	WK02TYF
43866	J101726		53154	YJ05XOR
43867	J101733		53205	YJ05XNV
43868	J101731		54602	RA04YHS
43869	J101706		56000	W4TRU
43870	J101722		62191	X685ADK, OIG1791
43871	J101717		62192	X686ADK, OIG1792
43872	J101716		62245	Y938CSF
43873	J101703		67600	SN53KKY
43874	J101730		69206	06D67526

Liveries

Unless stated below, all vehicles in this fleet carry FirstGroup corporate livery:

Eden Project: 11036-11038, 11085, 11087, 42801, 42802

ftr: 19010

Allover white: 20357, 20358, 23313, 36300, 42623, 44601, 44932-44934, 47535-47538, 47540-47543, 47572, 55101-55104, 55108, 69227

First Coaching: 20502, 20504, 23009-23011, 23014, 56001, 56003

Two-tone blue: 20556

Truronian: 20557, 20558

Newells Travel: 20561

Webber: 21126

Schoolbus: 21165, 68503, 68505, 68513, 68521, 68534, 68552, 68555, 68567, 68569-68571

Buses of Somerset (two-tone green): 23012, 23317, 23324, 32027, 32818, 32844, 32866, 32872-32874, 32936, 32954, 32961, 33377-33382, 40570, 40582-40585, 43822, 43823, 44922-44924, 45111, 45113-45115, 48270, 48272, 48273, 53503-53505, 53701, 54602, 67701-67710, 69012, 69013, 69017, 69018

Greyhound: 23315, 23316, 23318, 23322, 23325

Riviera Connection: 32709, 32713, 32714, 32717, 32755

Traditional Western National: 32716

Mayflower Link: 32808, 32846, 33175

Blue and cream: 33111, 33112

Tinner: 33450-33469

Blue Kernow: 33470-33479

Allover purple: 40581

First Training: 42358

Great Western Railway: 42860

Corlink: 43811

Truronian Coaches: 56000, 57000

Western Greyhound: 64049

Truro Park & Ride: 64050-64057

South Yorkshire

Garages

DO	Doncaster - 32-38 Duke Street, Doncaster, DN1 3EB
OG	Olive Grove - Olive Grove Garage, Olive Grove Road, Sheffield, S2 3GA
RO	Rotherham - Rotherham Garage, Midland Road, Rotherham, S61 1TF

30564-31786		Volvo B7TL		Alexander ALX400			H49/27F	
				* - H49/29F, $ - H49/28F				

30564*	WU02KVE	DO	30937$	X358VWT	OG	31144	YU52VYW	RO
30565*	WU02KVF	DO	30938$	X359VWT	OG	31145	YU52VYX	RO
30567*	WU02KVH	DO	31129	YU52VYE	OG	31148	YU52VZA	DO
30568*	WU02KVJ	DO	31130	YU52VYF	OG	31781	YN53EOF	DO
30569*	WU02KVK	DO	31131	YU52VYG	OG	31782	YN53EOG	DO
30570*	WU02KVL	DO	31132	YU52VYH	OG	31783	YN53EOH	DO
30575*	WU02KVS	DO	31133	YU52VYJ	OG	31784	YN53EOJ	RO
30577*	WU02KVV	DO	31134	YU52VYK	OG	31785	YN53EOK	RO
30578*	WU02KVW	RO	31135	YU52VYL	OG	31786	YN53EOL	RO
30884*	W739DWX	DO	31142	YU52VYT	RO			

Pictured between Doncaster town centre and the bus station is First South Yorkshire 30884, an Alexander ALX400-bodied Volvo B7TL about to complete its journey

32108-32220		Volvo B7TL		Plaxton President			H42/23F	
				* - H39/20F				

32108*	LT02ZCY	RO	32215	LT52WTY	RO	32219	LT52WUC	RO
32109*	LT02ZDH	RO	32216	LT52WTZ	RO	32220	LT52WUD	RO
32110*	LT02ZDJ	RO	32217	LT52WUA	RO			
32111*	LT02ZDK	RO	32218	LT52WUB	RO			

32263-32276		Volvo B7TL		Alexander ALX400 * - H45/19F			H45/21F	
32263*	LT52WWJ	OG	32269	LT52WWP	DO	32274	LT52WXD	DO
32264*	LT52WWK	OG	32270	LT52WWR	DO	32275	KDZ5104	DO
32265*	LT52WWL	OG	32271	LT52WWS	DO	32276	LT52WXF	DO
32267	LT52WWN	OG	32272	LT52WWU	u			
32268	LT52WWO	OG	32273	LT52WXC	DO			

32308-32312		Volvo B7TL		Plaxton President			H42/21F	
32308	LK03NHH	OG	32310	LK03NHL	OG	32312	LK03NHN	OG
32309	LK03NHJ	OG	32311	LK03NHM	OG			

32957	X957HLT	Dennis Trident SFD113	Plaxton President 9.9m	H39/20F	DO
33031	LK51UYN	Dennis Trident SFD339	Plaxton President 10.5m	H42/22F	u
33032	LK51UYO	Dennis Trident SFD339	Plaxton President 10.5m	H42/22F	u

33041-33071		Dennis Trident SFD136		Plaxton President 9.9m * - H39/20D			H39/20F	
33041	LN51DWF	DO	33065	LN51GKZ	DO	33070	LN51GLY	u
33052	LN51GKJ	DO	33069	LN51GLV	DO	33071*	LN51GKA	u

33082	LN51GNV	Dennis Trident SFD336	Plaxton President 10.5m	H42/22F	DO
33083	LN51GNX	Dennis Trident SFD336	Plaxton President 10.5m	H42/22F	u

Seen here is First South Yorkshire 33863, an ADL Enviro 400, pictured while leaving Sheffield Bus Station out of service

109

33124-33230		Dennis Trident SFD136		Plaxton President 9.9m * - H39/23F			H39/20F	
33124	LT02NVM	u	33127	LT02NVP	u	33230*	LT52WXH	u
33125	LT02NVN	u	33128	LT02NVR	u			

33858-33872		ADL E40D SFD4DS		ADL Enviro 400 10.8m			H45/30F	
33858	SL14DFD	OG	33863	SL14LMF	OG	33868	SL14LMU	OG
33859	SL14DFE	OG	33864	SL14LMJ	OG	33869	SL14LMV	OG
33860	SL14DFF	OG	33865	SL14LMK	OG	33870	SL14LMY	OG
33861	SL14DFG	OG	33866	SL14LMM	OG	33871	SL14LNA	OG
33862	SL14DFK	OG	33867	SL14LMO	OG	33872	SL14LNC	OG

35101-35138		Wright Streetdeck		Wright Streetdeck			H45/28F	
35101	SN64CSF	RO	35123	SM65EFK	RO	35131	SM65GGE	RO
35102	SN64CSO	RO	35124	SM65EFL	RO	35132	SM65GGF	RO
35117	SM65EFD	RO	35125	SM65EFN	RO	35133	SM65LMV	RO
35118	SM65EFE	RO	35126	SM65GFV	RO	35134	SM65LMX	RO
35119	SM65EFF	RO	35127	SM65GFX	RO	35135	SM65LMY	RO
35120	SM65EFG	RO	35128	SM65GFY	RO	35136	SM65LNA	RO
35121	SM65EFH	RO	35129	SM65GFZ	RO	35137	SM65LNC	RO
35122	SM65EFJ	RO	35130	SM65GGA	RO	35138	SM65LND	RO

Pictured between Doncaster town centre and the Bus Station is First South Yorkshire 35101, the first Wright Streetdeck to be delivered to FirstGroup, pictured about to complete its journey from Sheffield on route X78

37103-37529		Volvo B9TL		Wright Eclipse Gemini			H45/29F	
37103	YK07AYA	OG	37104	YK07AYB	OG	37105	YK07AYC	OG

37106	YK07AYD	OG	37235	YN08LCO	DO	37486	YN08NMJ	OG
37107	YK07AYE	OG	37236	YN57RKJ	DO	37487	YN08NMK	OG
37108	YK07AYF	OG	37237	YN08LCP	DO	37488	YN08NMM	OG
37109	YK07AYG	OG	37257	YN07MKX	DO	37489	YN08NMU	OG
37110	YK07AYH	OG	37259	YN07MLE	DO	37490	YN08NMV	OG
37111	YK07AYJ	OG	37261	YN07MLJ	DO	37491	YN08NMX	OG
37112	YK07AYL	OG	37262	YN07MLK	DO	37492	YN08NMY	OG
37113	YK07AYM	OG	37263	YN07MLL	DO	37493	YN08PLF	OG
37114	YK07AYN	OG	37264	YN07MLO	OG	37494	YN58ERX	DO
37115	YK07AYO	OG	37265	YN07MLU	OG	37495	YN08PLO	OG
37116	YK07AYP	OG	37472	YN08NLL	OG	37496	YN08PLU	OG
37117	YK07AYS	OG	37473	YN08NLM	OG	37497	YN58ERY	OG
37118	YK07AYT	OG	37474	YN08NLO	OG	37498	YN08PLX	OG
37119	YK07AYU	OG	37475	YN08NLP	OG	37499	YN08PLY	OG
37120	YK07AYV	OG	37476	YN08NLR	OG	37509	YN58ERZ	OG
37121	YK07AYW	OG	37477	YN08NLT	OG	37510	YN58ESF	OG
37122	YK07AYX	OG	37478	YN08NLU	OG	37511	YN58ESG	OG
37228	YN57RJU	DO	37479	YN08NLV	OG	37512	YN58ESO	OG
37229	3910WE	OG	37480	YN08NLX	OG	37513	YN58ESU	OG
37230	YN08LCK	DO	37481	YN08NLY	OG	37514	YN58ESV	OG
37231	YN08LCL	DO	37482	YN08NLZ	OG	37515	YN58ESY	OG
37232	YN57RJZ	DO	37483	YN08NMA	OG	37516	YN58ETA	OG
37233	YN57RKA	DO	37484	YN08NME	OG	37517	YN58ETD	OG
37234	YN08LCM	DO	37485	YN08NMF	OG	37518	YN58ETE	OG

The X78 between Rotherham and Doncaster leaves the main road and serves the centres of some of the larger villages. Making one such detour is First South Yorkshire 37231, a Wright Eclipse Gemini-bodied Volvo B9TL, seen here in Conisbrough. This vehicle also carries a commemorative Rotherham Corporation livery, one of four commemorative liveries applied to vehicles in this fleet

37519	YN58ETF	OG	37523	YN58ETO	OG	37528	YN58ETX	OG
37520	YN58ETJ	OG	37524	YN58ETR	OG	37529	YN58ETY	OG
37521	YN58ETK	OG	37526	YN58ETU	OG			
37522	YN58ETL	OG	37527	YN58ETV	OG			

47482-47490		Wright Streetlite DF		Wright Streetlite 10.8m		B37F	
47482	SN64CNO	DO	47485	SN64CNX	DO	47488	SN64COA	DO
47483	SN64CNU	DO	47486	SN64CNY	DO	47489	SN64COH	DO
47484	SN64CNV	DO	47487	SN64CNZ	DO	47490	SN64COJ	DO

53401	TO54TRU	Optare Solo M880	Optare Solo 8.8m	B29F	DO
53703	LK05DXR	Optare Solo M780	Optare Solo 7.8m	B21F	DO
53807	WX05RSV	Optare Solo M850SL	Optare Solo 8.5m	B28F	DO
53808	WX05RSY	Optare Solo M850SL	Optare Solo 8.5m	B28F	DO
53810	WX05RTO	Optare Solo M850SL	Optare Solo 8.5m	B28F	DO
60368	R578SBA	Volvo B10BLE	Wright Renown	B41F	ROt
60406	Y774TNC	Volvo B7L	Wright Eclipse	B41F	DO
60458	G603NWA	Volvo B10M-55	Alexander PS	B51F	ROt

60621-60681		Volvo B10BLE	Wright Renown	B41F	
			* - B44F		

60621*	R784WKW	RO	60630	S812RWG	OG	60681	T863MAK	ROt
60622*	R785WKW	u	60632	S814RWG	ROt			
60626*	R789WKW	RO	60676	T858MAK	u			

Rotherham Bus Station is the location for this shot of First South Yorkshire 60739, a Wright Eclipse-bodied Volvo B7L, seen while on route 39, a circular route serving Kimberworth Park

60703-61662		Volvo B7L			Wright Eclipse			B41F
60703	Y661UKU	OG	60731	MV02VDD	RO	60901	YJ51RFO	DO
60704	MV02VAA	OG	60733	MV02VDF	RO	60902	YG02DHK	DO
60705	MV02VAD	OG	60734	MV02VDG	RO	61192	YU52VXH	DO
60706	MV02VAE	RO	60735	MV02VDJ	RO	61193	YU52VXJ	DO
60707	MV02VAF	OG	60736	MV02VDK	OG	61194	YU52VXK	DO
60708	MV02VAH	OG	60737	MV02VDL	OG	61195	YU52VXL	DO
60709	MV02VAJ	OG	60738	MV02VDM	RO	61196	YU52VXM	DO
60710	MV02VAK	OG	60739	MV02VDN	RO	61197	YU52VXN	DO
60711	MV02VAM	OG	60740	MV02VDO	RO	61198	YU52VXO	DO
60712	MV02VAO	OG	60741	MV02VDP	RO	61199	YU52VXP	DO
60713	MV02VAU	OG	60742	MV02VDR	RO	61200	YU52VXR	DO
60714	MV02VBF	OG	60743	MV02VDT	RO	61201	YU52VXS	DO
60715	MV02VBG	OG	60744	MV02VDX	RO	61202	YU52VXT	DO
60716	MV02VBJ	OG	60745	MV02VDY	RO	61203	YU52VXV	DO
60717	MV02VBK	OG	60885	YJ51PZW	OG	61204	YU52VXW	DO
60718	MV02VBL	OG	60886	YJ51PZX	OG	61205	YU52VXX	w
60719	MV02VBM	OG	60887	YJ51PZY	OG	61206	YU52VXY	DO
60720	MV02VBN	RO	60888	YJ51RDZ	DO	61207	JDZ2339	DO
60721	MV02VBO	RO	60889	YJ51RHE	DO	61208	JDZ2340	DO
60722	MV02VBP	RO	60890	YJ51RHK	OG	61209	JDZ2391	DO
60724	MV02VCD	RO	60891	YJ51RGZ	OG	61211	NDZ3164	DO
60725	MV02VCE	OG	60892	YJ51RHF	OG	61631	SH51MKF	OG
60726	MV02VCF	RO	60893	YJ51RGY	OG	61633	SH51MKJ	OG
60727	MV02VCG	RO	60894	YJ51REU	OG	61636	SJ51DHD	u
60728	MV02VCJ	RO	60898	YJ51RFX	DO	61638	SJ51DHF	OG
60729	MV02VCK	RO	60899	YJ51RFL	DO	61639	SJ51DHG	u
60730	MV02VCL	RO	60900	YJ51RFN	DO	61662	SJ51DKK	u

62232-62244		Volvo B10BLE			Wright Renown			B41F
62232	Y937CSF	u	62237	Y945CSF	u	62243	Y953CSF	u
62234	Y943CSF	u	62239	Y948CSF	u	62244	Y952CSF	u
62235	Y946CSF	u	62240	Y949CSF	u			

63001-63388		Wright Streetlite Max			Wright Streetlite 11.5m			B41F
63001	SM13NDJ	OG	63021	SK63KGX	OG	63041	LK62HJX	RO
63002	SM13NDK	OG	63022	SK63KGY	OG	63119	SN14DVM	OG
63003	SM13NDL	OG	63023	SK63KGZ	OG	63120	SN14DVO	OG
63004	SM13NDN	OG	63024	SK63KHA	OG	63121	SN14DVP	OG
63005	SM13NDO	OG	63025	SK63KHB	OG	63122	SN14DVR	OG
63006	SM13NDU	OG	63026	SK63KHC	OG	63123	SN14DVT	OG
63007	SM13NDV	OG	63027	SK63KHD	OG	63124	SN14DVU	OG
63008	SM13NDX	OG	63028	SK63KHE	OG	63125	SN14DVV	OG
63009	SM13NDY	OG	63029	SK63KHF	OG	63126	SN14DVW	OG
63010	SM13NDZ	OG	63030	SK63KHG	OG	63127	SN14DVX	OG
63011	SM13NEF	OG	63031	SN63KHH	OG	63128	SN14DVY	OG
63012	SM13NEJ	OG	63032	SK63KHJ	OG	63129	SN14DVZ	OG
63013	SM13NEN	OG	63033	SK63KHL	OG	63130	SN14DWC	OG
63014	SM13NEO	OG	63034	SK63KHM	OG	63131	SN14DWD	OG
63015	SM13NEU	OG	63035	SK63KHO	OG	63132	SN14DWE	OG
63016	SM13NEY	OG	63036	SK63KHP	OG	63133	SN14DWF	OG
63017	SK63KGO	OG	63037	SK63KHR	OG	63134	SN14DWG	OG
63018	SK63KGP	OG	63038	LK62HJD	RO	63135	SN14DWJ	OG
63019	SK63KGU	OG	63039	LK62FUJ	RO	63136	SN14DWK	OG
63020	SK63KGV	OG	63040	LK62HKG	RO	63137	SN14DWL	OG

The crossing over the tram tracks in Sheffield city centre is the setting for Wright Streetlite 63018 operating on route 200 to Hemsworth

63138	SN14DWM	OG	63371	SL16RBF	RO	63381	SL16RCV	DO
63139	SN14DWO	OG	63372	SL16RBO	DO	63382	SL16RCX	RO
63140	SN14DWP	OG	63373	SL16RBU	DO	63383	SL16RCY	DO
63141	SN14DWU	OG	63374	SL16RBV	DO	63384	SL16RCZ	DO
63142	SN14DWV	OG	63375	SL16RBX	DO	63385	SL16RDO	DO
63143	SN14DWW	OG	63376	SL16RBY	DO	63386	SL16RDU	DO
63144	SN14DWX	OG	63377	SL16RBZ	DO	63387	SL16RDV	DO
63145	SN14DWY	OG	63378	SL16RCF	DO	63388	SL16RDX	DO
63369	SL16RAU	RO	63379	SL16RCO	DO			
63370	SL16RAX	DO	63380	SL16RCU	RO			

66168	W368EOW	Volvo B10BLE	Wright Renown	B44F	u
66732	WX54XCT	Volvo B7RLE	Wright Eclipse Urban	B43F	DO
66733	WX54XCU	Volvo B7RLE	Wright Eclipse Urban	B43F	DO

67141-67150		ADL E20D SFDDLA	ADL Enviro 200 MMC 11.5m	B45F

67141	YY16YLN	OG	67145	YY16YLS	OG	67149	YY16YLW	OG
67142	YY16YLO	OG	67146	YY16YLT	OG	67150	YY16YLX	OG
67143	YY16YLP	OG	67147	YY16YLU	OG			
67144	YY16YLR	OG	67148	YY16YLV	OG			

69020-69465		Volvo B7RLE	Wright Eclipse Urban	B43F
			* B44F	

69020	SF55UAN	OG	69024	SF55UAS	OG	69028	SF55UAW	OG
69022	SF55UAP	OG	69025	SF55UAT	OG	69029	SF55UAX	OG
69023	SF55UAR	OG	69026	SF55UAU	OG	69030	SF55UAY	OG

69031	SF55UAZ	OG	69050	SF55UBL	OG	69213	MX06YXS	DO
69032	SF55UBA	OG	69051	SF55UBM	OG	69214	MX06YXT	DO
69033	SF55UBT	OG	69052	SF55UBN	OG	69215	MX56AED	DO
69043	SF55UBC	OG	69053	SF55UBO	OG	69216	MX56AEE	DO
69044	SF55UBD	OG	69054	SF55UBP	OG	69217	MX56AEF	DO
69045	SF55UBE	OG	69055	SF55UBR	OG	69461*	YN09HFH	DO
69046	SF55UBG	OG	69056	SF55UBS	OG	69462*	YN09HFJ	DO
69047	SF55UBH	OG	69210	MX06VPL	DO	69463*	YN09HFK	DO
69048	SF55UBJ	OG	69211	MX06VPM	DO	69464*	YN09HFL	DO
69049	SF55UBK	OG	69212	MX06VPN	DO	69465*	YN09HFM	DO

Rotherham Bus Station is the location for 69054, a Wright Eclipse Urban-bodied Volvo B7RLE, seen while on route 37 heading for Ravenfield

Previous registrations

32275	LT52WXE	61208	YU52YVA
37229	YN08LCJ	61209	YU52YVB
60703	Y900FML	61211	YU52VYD
61207	YU52VXZ		

Liveries
Unless stated below, all vehicles in this fleet carry FirstGroup corporate livery;
Steel Link: 35117-35138
Sheffield Corporation: 37229, 37528
Doncaster Corporation: 37230
Rotherham Corporation: 37231
First Training: 60368, 60458, 60681

West of England

Garages

BH	Bath - Weston Island, Lower Bristol Road, Twerton, Bath, BA2 9ES
HE	Hengrove - Roman Farm Road, Bristol, BS4 1UJ
LH	Lawrence Hill - Easton Road, Bristol, BS5 0DZ
MS	Marlborough Street - Bristol Bus Station, Marlborough Street, Bristol, BS1 3NU
WS	Wells - Priory Road, Wells, BA5 1SZ
WM	Weston Super Mare - Searle Crescent, Weston-Super-Mare, BS23 3YX

10035-10179   Volvo B7LA   Wright Eclipse Fusion   AB56D
                                             * - ADP56D

10035	W118CWR	w	10174	WX55HVZ	BH	10177	WX55HWC	BH
10036	W119CWR	BH	10175	WX55HWA	BH	10178	WX55HWD	BH
10037	W122CWR	BH	10176	WX55HWB	u	10179	WX55HWE	u

See in Bath City Centre is 10035, a Wright Eclipse Fusion-bodied Volvo B7LA, while on route U1 to Lower Oldfield Park, for which this special maroon livery is carried by vehicles used on special university services for Bath University

30857-32292   Volvo B7TL   Alexander ALX400   H49/27F
                                             * - H49/29F, $ - H45/25F, % - H49/28F

30857*	W712CWR	w	32006	KFX691	WM	32015	WYY752	BH
30866*	W721CWR	w	32007	TPR354	BH	32016*	W816PAE	w
30867*	W722CWR	w	32008	W808PAE	LH	32018*	W818PAE	w
30870*	W726CWR	w	32009	W809PAE	LH	32019*	W819PAE	w
32001	620HOD	BH	32011	W811PAE	LH	32021*	W821PAE	w
32002	RKZ4760	BH	32012	W812PAE	LH	32022*	W822PAE	w
32003	PSU630	WM	32013	W813PAE	LH	32024*	W824PAE	w
32004	W804PAE	LH	32014	NTL655	WM	32069	KP51VZT	BH

116

32070	KP51VZW	LH	32099	KP51WDB	BH	32280%	WR03YZM	BH
32073	KP51VZZ	LH	32251$	LT52WVO	LH	32281%	WR03YZN	BH
32074	KP51WAJ	LH	32252$	LT52WVP	LH	32282%	WR03YZP	BH
32075	KP51WAO	u	32253$	LT52WVY	LH	32283%	WR03YZR	BH
32076	KP51WAU	u	32254$	LT52WVZ	LH	32284%	WR03YZT	BH
32083	KP51WBT	BH	32255$	LT52WWA	LH	32285%	WR03YZU	BH
32084	KP51WBU	LH	32256$	LT52WWB	LH	32286%	WR03YZV	BH
32090	KP51WCG	LH	32257$	LT52WWC	LH	32287%	WR03YZW	BH
32093	KP51WCO	LH	32258$	LT52WWD	LH	32288%	WR03YZX	LH
32094	KP51WCR	LH	32259$	LT52WWE	LH	32289%	WR03YZY	LH
32095	KP51WCW	LH	32277	KP51WDF	LH	32290%	WR03YZZ	LH
32096	KP51WCX	HE	32278	YU52VYM	MH	32291%	WR03ZBC	LH
32098	KP51WDD	MH	32279%	WR03YZL	BH	32292%	WR03ZBD	LH

32328-32360		Volvo B7TL			Wright Eclipse Gemini		H41/28F	
					$ - H38/25F			
32328	LK53LYH	LH	32339	LK53LYZ	HE	32351$	LK53LZO	LH
32329	LK53LYJ	LH	32340	LK53LZA	HE	32352$	LK53LZP	LH
32330	LK53LYO	LH	32341	LK53LZB	HE	32353$	LK53LZR	HE
32331	LK53LYP	HE	32342	LK53LZC	HE	32354$	LK53LZT	LH
32332	LK53LYR	HE	32343	LK53LZD	HE	32355$	LK53LZU	LH
32333	LK53LYT	LH	32344	LK53LZE	HE	32356$	LK53LZV	LH
32334	LK53LYU	LH	32345	LK53LZF	HE	32357$	LK53LZW	LH
32335	LK53LYV	HE	32346	LK53LZG	HE	32358$	LK53LZX	LH
32336	LK53LYW	HE	32347	LK53LZH	HE	32359$	LK53MBF	LH
32337	LK53LYX	HE	32349$	LK53LZM	MH	32360$	LK04HYP	LH
32338	LK53LYY	HE	32350$	LK53LZN	LH			

32636-32691		Volvo B7TL			Wright Eclipse Gemini		H45/29F	
32636	WX05UAF	BH	32686	WX56HKB	MH	32689	WX56HKE	MH
32637	WX05UAG	BH	32687	WX56HKC	LH	32690	WX56HKF	MH
32638	WU54EHO	BH	32688	WX56HKD	LH	32691	WX56HKG	MH

32931-32950		Dennis Trident SFD313			Alexander ALX400 10.5m		H45/27F	
					* - H45/24F			
32931	W931ULL	w	32940	W840VLO	w	32946	W946ULL	w
32937	W937ULL	w	32941*	W941ULL	w	32950	W132VLO	w
32939	W939ULL	w	32942*	W942ULL	w			

33411-33419		Dennis Trident SFD45M			Alexander Enviro 400 10.8m		H39/32F	
33411	WA56FUB	WM	33414	WA56FTK	WM	33417	WA56FTP	WM
33412	WA56FUD	WM	33415	WA56FTN	WM	33418	WA56FTT	WM
33413	WA56FUE	WM	33416	WA56FTO	WM	33419	WA56FTU	WM

33488	YX66WGO	ADL E40D SFDB32		ADL Enviro 400MMC 10.5m		H45/29F	MH
33489	YX66WGP	ADL E40D SFDB32		ADL Enviro 400MMC 10.5m		H45/29F	MH
33490	YX66WGU	ADL E40D SFDB32		ADL Enviro 400MMC 10.5m		H45/29F	MH

33506-33571		Dennis Trident SFD16M			Alexander Enviro 400 10.2m		H41/28F	
					* - H41/26F			
33506	LK08FKY	HE	33550	SN58CFV	WM	33560*	SN58CGV	WM
33508*	LK08FLA	WM	33554	SN58CGE	HE	33564*	SN58CHC	WM
33547	SN58CFO	HE	33556	SN58CGG	HE	33565	SN58CHD	WM

33566*	SN58CHF	WM	33569	SN58CHJ	WM	33571	SN58CHL	HE

33658-33754		ADL E40D SFD4DS		ADL Enviro 400 10.8m			H45/30F	
33658	SN12ADX	u	33662	SN12AED	HE	33667	SN12AEK	u
33659	SN12ADZ	HE	33664	SN12AEF	u	33685	SN12AFU	HE
33660	SN12AEA	u	33665	SN12AEG	HE	33750	SN12AOK	HE
33661	SN12AEA	u	33666	SN12AEJ	u	33754	SN12AOP	HE

33790-33802		ADL E40D SFDB32		ADL Enviro 400MMC 10.5m			H45/29F	
33790	YX66WKT	LH	33795	YX66WKZ	LH	33800	YX66WLE	LH
33791	YX66WKU	LH	33796	YX66WLA	LH	33801	YX66WLF	LH
33792	YX66WKV	LH	33797	YX66WLB	LH	33802	YX66WLG	LH
33793	YX66WKW	LH	33798	YX66WLC	LH			
33794	YX66WKY	LH	33799	YX66WLD	LH			

33825-33830		ADL E40D SFD4DS		ADL Enviro 400 10.8m			H45/30F	
33825	SN63MYH	WM	33827	SN63MYK	WM	33829	SN63MYM	WM
33826	SN63MYJ	WM	33828	SN63MYL	WM	33830	SN63MYO	WM

Making its way through The Centre in Bristol is 33826, an ADL Enviro 400, seen while on route X1 to Weston-Super-Mare, in the striking "Express Yourself" livery

33924-33930		ADL E40D SFDB32		ADL Enviro 400MMC 10.5m			H45/30F	
33924	YX66WKL	LH	33927	YX66WKO	LH	33930	YX66WKS	LH
33925	YX66WKM	LH	33928	YX66WKP	LH			
33926	YX66WKN	LH	33929	YX66WKR	LH			

33931-33950		ADL E40D SFDA12		ADL Enviro 400MMC 11.4m			H49/31D	
33931	YX66WDT	HE	33938	YX66WEC	HE	33945	YX66WEU	BH
33932	YX66WDU	HE	33939	YX66WEF	HE	33946	YX66WEV	BH
33933	YX66WDV	HE	33940	YX66WEH	HE	33947	YX66WEW	BH
33934	YX66WDW	HE	33941	YX66WEJ	HE	33948	YX66WFA	BH
33935	YX66WDY	HE	33942	YX66WEK	HE	33949	YX66WFB	BH
33936	YX66WDZ	HE	33943	YX66WEO	BH	33950	YX66WFC	BH
33937	YX66WEA	HE	33944	YX66WEP	BH			

Loading up at Brislington Park and Ride site is 33937, a ADL Enviro 400MMC in the special blue livery for this service

33951-33973		ADL E40D SFDB32		ADL Enviro 400MMC 10.5m			H45/29F	
33951	SN65ZBZ	LH	33959	SN65ZCT	LH	33967	SN65ZDD	LH
33952	SN65ZCA	LH	33960	SN65ZCU	LH	33968	SN65ZDE	LH
33953	SN65ZCE	LH	33961	SN65ZCV	LH	33969	SN65ZDF	LH
33954	SN65ZCF	LH	33962	SN65ZCX	LH	33970	SN65ZDG	LH
33955	SN65ZCJ	LH	33963	SN65ZCY	LH	33971	SN65ZDH	LH
33956	SN65ZCK	LH	33964	SN65ZCZ	LH	33972	SN65ZDJ	LH
33957	SN65ZCL	LH	33965	SN65ZDA	LH	33973	SN65ZDK	LH
33958	SN65ZCO	LH	33966	SN65ZDC	LH			

35103-35167		Wright Streetdeck		Wright Streetdeck			H45/28F	
35103	SM15WCR	HE	35109	SO15CUJ	HE	35115	SO15CUY	HE
35104	SM15WCT	HE	35110	SO15CUK	HE	35116	SO15CVA	HE
35105	SO15CUA	HE	35111	SO15CUU	HE	35139	SN65OMF	HE
35106	SO15CUC	HE	35112	SO15CUV	HE	35140	SN65OMH	HE
35107	SO15CUG	HE	35113	SO15CUW	HE	35141	SN65OMJ	HE
35108	SO15CUH	HE	35114	SO15CUX	HE	35142	SN65OMK	HE

35143	SN65OML	HE	35149	SN65OMT	HE	35164	SK65PWJ	WE
35144	SN65OMM	HE	35150	SN65OMU	HE	35165	SK65PWL	WE
35145	SN65OMO	HE	35160	SK65PVY	WE	35166	SK65PWN	WE
35146	SN65OMP	HE	35161	SK65PVZ	WE	35167	SK65PWO	WE
35147	SN65OMR	HE	35162	SK65PWE	WE			
35148	SN65OMS	WE	35163	SK65PWF	WE			

Seen here by Temple Meads Station in Bristol is Wright Streetdeck 35110, pictured while on route 70 to University of West England, showing the fuchsia-fronted variation of corporate livery carried by the vehicle

37001-37020		Volvo B7TL			Wright Eclipse Gemini			H45/29F
37001	WX55VHK	HE	37008	WX55VHT	HE	37015	WX55VJC	MH
37002	WX55VHL	HE	37009	WX55VHU	HE	37016	WX55VJD	MH
37003	WX55VHM	MH	37010	WX55VHV	HE	37017	WX55VJE	MH
37004	WX55VHN	MH	37011	WX55VHW	MH	37018	WX55VJF	MH
37005	WX55VHO	MH	37012	WX55VHY	MH	37019	WX55VJG	LH
37006	WX55VHP	MH	37013	WX55VHZ	MH	37020	WX55VJJ	LH
37007	WX55VHR	MH	37014	WX55VJA	MH			

37315-37772		Volvo B9TL			Wright Eclipse Gemini			H45/29F
37315	WX57HJO	HE	37324	WX57HKE	LH	37333	WX57HKO	LH
37316	WX57HJU	HE	37325	WX57HKF	LH	37334	WX57HKP	LH
37317	WX57HJV	HE	37326	WX57HKG	LH	37335	WX57HKT	LH
37318	WX57HJY	HE	37327	WX57HKH	LH	37336	WX57HKU	LH
37319	WX57HJZ	LH	37328	WX57HKJ	LH	37337	WX57HKV	LH
37320	WX57HKA	LH	37329	WX57HKK	LH	37338	WX57HKW	LH
37321	WX57HKB	LH	37330	WX57HKL	LH	37339	WX57HKY	LH
37322	WX57HKC	LH	37331	WX57HKM	LH	37340	WX57HKZ	LH
37323	WX57HKD	LH	37332	WX57HKN	LH	37341	WX57HLA	LH

37342	WX57HLC	LH		37597	WX58JXF	HE		37624	WX58JYK	LH
37343	WX57HLD	LH		37598	WX58JXG	HE		37625	WX58JYL	LH
37344	WX57HLE	LH		37599	WX58JXH	HE		37626	WX58JYN	LH
37345	WX57HLF	LH		37600	WX58JXJ	HE		37627	WX58JYO	LH
37346	WX57HLG	LH		37601	WX58JXK	HE		37628	WX58JYP	LH
37347	WX57HLH	LH		37602	WX58JXL	HE		37629	WX58JYR	LH
37348	WX57HLJ	LH		37603	WX58JXM	HE		37630	WX58JYS	LH
37349	WX57HLK	LH		37604	WX58JXN	HE		37631	WX58JYT	LH
37350	WX57HLM	LH		37605	WX58JXO	HE		37632	WX58JYU	LH
37351	WX57HLN	HE		37606	WX58JXP	HE		37757	WX09KBK	BH
37352	WX57HLO	HE		37607	WX58JXR	LH		37758	WX09KBN	BH
37353	WX57HLP	LH		37608	WX58JXS	HE		37759	WX09KBO	BH
37354	WX57HLR	LH		37609	WX58JXT	HE		37760	WX09KBP	BH
37355	WX57HLU	LH		37610	WX58JXU	HE		37761	WX09KBU	BH
37356	WX57HLV	LH		37611	WX58JXV	HE		37762	WX09KBV	BH
37357	WX57HLW	LH		37612	WX58JXW	HE		37763	WX09KBY	BH
37358	WX57HLY	BH		37613	WX58JXY	LH		37764	WX09KBZ	BH
37587	WX58JWU	HE		37614	WX58JXZ	LH		37765	WX09KCA	BH
37588	WX58JWV	HE		37615	WX58JYA	LH		37766	WX09KCC	BH
37589	WX58JWW	HE		37616	WX58JYB	LH		37767	WX09KCE	BH
37590	WX58JWY	HE		37617	WX58JYC	LH		37768	WX09KCF	HE
37591	WX58JWZ	HE		37618	WX58JYD	LH		37769	WX09KCG	HE
37592	WX58JXA	HE		37619	WX58JYE	LH		37770	WX09KCJ	HE
37593	WX58JXB	HE		37620	WX58JYF	LH		37771	WX09KCK	LH
37594	WX58JXC	HE		37621	WX58JYG	LH		37772	WX09KCN	LH
37595	WX58JXD	HE		37622	WX58JYH	LH				
37596	WX58JXE	HE		37623	WX58JYJ	LH				

Seen on the outskirts of Bath here is First West of England 37766, a Wright Eclipse Gemini-bodied Volvo B9TL route X39 from Bristol

Having just left Newbridge Park & Ride is ADL Enviro E400 hybrid 39138 making its way into Bath city centre showing the special livery carried by this vehicle

39005	LK58ECZ	Wright Hybrid			Wright Gemini 2			H41/28F	BH

39133-39141		ADL E40H SFD4BU			ADL Enviro 400 10.8m			H45/30F	
39133	SN62AWA	BH		39137	SN62AWO	BH		39140	SN62AXB	BH
39134	SN62AWF	BH		39138	SN62AWR	BH		39141	SN62AXC	BH
39135	SN62AWG	BH		39139	SN62AWY	BH				

39191	SN65ZGS	ADL E40HVE SFD824	ADL Enviro 400MMC 10.4m	H39/25D	HE
39192	SN65ZGT	ADL E40HVE SFD824	ADL Enviro 400MMC 10.4m	H39/25D	HE
40786	R290GHS	Dennis Dart SLF SFD322	Plaxton Pointer 2 10.7m	B37F	u
41162	R162TLM	Dennis Dart SLF SFD112	Marshall Capital 9.3m	B33F	w
41399	X399HLR	Dennis Dart SLF SFD212	Marshall Capital 10.2m	B27F	u
41420	LN51DXD	Dennis Dart SLF SFD2B2	Marshall Capital 10.2m	B28D	HEt
41423	LN51DXG	Dennis Dart SLF SFD2B2	Marshall Capital 10.2m	B28D	HEt
42703	R703BAE	Dennis Dart SLF SFD112	Plaxton Pointer 2 9.3m	B29F	w
42705	R705BAE	Dennis Dart SLF SFD112	Plaxton Pointer 2 9.3m	B29F	w
42709	R709BAE	Dennis Dart SLF SFD112	Plaxton Pointer 2 9.3m	B29F	w
42721	S721AFB	Dennis Dart SLF SFD322	Plaxton Pointer 2 10.7m	B37F	WEt
42730	T730REU	Dennis Dart SLF SFD322	Alexander ALX200 10.7m	B37F	w
42731	T731REU	Dennis Dart SLF SFD322	Alexander ALX200 10.7m	B37F	w
42734	V734FAE	Dennis Dart SLF SFD322	Alexander ALX200 10.7m	B35F	WE
42824	S824WYD	Dennis Dart SLF SFD212	East Lancs Spryte 10.2m	B35F	w

42895-42969		Dennis Dart SLF SFD3CA			Alexander Pointer 2 10.7m			B37F	
					* - B36F, $ - B38F				
42895	WX05RUW	WM		42896	WX05RUY	MH		42897	WX05RVA	BH

42898	WX05RVC	MH	42910	WX05RVU	BH	42959	WX06OMS	HE
42899	WX05RVE	BH	42915	WX05RWE	BH	42960	WX06OMT	HE
42900	WX05RVF	BH	42916	WX05RWF	BH	42961	WX06OMU	HE
42901	WX05RVJ	MH	42925*	SN05EAC	BH	42962	WX06OMV	MH
42902	WX05RVK	LH	42939	WX05SVE	BH	42963	WX06OMW	MH
42903	WX05RVL	BH	42947$	WA56FTX	WM	42964	WX06OMY	MH
42904	WX05RVM	BH	42948$	WA56FTY	WM	42965	WX06OMZ	MH
42905	WX05RVN	u	42955	WX06OMM	BH	42966	WX06ONA	MH
42906	WX05RVO	BH	42956	WX06OMO	BH	42967	WX06ONB	HE
42907	WX05RVP	BH	42957	WX06OMP	LH	42968	WX06ONC	LH
42909	WX05RVT	BH	42958	WX06OMR	HE	42969$	WA56FTZ	MH

Seen here in Bath is First West of England 42916, a Dennis Dart SLF with Alexander Pointer 2 bodywork, pictured while on route 13 heading for Foxhill

| 43849 | SN05HEJ | Dennis Dart SLF SFD6BA | Alexander Pointer 8.8m | | B29F | LH |

44520-44526		ADL E20D SFD8D1	ADL Enviro 200 10.2m		B33F	
44520	YX62DVM	BH	44523	YX62DWO	BH	44526	YX62DXH	BH
44521	YX62DWG	BH	44524	YX62DXC	BH
44522	YX62DWM	BH	44525	YX62DXF	BH

44902	WX08LNN	Dennis E200Dart SFD151	Alexander Enviro 200 9.4m	B29F	BH
44903	WX08LNO	Dennis E200Dart SFD111	Alexander Enviro 200 9.4m	B29F	BH
44904	WX08LNP	Dennis E200Dart SFD121	Alexander Enviro 200 9.4m	B29F	BH

44905-44915		Dennis E200Dart SFD151	Alexander Enviro 200 9.4m	B28F	
44905	YX09AFN	WM	44907	YX09AFU	WM	44909	YX09AFY	WM
44906	YX09AFO	WM	44908	YX09AFV	WM	44910	YX09AFZ	WM

44911	YX09AGO	WM	44913	YX09AGV	BH	44915	YX09AHA	WM
44912	YX09AGU	WE	44914	YX09AGZ	WM			

47435-47571		Wright Streetlite DF		Wright Streetlite 10.8m			B37F	
47435	SK63KNG	HE	47455	SK63KKR	HE	47553	SN14FGE	WM
47436	SK63KNH	HE	47456	SK63KKS	HE	47554	SN14FGF	WM
47437	SK63KNJ	u	47457	SK63KKU	HE	47555	SN14FGG	WM
47438	SK63KNL	HE	47458	SK63KKV	HE	47556	SN14FGJ	WM
47439	SK63KNM	HE	47459	SK63KKW	HE	47557	SN14FGK	WM
47440	SK63KNN	HE	47460	SK63KKX	HE	47558	SN14FGM	WM
47441	SK63KNO	u	47461	SK63KKY	HE	47559	SN64CLF	LH
47442	SK63KNP	HE	47462	SK63KKZ	HE	47560	SN64CLJ	LH
47443	SK63KNR	HE	47463	SK63KLA	HE	47561	SN64CLO	LH
47444	SK63KNS	u	47464	SK63KLC	HE	47562	SN64CLU	LH
47445	SK63KNU	HE	47465	SK63KLD	HE	47563	SN64CLV	LH
47446	SK63KNV	HE	47544	SN14FFU	BH	47564	SN64CLX	LH
47447	SK63KNX	HE	47545	SN14FFV	BH	47565	SN64CLY	LH
47448	SK63KNY	HE	47546	SN14FFW	BH	47566	SN64CLZ	LH
47449	SK63KKJ	HE	47547	SN14FFX	BH	47567	SN64CME	HE
47450	SK63KKL	HE	47548	SN14FFY	BH	47568	SN64CMF	HE
47451	SK63KKM	HE	47549	SN14FFZ	BH	47569	SN64CMK	HE
47452	SK63KKN	HE	47550	SN14FGA	BH	47570	SN64CMO	HE
47453	SK63KKO	HE	47551	SN14FGC	WM	47571	SN64CMU	HE
47454	SK63KKP	HE	47552	SN14FGD	WM			

Vehicles on Route 8 turn into Temple Meads station approach on their way into Bristol City Centre. 47439, a Wright Streetlite DF is seen here in summer sunshine.

48217	W817PFB	Volvo B6BLE	Wright Crusader 2	B35F
48223	W823PFB	Volvo B6BLE	Wright Crusader 2	B35F

| 50318 | YN53ELO | Optare M850 | | Optare Solo 8.5m | | | B27F | w |

53806-53820		Optare M850SL		Optare Solo Slimline 8.5m			B26F	
53806	WX05RSU	BH	53813	WX05RTZ	BH	53817	WX05RUO	BH
53809	WX05RSZ	BH	53814	WX05RUA	BH	53818	WX05RUR	BH
53811	WX05RTU	BH	53815	WX05RUC	BH	53819	WX05RUU	BH
53812	WX05RTV	BH	53816	WX05RUJ	BH	53820	WX05RUV	BH

54601	FA04YGX	Ford Transit	Ford	M16	HEa
60911	YG02DLO	Volvo B7L	Wright Eclipse	B41F	WE
60914	YG02DKO	Volvo B7L	Wright Eclipse	B36F	HE
61212	L64UOU	Volvo B10M-62	Plaxton Expressliner 2	C49FT	t
62157	R331GHS	Volvo B10BLE	Wright Renown	B41F	w
62185	W586RFS	Volvo B10BLE	Alexander ALX300	B44F	w
62198	X693ADK	Volvo B10BLE	Wright Renown	B43F	w
62199	X694ADK	Volvo B10BLE	Wright Renown	B43F	w

63068-63078		Wright Streetlite Max		Wright Streetlite 11.5m			B41F	
63068	SN13NAE	BH	63072	SM13NBD	BH	63076	SM13NBJ	BH
63069	SN13NAO	BH	63073	SM13NBE	BH	63077	SM13NBK	BH
63070	SM13NBA	BH	63074	SM13NBF	BH	63078	SM13NBL	BH
63071	SM13NBB	BH	63075	SM13NBG	BH			

53812, an Optare Solo, is leaving Bath city centre for a jouney on route 4 to Kingsway

65724	LK55ABZ	Scania L94UB	Wright Solar	B39F	BH
65725	LK55ACF	Scania L94UB	Wright Solar	B39F	BH
65726	LK55ACJ	Scania L94UB	Wright Solar	B39F	BH

66105-66172		Volvo B10BLE		Wright Renown			B47F	
66104	R904BOU	MH	66120	R920COU	w	66173%	W373EOW	WE
66105	R905BOU	w	66160*	S360XCR	WE	66174$	W374EOW	WM
66108	R908BOU	WM	66162*	S362XCR	MH	66206*	S806RWG	WE
66117	R917BOU	w	66163*	S363XCR	w	66207*	S807RWG	WM
66118	R918BOU	w	66171$	W371EOW	WE			

66301-66356		Volvo B7L		Wright Eclipse			B41F	
66301	KV02VVC	HE	66335	MV02VCA	LH	66352	MV02VEF	BH
66325	MV02VAY	LH	66336	MV02VCC	HE	66353	MV02VEH	BH
66326	MV02VBA	LH	66337	MV02VCM	LH	66354	MV02VEK	BH
66327	MV02VBB	LH	66342	MV02VCU	HE	66355	MV02VEL	BH
66330	MV02VBE	LH	66345	MV02VCY	MH	66356	MV02VEM	BH
66332	MV02VBX	LH	66346	MV02VCZ	LH			

These Wright Eclipse-bodied Volvo B7L have passed through many of the first fleets. Here is 66355 leaving Bath centre on route 5 to Whiteway

66719-66993		Volvo B7RLE		Wright Eclipse Urban * - B34D, $ - B44F			B43F	
66719	WX54XDC	MH	66728	WX54XCN	MH	66885	MX05CLF	MH
66720	WX54XDE	WE	66729	WX54XCO	MH	66886	MX55HHL	MH
66721	WX54XDF	WE	66730	WX54XCP	BH	66934	WX55UAA	MH
66722	WX54XDG	BH	66731	WX54XCR	BH	66935	WX55UAB	HE
66723	WX54XDH	WE	66734	WX54XCV	MH	66936	WX55UAC	MH
66724	WX54XDJ	WM	66881	MX05CKP	BH	66937	WX55UAD	BH
66725	WX54XDK	WM	66882	MX55HHR	BH	66938	WX55TVZ	MH
66726	WX54XDL	WM	66883	MX55HHP	BH	66939	WX55TZA	MH
66727	WX54XCM	BH	66884	MX55HHO	BH	66940	WX55TZB	MH

66941	WX55TZC	MH	66956	WX55TZT	WM	69253$	YJ07WFV	MH
66942	WX55TZD	MH	66992*	DC06FNG	BH			
66943	WX55TZE	MH	66993*	DC06FNH	BH			

A rarity is the dual doored Volvo B7RLE. 2 of them are allocated to Bath depot and 66992, showing the pink-based "mTickets" mobile device-based ticketing for FirstGroup buses is leaving Bath heading for the university

| 69437-69511 | | Volvo B7RLE | | | Wright Eclipse Urban 2 | | | DP37F |
| | | | | | * - B43F, $ - B44F | | | |

69437*	WX59BYO	WE	69447*	WX59BZA	WE	69504	BJ10VGF	HE
69438*	WX59BYP	WE	69448*	WX59BZB	MH	69505	BJ10VGG	HE
69439*	WX59BYR	WE	69457$	WX59BZL	MH	69506	BJ11XHY	HE
69440*	WX59BYS	WE	69458$	WX59BZM	MH	69507	BJ11EBV	HE
69441*	WX59BYT	WE	69500	BJ10VGA	HE	69508	BJ11EBY	HE
69442*	WX59BYU	WE	69501	BJ10VGC	HE	69509	BJ11XHZ	HE
69443*	WX59BYV	WE	69502	BJ10VGD	HE	69510	BJ11EBU	HE
69446*	WX59BYZ	WE	69503	BJ10VGE	HE	69511	BJ11EBZ	HE

Previous registrations

32001	W801PAE		32014	W814PAE
32002	W802PAE		32015	W815PAE
32003	W803PAE		61212	L64UOU, TDZ3265
32006	W806PAE		66992	RKZ4761
32007	W807PAE		66993	RKZ4760

Seen here at on the approach to Temple Meads is First West of England 69437, a Wright Eclipse Urban 2-bodied Volvo B7RLE, pictured while on route 376 to Wells

Liveries

Unless stated below, all vehicles in this fleet carry FirstGroup corporate livery:

Bath Unibus: 10035, 10175, 10177, 10178, 32001-32003, 32006, 32007, 32014, 32015, 32069, 32075, 32083, 33943-33950

Allover white: 10036, 10037, 33415, 44902-44904, 55105

First Express: 32684, 32685, 32688, 33488-33490, 35160-35167

Bristol Park & Ride: 33411-33414, 33416-33419, 33942, 66352-66356

Portway Park & Ride: 33931-33934

Brislington Park & Ride: 33936-33941

Bath Park & Ride: 39133-39140

ElectriCity: 39191, 39192

First Coaching: 61212

Badgerline: 66725, 66726

Mendip Explorer: 69446, 69458

West Yorkshire

Garages

BD	Bradford - Bowling Back Lane, Bradford, BD4 8SP
HD	Huddersfield - Old Fieldhouse Lane, Deighton, Huddersfield, HD2 1AG
HX	Halifax - Skircoat Road, Halifax, HX1 2RF
LB	Bramley - Henconner Lane, Bramley, Leeds, LS13 4LD
LH	Hunslet Park - Donisthorpe Street, Leeds, LS10 1PL
YK	York - 7 James Street, York, YO10 3WW

11101-11115			Mercedes-Benz O530G			Mercedes Benz Citaro		AB51D
11101	BG58OLR	YK	11106	BG58OMA	YK	11111	BG58OMF	YK
11102	BG58OLT	YK	11107	BG58OMB	YK	11112	BG58OMH	YK
11103	BG58OLU	YK	11108	BG58OMC	YK	11113	BG58OMJ	YK
11104	BG58OLV	YK	11109	BG58OMD	YK	11114	BG58OMK	YK
11105	BG58OLX	YK	11110	BG58OME	YK	11115	BG58OML	YK

A batch of 15 Mercedes-Benz Citaro artics operate on York Park & Ride services. Seen here having just left York Station and with the city walls behind it is 11113, showing the silver-based Park & Ride livery.

19001-19028			Volvo B7LA			Wright Streetcar * - AB37D		AB42D •
19001	YK06AOU	w	19009	YK06AUL	w	19018	YJ56EAG	w
19002	YK06ATV	w	19011	YK06AUC	w	19019*	YJ07LVL	w
19003	YK06ATU	w	19012	YJ06XLR	w	19020*	YJ07LVM	w
19004	MH06ZSW	w	19013	YJ06XLS	w	19021*	YJ07LVN	w
19005	YK06ATX	w	19014*	YJ56EAA	w	19022*	YJ07LVO	w
19006	MH06ZSP	w	19015	YJ56EAC	w	19023*	YJ07LVR	w
19007	YK06ATY	w	19016	YJ56EAE	w	19024*	YJ07LVS	w
19008	YK06ATZ	w	19017	YJ56EAF	w	19025*	YJ07LVT	w

| 19026* | YJ07LVU | w | | 19027* | YJ07LVV | w | | 19028* | YJ07LVW | w |

| 30561-30576 | | Volvo B7TL | | | Alexander ALX400 | | | H49/29F | | |
| | | | | | * - H49/28F | | | | | |

30561	X856UOK	HX		30571	WU02KVM	BD		30574	WU02KVR	BD
30562*	X857UOK	HD		30572	WU02KVO	BD		30576	WU02KVT	BD
30563*	X858UOK	BD		30573	WU02KVP	BD				

| 30796-30840 | | Volvo Olympian | | | Alexander Royale | | | H43/29F | | |

| 30796 | R616JUB | w | | 30805 | R625JUB | w | | 30834 | S654FWY | t |
| 30800 | R620JUB | u | | 30809 | R629JUB | w | | | | |

| 30847-31141 | | Volvo B7TL | | | Alexander ALX400 | | | H49/29F | | |
| | | | | | * - H49/28F, $ - H49/27F | | | | | |

30847	W702CWR	w		30868	W723CWR	BD		30906	W761DWX	HX
30848	W703CWR	w		30869	W724CWR	BD		30907	W762DWX	HX
30850	W705CWR	w		30883	W738DWX	BD		30908	X763VUA	LB
30852	W707CWR	w		30885	W772DWX	BD		30909	X764VUA	LB
30854	W709CWR	w		30890	W745DWX	u		30910	W778DWX	BD
30855	W667CWT	w		30891	W746DWX	w		30911	X766VUA	LB
30856	W711CWR	w		30893	W748DWX	u		30913	W768DWX	BD
30858	W713CWR	w		30895	W773DWX	BD		30914	W769DWX	BD
30859	W714CWR	w		30896	W751DWX	w		30916	W771KBT	HD
30860	W715CWR	w		30897	W752DWX	BD		30917	W772KBT	HD
30863	W718CWR	w		30904	W759DWX	BD		30918	W773KBT	HD
30864	W719CWR	w		30905	W776DWX	HX				

At the exit from Huddersfield Bus Station is First West Yorkshire 30953, a Volvo B7TL with Alexander ALX400 bodywork, seen while on route 323 to Marten Nest

30919	W774KBT	HD	30939	Y794XNW	u	30953	YJ51RSU	HD
30920	W787KBT	HD	30942	Y797XNW	u	31137$	YU52VYN	BD
30921	W776KBT	HD	30943	Y798XNW	HD	31138$	YU52VYO	BD
30929	X797NWR	LB	30949	YJ51RRX	HD	31139$	YU52VYP	HX
30930	X798NWR	HX	30950	YJ51RRY	HD	31140$	YU52VYR	HX
30931*	X351VWT	HX	30951	YJ51RRZ	HD	31141$	YU52VYS	YK
30933*	X353VWT	LB	30952	YJ51RSO	HD			

31677	P613WSU	Volvo Olympian		Alexander Royale		H42/29F	w

31760-31775		Volvo Olympian		Alexander RH		H47/29F	

31760	R921WOE	w	31767	R931WOE	BD	31775	R940YOV	w
31762	R923WOE	w	31768	R932YOV	w			
31766	R930WOE	BD	31769	R933YOV	BD			

31776-31780		Volvo B7TL		Alexander ALX400		H49/27F	

31776	YN53EOA	HX	31778	YN53EOC	HX	31780	YN53EOE	HX
31777	YN53EOB	HD	31779	YN53EOD	HX			

31790	YN53EFH	Volvo B7TL	Wright Eclipse Gemini	H45/29F	BD
31791	YN53EFJ	Volvo B7TL	Wright Eclipse Gemini	H45/29F	BD
31807	R929WOE	Volvo Olympian	Alexander RH	H47/29F	w
31808	R936YOV	Volvo Olympian	Alexander RH	H47/29F	w

32071-32092		Volvo B7TL		Alexander ALX400		H49/27F	

32071	KP51VZX	HD	32080	KP51WBK	BD	32089	KP51WCF	BD
32072	KP51VZY	HD	32082	KP51WBO	BD	32091	KP51WCJ	BD
32077	KP51WBD	BD	32085	KP51WBV	HD	32092	KP51WCN	BD
32078	KP51WBG	BD	32086	KP51WBY	BD			
32079	KP51WBJ	BD	32088	KP51WCA	BD			

32222	LT52WUG	Volvo B7TL	Plaxton President	H42/22F	YK
32223	LT52WUH	Volvo B7TL	Plaxton President	H42/22F	YK
32224	LT52WUJ	Volvo B7TL	Plaxton President	H42/22F	YK

32249-32266		Volvo B7TL		Alexander ALX400		H45/21F	
				* - H45/19F			

32249	LT52WVM	YK	32260	LT52WWF	YK	32262	LT52WWH	YK
32250	LT52WVN	YK	32261*	LT52WWG	YK	32266	LT52WWM	YK

32431-32697		Volvo B7TL		Wright Eclipse Gemini		H45/29F	

32431	YW04VAU	LB	32444	YJ04FYR	LB	32464	YJ04FZN	LB
32432	YJ04FYB	LB	32445	YJ04FYS	LB	32465	YJ04FZP	LB
32433	YJ04FYC	LB	32446	YJ04FYT	LB	32466	YJ04FZR	LB
32434	YJ04FYD	LB	32447	YJ04FYU	LB	32467	YJ04FZS	LB
32435	YJ04FYE	LB	32448	YJ04FYV	LB	32468	YJ04FZT	LB
32436	YJ04FYF	LB	32449	YJ04FYW	LB	32469	YJ04FZU	LB
32437	YJ04FYG	LB	32450	YJ04FYX	LB	32470	YJ04FZV	LB
32438	YJ04FYH	LB	32451	YJ04FYY	LB	32471	YJ04FZX	LB
32439	YJ04FYK	LB	32452	YJ04FYZ	LB	32472	YJ04FZY	LB
32440	YJ04FYL	LB	32460	YJ04FZH	LH	32473	YJ04FZZ	LB
32441	YJ04FYM	LH	32461	YJ04FZK	LB	32503	YJ54XTO	HD
32442	YJ04FYN	LB	32462	YJ04FZL	LB	32504	YJ54XTP	HD
32443	YJ04FYP	LB	32463	YJ04FZM	LB	32505	YJ54XTR	HD

32506	YJ54XTT	HD	32521	YJ54XUM	HX	32536	YJ54XVD	HX
32507	YJ54XTU	HD	32522	YJ54XUN	HX	32537	YJ05VUX	HX
32508	YJ54XTV	HD	32523	YJ54XUO	HX	32538	YJ05VUW	BD
32509	YJ54XTW	HD	32524	YJ54XUP	HX	32539	YJ05VWG	HX
32510	YJ54XTX	HD	32525	YJ54XUR	HX	32540	YJ05VWE	HX
32511	YJ54XTZ	HD	32526	YJ54XUT	HX	32541	YJ05VWF	HX
32512	YJ54XUA	HD	32527	YJ54XUU	HX	32542	YJ05VWH	HX
32513	YJ54XUB	HD	32528	YJ54XUV	BD	32684	WX56HJZ	LH
32514	YJ54XUC	HD	32529	YJ54XUW	BD	32685	WX56HKA	LH
32515	YJ54XUD	HD	32530	YJ54XUX	HX	32692	YJ06XLK	HX
32516	YJ54XUE	HD	32531	YJ54XUY	HX	32693	YJ06XLL	HX
32517	YJ54XUF	HD	32532	YJ05VUY	HX	32694	YJ06XLM	HX
32518	YJ54XUG	HD	32533	YJ54XVA	BD	32695	YJ06XLN	HX
32519	YJ54XUH	HD	32534	YJ54XVB	BD	32696	YJ06XLO	HX
32520	YJ54XUK	HX	32535	YJ54XVC	HX	32697	YJ06XLP	LH

33480-33487   ADL E40D SFDB32   ADL Enviro 400MMC 10.5m   H45/29F

33480	YX66WKC	LB	33483	YX66WJG	LB	33486	YX66WKJ	LB
33481	YX66WKD	LB	33484	YX66WKG	LB	33487	YX66WKK	LB
33482	YX66WKE	LB	33485	YX66WKH	LB			

33873-33890   ADL E40D SFD4DS   ADL Enviro 400 10.8m   H45/30F

33873	SN14TUY	LB	33879	SN14TVJ	LB	33885	SN14TVT	LB
33874	SN14TVA	LB	33880	SN14TVK	LB	33886	SN14TVU	LB
33875	SN14TVC	LB	33881	SN14TVL	LB	33887	SN14TVV	LB
33876	SN14TVD	LB	33882	SN14TVM	LB	33888	SL14DBO	LB
33877	SN14TVE	LB	33883	SN14TVO	LB	33889	SL14DBU	LB
33878	SN14TVF	LB	33884	SN14TVP	LB	33890	SL14DBV	LB

34214   S214LLO   Volvo Olympian   NC Palatine 1   H47/31F   w

35202-35238   Wright Streetdeck   Wright Streetdeck   H45/28F

35202	SL16PZZ	LH	35215	SL16RGO	LB	35228	SL16YOP	LB
35203	SL16RDY	LH	35216	SL16RGU	LB	35229	SL16YOR	BD
35204	SL16RDZ	LH	35217	SL16RGV	LB	35230	SL16YOT	BD
35205	SL16REU	LH	35218	SL16RGX	LB	35231	SL16YOV	BD
35206	SL16RFE	LH	35219	SL16RGY	LB	35232	SL16RHE	BD
35207	SL16RFF	LH	35220	SL16RGZ	LB	35233	SL16RHF	BD
35208	SL16RFJ	LH	35221	SL16RHA	LB	35234	SL16RHJ	BD
35209	SL16RFK	LH	35222	SL16YOH	LB	35235	SL16YOW	BD
35210	SL16RFN	LH	35223	SL16YOJ	LB	35236	SL16YOY	BD
35211	SL16RFO	LH	35224	SL16YOK	LB	35237	SL16YPA	BD
35212	SL16RFX	LH	35225	SL16YOM	LB	35238	SL16YPC	BD
35213	SL16RFY	LH	35226	SL16YON	LB			
35214	SL16RFZ	LB	35227	SL16YOO	LB			

36203-36278   Volvo B9TL   Wright Eclipse Gemini 2   H45/27F

36203	BN12WOD	LH	36210	BJ12VWS	LH	36217	BJ12VXA	LH
36204	BN12WOH	LH	36211	BJ12VWT	LH	36218	BJ12VXB	LH
36205	BN12WOJ	LH	36212	BJ12VWU	LH	36219	BJ12VXC	LH
36206	BN12WOM	LH	36213	BJ12VWV	LH	36220	BJ12VXD	LH
36207	BJ12VWO	LH	36214	BJ12VWW	LH	36221	BJ12VXE	LH
36208	BJ12VWP	LH	36215	BJ12VWX	LH	36222	BD12SZY	LH
36209	BJ12VWR	LH	36216	BJ12VWY	LH	36223	BD12SZZ	LH

In 2012, FirstGroup operated a number of special services for the London Olympics, consisted of a number of ADL Enviro 400s and Wright Eclipse Gemini 2-bodied Volvo B9TLs. After the Olympics, 76 of the latter made their way to West Yorkshire. One such vehicle, 36223, is seen here just short of its destination of Leeds Bus Station

36224	BD12TAU	LH	36243	BN12WPE	LH	36262	BG12YJU	LH
36225	BD12TAV	LH	36244	BN12WPF	LH	36263	BG12YJV	LH
36226	BD12TBO	LH	36245	BN12WPJ	LH	36264	BG12YJW	LH
36227	BD12TBU	LH	36246	BJ12VNR	LH	36265	BG12YJX	LH
36228	BD12TBV	LH	36247	BJ12VNS	LH	36266	BG12YJY	LH
36229	BD12TBX	LH	36248	BG12UKM	LH	36267	BG12YJZ	LH
36230	BD12TBY	LH	36249	BF12KWU	LH	36268	BG12YKA	LH
36231	BD12TBZ	LH	36250	BG12YJF	LH	36269	BG12YKB	LH
36232	BD12TCV	LH	36251	BG12YJH	LH	36270	BG12YKC	LH
36233	BD12TCU	LH	36252	BG12YJJ	LH	36271	BG12YKD	LH
36234	BD12TCY	LH	36253	BG12YJK	LH	36272	BG12YKE	LH
36235	BD12TCX	LH	36254	BG12YJL	LH	36273	BG12YKF	LH
36236	BN12WOR	LH	36255	BG12YJM	LH	36274	BD12TDV	LH
36237	BN12WOU	LH	36256	BG12YJN	LH	36275	BD12TCO	LH
36238	BN12WOV	LH	36257	BG12YJO	LH	36276	BD12TCK	LH
36239	BN12WOX	LH	36258	BG12YJP	LH	36277	BD12TDO	LH
36240	BN12WOY	LH	36259	BG12YJR	LH	36278	BD12TCZ	LH
36241	BN12WPA	LH	36260	BG12YJS	LH			
36242	BN12WPD	LH	36261	BG12YJT	LH			

37021-37062		Volvo B7TL			Wright Eclipse Gemini			H45/29F
37021	YJ06XKK	u	37025	YJ06XKO	LH	37029	YJ06XKU	HD
37022	YJ06XKL	u	37026	YJ06XKP	u	37030	YJ06XKV	HD
37023	YJ06XKM	LH	37027	YJ06XKS	u	37031	YJ06XKW	u
37024	YJ06XKN	LH	37028	YJ06XKT	HD	37032	YJ06XKX	HD

37033	YJ06XKY	HD	37043	YJ06XLT	LH	37053	YJ06XMD	HX
37034	YJ06XKZ	HX	37044	YJ06XLU	LH	37054	YJ06XME	HX
37035	YJ06XLA	HX	37045	YJ06XLV	YK	37055	YJ06XMF	BD
37036	YJ06XLB	LH	37046	YJ06XLW	HD	37056	YJ06XMG	BD
37037	YJ06XLC	LH	37047	YJ06XLX	HD	37057	YJ06XMH	BD
37038	YJ06XLD	LH	37048	YJ06XLY	HX	37058	YJ06XMK	BD
37039	YJ06XLE	LH	37049	YJ06XLZ	HD	37059	YJ06XML	BD
37040	YJ06XLF	LH	37050	YJ06XMA	HD	37060	YJ06XMM	LH
37041	YJ06XLG	LH	37051	YJ06XMB	HX	37061	YJ06XMO	LH
37042	YJ06XLH	LH	37052	YJ06XMC	HX	37062	YJ06XMP	LH

As part of commemorations, First West Yorkshire repainted one of their buses, Wright Eclipse Gemini 37048, into a variation of corporate livery, based on the colours of Halifax Corporation. Leaving Halifax Bus Station it is on route 508 to Leeds

37063-37756		Volvo B9TL		Wright Eclipse Gemini			H45/29F	
37063	YK57EZS	LB	37076	YJ08GVM	BD	37089	YJ08GWC	BD
37064	YK57EZT	LB	37077	YJ08GVN	BD	37090	YJ08GWD	BD
37065	YK57EZU	YK	37078	YJ08GVO	BD	37091	YJ08GWE	BD
37066	YK57EZV	YK	37079	YJ08GVP	BD	37092	YJ08GWF	BD
37067	YK57EZW	YK	37080	YJ08GVR	BD	37093	YJ08GWG	BD
37068	YK57EZX	YK	37081	YJ08GVT	BD	37094	YJ08GWK	BD
37069	YK57EZZ	YK	37082	YJ08GVU	BD	37095	YJ08GWL	BD
37070	YK57FAA	YK	37083	YJ08GVV	BD	37096	YJ08GWM	BD
37071	YJ08GVE	BD	37084	YJ08GVW	BD	37097	YJ08GWN	BD
37072	YJ08GVF	BD	37085	YJ08GVX	BD	37098	YJ08GWO	BD
37073	YJ08GVG	BD	37086	YJ08GVY	BD	37099	YJ08GWP	BD
37074	YJ08GVK	BD	37087	YJ08GVZ	BD	37100	YJ08GWU	BD
37075	YJ08GVL	BD	37088	YJ08GWA	BD	37101	YJ08GWV	BD

Pictured here in Bradford is First West Yorkshire 37709, a Volvo B9TL with Wright Eclipse Gemini
bodywork, seen while on route 72 to Leeds Eastgate

37102	YJ08GWW	BD	37295	MX07BTZ	HD	37648	YJ58RNV	LB
37123	YK07AYY	LH	37296	MX07BUA	HD	37649	YJ58RNX	LB
37124	YK07AYZ	LH	37298	MX07BUF	HD	37650	YJ58RNY	LB
37125	YK57CJF	LH	37299	MX07BUH	HD	37651	YJ58RNZ	u
37126	YK57CJJ	LH	37300	MX07BUJ	HD	37652	YJ58ROH	u
37127	YK57CJO	LH	37302	MX57HEJ	HD	37653	YJ58ROU	u
37128	YK57CJU	LH	37359	WX57HLZ	YK	37654	YJ58RPO	LB
37129	YK57CJV	LH	37360	YJ58GNP	BD	37655	YJ58RPU	LB
37130	YK57CJX	LH	37361	YJ58GMO	BD	37656	YJ58RPV	LB
37131	YK57CJY	LH	37362	YJ58GNU	u	37657	YJ58RPX	LB
37132	YK57CJZ	LH	37363	YJ58GMU	BD	37658	YJ58RPY	LB
37246	YN07MKD	YK	37364	YJ58GNV	BD	37659	YJ58RPZ	LB
37247	YN07MKE	YK	37365	YJ58GNW	BD	37660	YJ58RRO	LB
37248	YN07MKF	YK	37366	YJ58GNX	BD	37661	YJ58RRU	LB
37249	YN07MKG	YK	37500	YN08PMO	HD	37662	YJ58RRV	LB
37250	YN07MKJ	YK	37501	YN08PMU	BD	37663	YJ58RRX	LB
37251	YN07MKK	YK	37502	YN08PMV	BD	37664	YJ58RRY	LB
37252	YN07MKL	YK	37503	YN08PMX	BD	37665	YJ58RRZ	LB
37253	YN07MKM	YK	37504	YN08PMY	BD	37666	YJ58RSO	LB
37254	YN07MKO	YK	37505	YN08PNE	BD	37667	YJ58RSU	LH
37255	YN07MKP	YK	37506	YN08PNF	BD	37668	YJ58RSV	LH
37256	YN07MKV	YK	37507	YN08PNJ	BD	37669	YJ58RSX	LH
37258	YN07MKZ	u	37508	YN08PNK	BD	37670	YJ58RSY	LH
37291	MX07BTO	HD	37525	YN58ETT	HD	37671	YJ58RSZ	LH
37292	MX07BTU	HD	37645	YJ58RNN	LB	37672	YJ58RTO	LH
37293	MX07BTV	HD	37646	YJ58RNO	LB	37673	YJ58RTU	LH
37294	MX07BTY	HD	37647	YJ58RNU	LB	37674	YJ58RTV	LH

37675	YJ58RTX	LH	37697	YJ09OAO	LH	37719	YJ09OBP	LB
37676	YJ09FVG	LH	37698	YJ09OAP	LH	37720	YJ09OBR	LB
37677	YJ09FVH	LH	37699	YJ09OAS	LH	37721	YJ09OBS	LB
37678	YJ09FVK	u	37700	YJ09OAU	LH	37722	YJ09OBT	LB
37679	YJ09FVL	u	37701	YJ09OAV	LH	37723	YJ09OBU	LB
37680	YJ09FVM	LB	37702	YJ09OAW	LH	37724	YJ09OBV	LB
37681	YJ09FVN	u	37703	YJ09OAX	LH	37725	YJ09OBW	LB
37682	YJ09FVO	LB	37704	YJ09OAY	LH	37726	YJ09OBX	LB
37683	YJ09FVP	LB	37705	YJ09OAZ	LH	37727	YJ09OBY	LB
37684	YJ09FVE	LB	37706	YJ09OBA	LB	37728	YJ09OBZ	LB
37685	YJ09FVF	LH	37707	YJ09OBB	LB	37729	YJ09OCA	LB
37686	YJ09NZY	LH	37708	YJ09OBC	LB	37730	YJ09OCB	LB
37687	YJ09OAA	LB	37709	YJ09OBD	LB	37731	YJ09OCC	LB
37688	YJ09OAB	LB	37710	YJ09OBE	LB	37732	YJ09OCD	BD
37689	YJ09OAC	LB	37711	YJ09OBF	LB	37733	YJ09OCE	u
37690	YJ09OAD	LH	37712	YJ09OBG	LB	37734	YJ09OCF	u
37691	YJ09OAE	LH	37713	YJ09OBH	LB	37735	YJ09OCG	BD
37692	YJ09OAG	LH	37714	YJ09OBK	LB	37752	YJ59KSO	LB
37693	YJ09OAH	LH	37715	YJ09OBL	LB	37753	YJ59KSU	LB
37694	YJ09OAL	LH	37716	YJ09OBM	LB	37754	YJ59KSV	LB
37695	YJ09OAM	LH	37717	YJ09OBN	LB	37755	YJ59KSY	LB
37696	YJ09OAN	LH	37718	YJ09OBO	LB	37756	YJ59KSZ	LB

39001-39004   Wright Hybrid   Wright Gemini 2   H41/28F

39001	LK58ECV	YK	39003	LK58ECX	YK
39002	LK58ECW	YK	39004	LK58ECY	YK

39201-39236   Volvo B5LH   Wright Eclipse Gemini 2   H41/23F

39201	BJ60BZA	LH	39223	BP11JWD	LH	39231	BP11JWK	LH
39202	BJ60BZB	LH	39224	BP11JWE	LH	39232	BP11JWO	LH
39203	BJ60BZC	LH	39225	BP11JWF	LH	39233	BP11JWU	LH
39204	BJ60BZD	LH	39226	BP11JWG	LH	39234	BP11JWV	LH
39205	BJ60BZE	LH	39227	BP11JWL	LH	39235	BP11JWX	LH
39206	BJ60BZF	LH	39228	BP11JWM	LH	39236	BP11JWW	LH
39221	BP11JWA	LH	39229	BP11JWN	LH			
39222	BP11JWC	LH	39230	BP11JWJ	LH			

39316-39323   ADL E40H   ADL Enviro 400MMC

39316	39319	39322
39317	39320	39323
39318	39321	

40571-40587   Volvo B6BLE   Wright Crusader 2   B38F

40571	YJ51RKO	YK	40575	YJ51RSX	YK	40579	YJ51RHV	LH
40572	YJ51RKU	YK	40576	YJ51RSY	LH	40587	YJ51RFZ	LH
40573	YJ51RKV	YK	40577	YJ51RHO	LH			
40574	YJ51RSV	YK	40578	YJ51RHU	w			

40973	YV03UOY	Dennis Dart SLF SFD3CA	Alexander Pointer 2 10.7m	B37F	HX
40975	YV03UOW	Dennis Dart SLF SFD3CA	Alexander Pointer 2 10.7m	B37F	HX
40976	YX03UOV	Dennis Dart SLF SFD3CA	Alexander Pointer 2 10.7m	B37F	HX
41282	T282JLD	Dennis Dart SLF SFD112	Marshall Capital 9.3m	B27F	w
41283	T283JLD	Dennis Dart SLF SFD112	Marshall Capital 9.3m	B27F	w

Above: *In Leeds City Centre is 39206 in the First West Yorkshire fleet, a Wright Eclipse Gemini 2-bodied Volvo B5LH hybrid, seen while on route 7A to Alwoodley*

Below: *With the backdrop of York minster and the city walls, 40571, a Volvo B6BLE with Wright Crusader 2 bodywork, is pictured while on route 6 to Clifton Moor*

47491-47500		Wright Streetlite DF		Wright Streetlite 10.8m			B37F	
47491	SN64CHC	HD	47495	SN64CHH	HD	47499	SN64CHO	HD
47492	SN64CHD	HD	47496	SN64CHJ	HD	47500	SN64CHV	HD
47493	SN64CHF	HD	47497	SN64CHK	HD			
47494	SN64CHG	HD	47498	SN64CHL	HD			

49901-49912		Optare Versa V1110EV		Optare Versa EV 11.1m			B36F	
49901	YJ14BHA	YK	49905	YJ14BHK	YK	49909	YJ15AYL	YK
49902	YJ14BHD	YK	49906	YJ14BHL	YK	49910	YJ15AYM	YK
49903	YJ14BHE	YK	49907	YJ15AYP	YK	49911	YJ15AYN	YK
49904	YJ14BHF	YK	49908	YJ15AYK	YK	49912	YJ15AYO	YK

A batch of 6 electric-powered Optare Versas joined the fleet in 2014, followed by a further 6 in 2015. All these vehicles are used on York Park & Ride services. 49903, is seen here on route 59 to Poppleton Bar Park & Ride site

50235-53101		Optare Solo M850		Optare Solo 8.5m			B26F	
				* - DP25F, $ - B29F				
50235	Y254HHL	w	50319*	YN53ELJ	HX	53034$	Y546XNW	w
50238	YT51EZX	HX	50407	YN03ZVX	HX	53035$	Y547XNW	BD

53301	YJ54BVA	Optare Solo M1020	Optare Solo 10.2m	B37F	HX
53302	YJ54BVB	Optare Solo M1020	Optare Solo 10.2m	B37F	HX
53303	YJ54BVC	Optare Solo M1020	Optare Solo 10.2m	B37F	HX

Starting life in London with First Essex Buses as their 501 for a London tendered route, Optare Solo 53101 made its way north to West Yorkshire. It is just about to reach its terminus in Bradford city centre before making its way back out to Tyersal.

60066-60214		Scania L94UB		Wright Floline * - B40F			B43F	
60066	T824SFS	LB	60172*	T919SSF	LH	60213	X269USH	LB
60067	T825SFS	LH	60212	Y633RTD	LH	60214	Y634RTD	LB

60361	R571YNC	Volvo B10BLE		Wright Renown			B41F	YKt
60467	G622NWA	Volvo B10M-55		Alexander PS			B51F	t
60472	G627NWA	Volvo B10M-55		Alexander PS			B37F	LBt

60637-60855		Volvo B10BLE		Wright Renown * - B41F, $ - B--F			B44F	
60637*	T819MAK	LBt	60839	V772UVY	BD	60849	W809DWX	HX
60638$	T820MAK	BDa	60842	W802DWX	HX	60850	W811DWX	HX
60658*	T840MAK	t	60843	W803DWX	HX	60851	W812DWX	HD
60665*	T847MAK	w	60844	W804DWX	HX	60852	W813DWX	BD
60668*	T850MAK	BDt	60845	W805DWX	HX	60853	W814DWX	BD
60827	V760UVY	HX	60846	W806DWX	HX	60854	W815DWX	BD
60832	V765UVY	w	60847	W807DWX	HX	60855	W816DWX	BD
60837	V770UVY	w	60848	W808DWX	HX			

60876-60928		Volvo B7L		Wright Eclipse * - B36F			B41F	
60876	Y445CUB	YK	60880	Y449CUB	LB	60883	YJ51PZU	LB
60877	Y446CUB	BD	60881	Y451CUB	LB	60884	YJ51PZV	YK
60878	Y447CUB	BD	60882	YJ51PZT	LB	60895	YJ51RFE	BD

60896	YJ51RFF	LB	60909	YG02DGZ	YK	60921	YG02DLN	YK
60897	YJ51RFY	LB	60910	YJ51RFK	BD	60922	YG02DHJ	YK
60903	YG02DHM	BD	60912*	YG02DLD	u	60923	YG02DHF	BD
60904	YG02DHL	BD	60913	YG02DLY	u	60924	YG02DHE	u
60905	YG02DHO	BD	60917	YG02DKV	BD	60925	YG02DHD	BD
60906	YG02DHN	BD	60918	YG02DLJ	BD	60926	YG02DGY	YK
60907	YG02DHV	BD	60919	YG02DLX	YK	60927	YG02DHC	YK
60908	YG02DHA	BD	60920	YG02DLU	YK	60928	YG02DHU	YK

61029-61041		Scania L94UB		Wright Floline			B43F	
61029	T428GUG	LB	61036	V135ESC	LH	61039	V138ESC	w
61034	V133ESC	LH	61037	V136ESC	LH	61040	V139ESC	LB
61035	V134ESC	LH	61038	V137ESC	LB	61041	V140ESC	LB

Passing Leeds Bus Station is First West Yorkshire 61029, a Wright Floline-bodied Scania L94UB, while on route 19A to East Garforth

61214-61227		Scania L94UB		Wright Solar			B43F	
61214	YM52UVK	LB	61216	YM52UVN	LB	61226	YM52UWB	LB
61215	YM52UVL	LB	61219	YM52UVR	LB	61227	YM52UWD	LB

61289	S809RWG	Volvo B10BLE	Wright Renown	B41F	HX
61363	L304VSU	Volvo B10B-58	Alexander Strider	B51F	LBt
61594	SA02BZL	Volvo B7L	Wright Eclipse	B41F	BD
62355	SN51MSV	Scania L94UB	Wright Solar	B43F	LB

63277-63295		Wright Streetlite Max		Wright Streetlite 11.5m			B41F	
63277	SL16YVP	BD	63279	SL15ZFJ	BD	63281	SL15ZFM	BD
63278	SL15ZFH	BD	63280	SL15ZFK	BD	63282	SL15ZFN	BD

63283	SL15ZFO	BD	63288	SN65OLX	BD	63293	SL15ZFZ	HX
63284	SL15ZFP	BD	63289	SL15ZFV	HX	63294	SL15ZGA	HX
63285	SL15ZFR	BD	63290	SL15ZFW	HX	63295	SL15ZGB	HX
63286	SL15ZFS	BD	63291	SL15ZFX	HX			
63287	SL15ZFT	BD	63292	SL15ZFY	HX			

Halifax has a batch of Wright Streetlites allocated for Red Arrow services, 63293 is to the longer Max specification and is showing the red front as part of its branding.

66324	MV02VAX	Volvo B7L	Wright Eclipse	B41F	LH
66339	MV02VCO	Volvo B7L	Wright Eclipse	B41F	BD
66347	MV02VDA	Volvo B7L	Wright Eclipse	B41F	LH
66651	K114PRV	Volvo B10B-58	NC Paladin	B51F	BDt
66652	M967GDU	Volvo B10B-58	Plaxton Verde	B51F	BDt

66707-66999   Volvo B7RLE   Wright Eclipse Urban   B40F
* - B44F, \$ - B43F

66707*	YK53GXR	LB	66742	YJ54XVR	LB	66756	YJ05KNX	BD
66708*	YK53GXT	LB	66743	YJ54XVT	LB	66757	YJ05KNY	BD
66709*	YK53GXU	LB	66744	YJ54XVU	HX	66758	YJ05KNZ	BD
66710*	YK53GXV	LB	66746	YJ54XVX	HX	66759	YJ05VVA	YK
66711$	YK04EZJ	HX	66747	YJ54XVY	HX	66760	YJ05VVB	YK
66712$	YK04EZL	LB	66748	YJ54XVZ	HX	66761	YJ05VVC	YK
66713$	YK04EZG	HX	66749	YJ54XWA	BD	66762	YJ05VVD	YK
66714$	YK04EZM	HD	66750	YJ05KOB	BD	66763	YJ05VVE	YK
66715$	YK04EZH	LH	66751	YJ05KOD	BD	66764	YJ05VVF	BD
66738	YJ54XVM	LB	66752	YJ05KOE	BD	66765	YJ05VVG	BD
66739	YJ54XVN	LB	66753	YJ05KOH	HD	66766	YJ05VVH	LB
66740	YJ54XVO	LB	66754	YJ05KNV	BD	66767	YJ05VVK	LB
66741	YJ54XVP	LB	66755	YJ05KNW	LB	66768	YJ05VVL	LB

66769	YJ05VVM	LB	66780	YJ05VVZ	HX	66789	YK05FOT	HX
66772	YJ05VVP	LB	66781	YK05FJJ	HX	66790	YA05SOU	HX
66773	YJ05VVR	HD	66782	YK05FLB	YK	66791	YK05FOP	HD
66774	YJ05VVS	HD	66783	YK05FJF	HX	66792	YA05SOJ	HD
66775	YJ05VVT	HD	66784	YK05FJE	HX	66995*	YJ07LWC	LB
66776	YJ05VVU	BD	66785	YK05FPA	HD	66996*	YJ07LWD	LB
66777	YJ05VVW	HX	66786	YK05FLC	LH	66997*	YJ07LWE	LH
66778	YJ05VVX	HX	66787	YK05FOV	HD	66998*	YJ07LWF	LH
66779	YJ05VVY	HX	66788	YK05FOU	LH	66999*	YK57FCL	BD

66758 in the First West Yorkshire fleet is a Wright Eclipse Urban-bodied Volvo B7RLE, seen here in Bradford while on route 612 to Shipley

68515-68548		BMC 1100FE		BMC			B55FL	
				* - B60F				
68515*	YJ54YCO	HX	68529	YA54WBO	HX	68547	YJ55CAV	HX
68516*	YJ54YCP	HX	68530	YA54WBN	HX	68548	YJ55CAU	HX
68527	YA54WBL	HX	68545	YJ05VWA	HX			
68528	YA54WBK	HX	68546	YJ55CAO	HX			

68603-68683		BMC 220 Condor		BMC			B57F	
68603	YK55AAJ	BD	68621	YK55AVF	BD	68635	YK06DYJ	HX
68606	YK55AUP	BD	68622	YK55AVG	BD	68638	YK06DNN	HX
68608	YJ06XFR	HX	68623	YK55AVJ	BD	68639	YK06DTZ	BD
68609	YK55AUU	HX	68625	YK55AVM	HX	68640	YJ06XEK	BD
68610	YK55AAN	HX	68626	YJ06WTX	BD	68641	YJ06XEL	HX
68614	YK55AUE	HD	68628	YJ06WTV	BD	68642	YK06ATO	HX
68615	YK55AUF	HX	68630	YJ06WTZ	BD	68643	YK06CZZ	HX
68616	YK55AUH	HD	68631	YJ06WUA	BD	68646	YK06DAA	BD

68648	YK06EHE	HX	68660	YJ56LLO	HX	68672	YJ56LRL	BD
68651	YJ56LJE	BD	68662	YJ56LNA	HX	68674	YJ56WGA	HX
68652	YJ56LJF	u	68663	YJ56LKE	HX	68675	YJ56ZMU	HX
68653	YJ56LJK	BD	68664	YJ56LJY	HX	68676	YK07FTU	HX
68654	YJ56LJN	HX	68667	YJ56LKC	HX	68677	YK07FUD	HX
68655	YJ56LJL	HX	68668	YJ56LKD	HX	68680	YK07FUA	HX
68656	YJ56LLG	HX	68669	YJ56LMX	HX	68682	YK07FTP	HD
68657	YJ56LLK	BD	68670	YJ56LRU	HX	68683	YK07FTT	HX
68659	YJ56LLN	HX	68671	YJ56LRN	BD			

68684-68700   BMC 225 Condor   BMC   B57F
* - B55F

68684	YJ57VYX	HD	68691	YJ08XCP	HD	68697	YJ07XMB	HD
68685	YJ57VTV	HD	68692	YJ08XCN	HD	68698	YJ07XWG	BD
68686	YJ57VVA	HD	68693	YJ08XCS	HD	68699	YK07FTX	HD
68687	YJ57VYY	HD	68694*	YK07BJX	HD	68700	YJ07WBL	BD
68689	YJ08XCR	HD	68695*	YK07BJY	HD			
68690	YJ08XCO	HD	68696*	YK07BJZ	HD			

68701-68709   BMC 220 Condor   BMC   B57F

68701	YK55JCN	HX	68704	YJ56ZTM	u	68707	YJ57WKB	HX
68702	YK06EFR	HX	68705	YJ57NFF	HX	68708	YJ07XND	HX
68703	YK06EFS	HX	68706	YJ57WKC	HX	68709	YJ07FLP	BD

68710	YJ07XWF	BMC 225 Condor	BMC	B57F	BD
68711	YJ07WBK	BMC 225 Condor	BMC	B57F	BD

69000-69485   Volvo B7RLE   Wright Eclipse Urban   B44F
* - B43F

69000*	YK54ENP	LB	69319	YJ09FWO	BD	69349	YJ08CFD	LB
69001*	YK54ENL	YK	69320	YJ09FWP	BD	69350	YJ08CFE	LB
69002*	YK54ENM	YK	69321	YJ09FWR	BD	69358	YJ08ZGL	YK
69003*	YK54ENN	YK	69322	YJ09FWS	BD	69359	YJ08ZGM	YK
69004*	YK54ENO	YK	69323	YJ09FWT	HD	69360	YJ08ZGN	YK
69268	YJ57YSK	LB	69324	YJ09FWU	HD	69361	YJ08ZGO	YK
69269	YJ57YSL	LB	69329*	YJ08CDE	HD	69362	YJ08ZGP	YK
69270	YN07WFW	BD	69330*	YJ08CDF	HD	69363*	YJ08XYB	YK
69271	YN07WFX	BD	69331*	YJ08CDK	LB	69364*	YJ08XYC	YK
69272	YN07WFY	BD	69332	YJ08CDN	LB	69365*	YJ08XYD	YK
69273	YN07WFZ	BD	69333	YJ08CDO	LB	69366*	YJ08XYE	YK
69274	YN07WGA	BD	69334	YJ08CDU	LB	69367*	YJ08XYF	YK
69275	YJ57YSN	YK	69335	YJ08CDV	LB	69368*	YJ08XYG	YK
69276	YJ57YSM	YK	69336	YJ08CDX	LB	69369*	YJ08XYH	YK
69277	YJ57YSO	YK	69337	YJ08CDY	LB	69370*	YJ08XYK	YK
69278	YJ57YSP	YK	69338	YJ08CDZ	LB	69371*	YJ08XYL	YK
69279	YJ57YSR	YK	69339	YJ08CEA	LB	69372*	YJ08XYM	YK
69299	YJ08GWX	BD	69340	YJ08CEF	LB	69373*	YJ08XYN	YK
69300	YJ08GWY	u	69341	YJ08CEK	LB	69374*	YJ08XYO	YK
69306	YJ09FWA	LH	69342	YJ08CEN	LB	69375*	YJ08XYP	YK
69307	YJ09FWB	HD	69343	YJ08CEO	LB	69376*	YJ08XYR	YK
69308	YJ09FWC	HD	69344	YJ08CEU	LB	69377*	YJ08XYS	YK
69315	YJ58RVA	BD	69345	YJ08CEV	LB	69378*	YJ08XYT	YK
69316	YJ09FWL	BD	69346	YJ08CEX	LB	69379*	YJ08XXW	YK
69317	YJ09FWM	BD	69347	YJ08CEY	LB	69412	YJ09FWZ	LH
69318	YJ09FWN	BD	69348	YJ08CFA	LB	69413	YJ09FXA	LH

Passing Leeds Bus Station while on route 74 to Middleton Asda is First West Yorkshire 69341, a Wright Eclipse Urban-bodied Volvo B7RLE

69414	YJ09FXB	LH		69469	YJ09NYD	BD		69478	YJ09NYR	BD
69415	YJ09FXC	LH		69470	YJ09NYF	BD		69479	YJ09NYS	BD
69416	YJ09FXD	LH		69471	YJ09NYG	BD		69480	YJ09NYT	HX
69417	YJ09FXE	LH		69472	YJ09NYH	BD		69481	YJ09NYU	HX
69418	YJ09FXF	LH		69473	YJ09NYK	BD		69482	YJ09NYV	HX
69419	YJ09FXG	HD		69474	YJ09NYM	BD		69483	YJ09NYW	HX
69466	YJ09NYA	BD		69475	YJ09NYN	BD		69484	YJ09NYX	HX
69467	YJ09NYB	BD		69476	YJ09NYO	BD		69485	YJ09NYY	HX
69468	YJ09NYC	BD		69477	YJ09NYP	HX				

69556-69587		Volvo B7RLE			Wright Eclipse Urban 2			B41F		
69556	BV13ZDH	HD		69567	BD13NFM	BD		69578	BD13OHT	HX
69557	BV13ZDJ	HD		69568	BD13NFN	BD		69579	BT13YVV	HX
69558	BV13ZDK	HD		69569	BD13NFR	BD		69580	BT13YVW	HX
69559	BV13YZZ	HD		69570	BD13NFV	BD		69581	BT13YVX	HX
69560	BG13VUD	HD		69571	BD13OHK	BD		69582	BT13YVY	LH
69561	BG13VUC	HD		69572	BD13OHL	BD		69583	BT13YVZ	HX
69562	BG13VUE	HD		69573	BD13OHN	BD		69584	BT13YWA	HX
69563	BD13NFL	HD		69574	BD13OHO	BD		69585	BT13YWB	HX
69564	BD13NFK	HD		69575	BD13OHP	BD		69586	BT13YWC	HX
69565	BD13NFO	HD		69576	BD13OHR	BD		69587	BT13YWD	HX
69566	BD13NFP	BD		69577	BD13OHS	BD				

Previous registrations

32431	K1FRL		60361	P571PBA

69578 in the First West Yorkshire fleet is a Wright Eclipse Urban 2-bodied Volvo B7RLE, seen here leaving Halifax Bus Station on route 512 to Mixenden, showing the red-fronted livery carried by the vehicle

Liveries

Unless stated below, all vehicles in this fleet carry FirstGroup corporate livery

York Park & Ride: 11101-11115, 49901-49911, 60912, 60913, 60917, 69365-69373

ftr: 19001, 19003, 19005, 19007-19009, 19011, 19012, 19014-19023, 19026, 19028

Hyperlink: 19004, 19006, 19013, 19024, 19025, 19027

Unilink: 31764, 31766

Express (blue and gold): 32505-32508, 33480-33487, 35229-35238, 37083-37087, 37672, 37673 , 37675

Zest (orange front on corporate livery): 32520-32527, 32539-32541

Elland Road Park & Ride: 36276-36278

Halifax version of corporate livery: 37048

University of York: 37065-37070, 37253-37256, 37359, 49912

Holme Valley Connection (red front on corporate livery): 37291-37296, 37298, 37299, 37302, 37500, 37525

Huddersfield Corporation: 37300

West Yorkshire Road Car: 37365

Yorkshire Rider: 37674

Bradford Corporation: 37732

First Hybrid: 39201-39206, 39221-39236, 39316-39323

Metro MyBus: 50319

First Training: 60361, 60467, 60472, 66651, 66652

Red Arrow (red front on corporate livery): 63289-63295, 66748, 66749, 66751, 66752, 66764, 66765, 69578, 69579

Schoolbus: 68515, 68516, 68527-68530, 68545-68548, 68603, 68606, 68608-68610, 68614-68616, 68621-68623, 68625, 68626, 68628, 68630, 68631, 68635, 68638-68643, 68646, 68648, 68651-68657, 68659, 68660, 68662-68664, 68667-68672, 68674-68677, 68680, 68682-68687, 68689-68711

Calder Connection (green front on corporate livery): 69480-69485

Croydon Tramlink

Depots and stabling points
Therapia Lane, Beddington

2530-2553		Bombardier CR4000 2-set sets		
2530	2535	2540	2545	2550
2531	2536	2541	2546	2551
2532	2537	2542	2547	2552
2533	2538	2543	2548	2553
2534	2539	2544	2549	

2554-2565		Stadler Rail Variobahn 2-car set	
2554	2557	2560	2563
2555	2558	2561	2564
2556	2559	2562	2565

Pictured here approaching West Croydon Bus Station while on Line 1 to Elmers End is Bombardier Tram 2552, one of the original trams delivered new for the Croydon Tramlink operation

Tram Lines in Croydon Tramlink network

Line 1   Elmers End to Wellesley Road (trams then continue via route 2 to Beckenham Junction)

Line 2   Beckenham Junction to Wellesley Road (trams then continue via route 1 to Elmers End)

Line 3   New Addington to Wimbledon

Line 4   Elmers End to Wimbledon

Above: *Seen here near West Croydon Bus Station is Stadler Rail Variobahn tram 2558, pictured while on Tram Line 4 to Elmers End, delivered in 2016 for increased services on the Croydon Tramlink network*

Below: *Seen at New Addington in an overall advert for Turkish Airlines is Bombardier Tram 2537.*

Great Western Railway (including Heathrow Connect)

Depots and stabling points

Old Oak Common, London	Landore, Swansea	Reading
Laira, Plymouth	Exeter	
St Philip's Marsh, Bristol	Long Rock, Penzance	

Class 08 BR/Electric English shunting locomotives

08 410	08 641	08 644	08 795	08 836
08 483	08 643	08 663	08 822	

Class 43 BREL HST locomotives

43 002	43 023	43 037	43 087	43 128
43 003	43 024	43 040	43 088	43 129
43 004	43 025	43 041	43 091	43 130
43 005	43 026	43 042	43 092	43 131
43 009	43 027	43 053	43 093	43 132
43 010	43 028	43 056	43 094	43 133
43 012	43 029	43 063	43 097	43 134
43 015	43 030	43 069	43 098	43 135
43 016	43 031	43 070	43 122	43 136
43 017	43 032	43 071	43 123	43 137
43 018	43 033	43 078	43 124	43 138
43 020	43 034	43 079	43 125	43 139
43 021	43 035	43 084	43 126	43 140
43 022	43 036	43 086	43 127	43 141

Seen near South Marston is Class 43 loco 43 156, heading towards Swindon in this striking photograph looking up an embankment

43 142	43 152	43 164	43 177	43 189
43 143	43 153	43 165	43 179	43 190
43 144	43 154	43 168	43 180	43 191
43 145	43 155	43 169	43 181	43 192
43 146	43 156	43 170	43 182	43 193
43 147	43 158	43 171	43 183	43 195
43 148	43 159	43 172	43 185	43 196
43 149	43 161	43 174	43 186	43 197
43 150	43 162	43 175	43 187	43 198
43 151	43 163	43 176	43 188	

Mk3 HST carriages

40101	40114	40707	40752	40900
40102	40115	40710	40755	40901
40103	40116	40713	40757	40902
40104	40117	40715	40801	40903
40105	40118	40716	40802	40904
40106	40119	40718	40803	41004
40107	40204	40721	40804	41006
40108	40205	40722	40806	41008
40109	40207	40727	40807	41010
40110	40210	40733	40808	41012
40111	40221	40734	40809	41016
40112	40231	40739	40810	41018
40113	40703	40743	40811	41020

Seen here at Newport is Class 43 loco 43 002, restored into Inter-City 125 colours from the 1970s. This loco has been named "Sir Kenneth Grange", who designed the shape of this iconic locomotive, and celebrates the 40th anniversary of the entry into service of the Inter-City 125 (courtesy of Kevin Cooper)

41030	41137	42006	42039	42073
41032	41138	42007	42040	42074
41034	41140	42008	42041	42075
41038	41142	42009	42042	42076
41052	41144	42010	42043	42077
41056	41146	42012	42044	42078
41059	41149	42013	42045	42079
41089	41158	42014	42046	42080
41094	41160	42015	42047	42081
41102	41161	42016	42048	42083
41103	41162	42019	42049	42085
41104	41166	42021	42050	42087
41106	41167	42023	42054	42089
41108	41169	42024	42055	42092
41110	41176	42025	42056	42093
41116	41180	42026	42060	42094
41122	41182	42027	42061	42095
41124	41183	42028	42062	42096
41126	41186	42029	42066	42098
41128	41187	42030	42067	42099
41130	41189	42031	42068	42101
41132	41192	42032	42069	42102
41134	42003	42033	42070	42103
41135	42004	42034	42071	42105
41136	42005	42035	42072	42107

Seen here at entering Buckfastleigh Station on the South Devon Railway is Class 43 loco 43 187, this has just worked a special over the heritage railway from Totnes. It is showing the now standard green GWR livery (photo courtesy of Kevin Cooper)

42138	42256	42333	42561	44034
42143	42257	42343	42562	44035
42144	42258	42344	42563	44036
42145	42259	42345	42564	44037
42166	42260	42346	42565	44038
42167	42261	42347	42566	44039
42168	42263	42348	42567	44040
42169	42264	42349	42568	44042
42173	42265	42350	42569	44043
42174	42266	42351	42570	44049
42175	42267	42353	42571	44055
42176	42268	42356	42572	44059
42177	42269	42360	42573	44060
42178	42271	42361	42574	44064
42183	42272	42362	42575	44066
42184	42273	42364	42576	44067
42185	42275	42365	42577	44068
42195	42276	42381	42578	44069
42196	42277	42382	42579	44074
42197	42279	42383	42580	44076
42200	42280	42501	42581	44078
42201	42281	42502	42582	44079
42202	42283	42503	42583	44081
42203	42284	42504	44000	44083
42204	42285	42505	44001	44086
42206	42287	42506	44002	44090
42207	42288	42507	44003	44091
42208	42289	42508	44004	44093
42209	42291	42509	44005	44097
42211	42292	42510	44007	44100
42212	42293	42511	44008	44101
42213	42294	42512	44009	46001
42214	42295	42513	44010	46002
42216	42296	42514	44011	46003
42217	42297	42515	44013	46004
42218	42299	42516	44014	46005
42221	42300	42517	44015	46006
42222	42301	42518	44016	46007
42224	42302	42519	44018	46008
42231	42303	42520	44020	46009
42232	42304	42551	44022	46010
42233	42305	42552	44023	46011
42236	42308	42553	44024	46012
42245	42310	42554	44025	46013
42247	42315	42555	44026	46014
42250	42317	42556	44028	46015
42251	42319	42557	44029	46016
42252	42321	42558	44030	46017
42253	42325	42559	44032	46018
42255	42332	42560	44033	

Class 57   Bush Traction diesel locomotives

57 602	57 603	57 604	57 605

Above: *Pictured arriving at St Germans is Class 57 loco 57 605, seen working a Par-Plymouth service (photo courtesy of Kevin Cooper)*

Below: *Seen here at Newton Abbot heading for Plymouth is 2-car Sprinter set 150 221*

Mk3 sleeper coaches for the Night Riviera Express service
* - kitchen buffet car, $ - sleeper car, % - open standard, & - unclassified brake

10219*	10534$	10590$	10612$	12161%
10225*	10563$	10594$	10616$	17173&
10232*	10584$	10596$	12100%	17174&
10532$	10589$	10601$	12142%	17175&

Class 143   Hunslet-Barclay and Walter Alexander Pacer sets

143 603	143 612	143 618	143 620
143 611	143 617	143 619	143 621

Class 150   BREL Sprinter 3-car sets

150 001	150 002

Class 150   BREL Sprinter 2-car sets

150 101	150 122	150 131	150 234	150 248
150 102	150 123	150 202	150 238	150 249
150 104	150 124	150 216	150 239	150 261
150 106	150 127	150 219	150 243	150 263
150 108	150 128	150 221	150 244	150 265
150 120	150 129	150 232	150 246	150 266
150 121	150 130	150 233	150 247	

Seen here passing Dawlish Warren is First Great Western single-car unit 153 361, coupled to two-car set 150 238, while operating to Paignton (courtesy of Kevin Cooper)

Pictured here approaching Southampton while on way to Cardiff is 2-car Express Sprinter set 158 766

Class 150	BREL Sprinter 3-car sets			
150 925	150 926	150 938		

Class 153	BREL Super Sprinter single-car units			
153 305	153 329	153 368	153 372	153 380
153 318	153 333	153 369	153 373	153 382
153 325	153 361	153 370	153 377	

Class 158	BREL Express Sprinter 2-car sets			
158 763	158 766			

Class 158	BREL Express Sprinter 3-car sets			
158 798	158 952	158 955	158 958	158 961
158 950	158 953	158 956	158 959	
158 951	158 954	158 957	158 960	

Class 165	BREL Networker Turbo 3-car sets		
165 101	165 105	165 109	165 113
165 102	165 106	165 110	165 114
165 103	165 107	165 111	165 116
165 104	165 108	165 112	165 117

Class 165	BREL Networker Turbo 2-car sets			
165 118	165 122	165 126	165 130	165 134
165 119	165 123	165 127	165 131	165 135
165 120	165 124	165 128	165 132	165 136
165 121	165 125	165 129	165 133	165 137

Class 166	BREL Networker Turbo Express 3-car sets			
166 201	166 206	166 211	166 216	166 221
166 202	166 207	166 212	166 217	
166 203	166 208	166 213	166 218	
166 204	166 209	166 214	166 219	
166 205	166 210	166 215	166 220	

Seen at Thatcham while heading for London Paddington is 3-car Networker Turbo Express set 166 214

Class 180	Alstom Adelante 5-car sets			
180 102	180 103	180 104	180 106	180 108

Class 360	Siemens Desiro 5-car sets			
360 201	360 202	360 203	360 204	360 205

Class 387	Bombardier Electrostar 4-car sets (currently under delivery)			
387 130	387 135	387 140	387 145	387 150
387 131	387 136	387 141	387 146	387 151
387 132	387 137	387 142	387 147	387 152
387 133	387 138	387 143	387 148	387 153
387 134	387 139	387 144	387 149	387 154

387 155	387 159	387 163	387 167	387 171
387 156	387 160	387 164	387 168	387 172
387 157	387 161	387 165	387 169	387 173
387 158	387 162	387 166	387 170	387 174

Class 800   Hitachi Intercity Express 5-car sets (currently on order)

800 001	800 009	800 017	800 025	800 033
800 002	800 010	800 018	800 026	800 034
800 003	800 011	800 019	800 027	800 035
800 004	800 012	800 020	800 028	800 036
800 005	800 013	800 021	800 029	
800 006	800 014	800 022	800 030	
800 007	800 015	800 023	800 031	
800 008	800 016	800 024	800 032	

Class 800   Hitachi Intercity Express 9-car sets (currently on order)

800 301	800 306	800 311	800 316	800 321
800 302	800 307	800 312	800 317	
800 303	800 308	800 313	800 318	
800 304	800 309	800 314	800 319	
800 305	800 310	800 315	800 320	

Class 802   Hitachi AT300 5-car sets (currently on order)

802 001	802 006	802 011	802 016	802 021
802 002	802 007	802 012	802 017	802 022
802 003	802 008	802 013	802 018	
802 004	802 009	802 014	802 019	
802 005	802 010	802 015	802 020	

Class 802   Hitachi AT300 9-car sets (currently on order)

802 101	802 104	802 107	802 110	802 113
802 102	802 105	802 108	802 111	802 114
802 103	802 106	802 109	802 112	

Named units and sets

43 002	Sir Kenneth Grange
43 003	Isambard Kingdom Brunel
43 017	Hannahs discoverhannahs.org
43 020	MTU Power, Passion, Partnership
43 021	David Austin—Cartoonist
43 024	Great Western Society 1961-2011 Didcot Railway Centre
43 025	The Institution of Railway Operators 2000-2010
43 027	Glorious Devon
43 030	Christian Lewis Trust
43 033	Driver Brian Cooper 15 June 1947—5th October 1999
43 034	TravelWatch SouthWest
43 037	Penydarren
43 040	Bristol St Philips Marsh
43 041	Meningitis Trust Support for Life
43 053	University of Worcester
43 056	The Royal British Legion

43 070	The Corps of Royal Electrical and Mechanical Engineers
43 087	11 Explosive Ordnance Disposal Regiment Royal Logistics Corps
43 097	Environment Agency
43 127	Sir Peter Parker 1924-2002 Cotswold Line 150
43 132	We Save the Children - Will you?
43 137	Newton Abbot 150
43 139	Driver Stan Martin 25 June 1950 - 6 November 2004
43 140	Landore Diesel Depot 1963 Celebrating 50 Years 2013
43 142	Reading Panel Signal Box 1965-2010
43 143	Stroud 700
43 147	Royal Marines Celebrating 350 Years
43 149	University of Plymouth
43 155	The Red Arrows 50 Seasons of Excellence
43 156	Dartington International Summer School
43 160	Sir Moir Lockhead OBE
43 165	Prince Michael of Kent
43 169	The National Trust
43 175	GWR - 175th Anniversary
43 179	Pride of Laira
43 185	Great Western
43 189	Railway Heritage Trust
43 198	Oxfordshire 2007
57 602	Restormel Castle
57 603	Tintagel Castle
57 604	Pendennis Castle
57 605	Totnes Castle

Common lines of operation

Class 43	London Paddington to Swindon, Bath, Bristol, Swansea, Paignton, Newquay, Cardiff, Cheltenham, Oxford, Worcester, Hereford, Plymouth and Penzance
Class 57	London Paddington to Penzance - Night Riviera Express (sleeper service)
Class 143	Exmouth to Paignton and Barnstaple
Class 150	Reading to Basingstoke Cardiff to Taunton Bristol to Weston-Super-Mare Plymouth to Penzance Severn Beach line Devon and Cornwall branch lines Bristol suburban services
Class 153	Cardiff to Taunton Bristol to Weston-Super-Mare Plymouth to Penzance Severn Beach line Devon and Cornwall branch lines

Class 158   Cardiff to Portsmouth and Taunton
               Brighton to Great Malvern
               Bristol to Weymouth

Class 165   London Paddington to Reading and Bedwyn
               Reading to Basingstoke and Newbury
               Thames Valley branch lines
               Oxford to Banbury

Class 166   London Paddington to Oxford and Bedwyn
               Reading to Redhill and Gatwick Airport

Class 180   London Paddington to Worcester, Great Malvern, Hereford and Oxford

Class 360   London Paddington to Heathrow Airport *(Heathrow Connect services)*

Class 387   London Paddington to Hayes & Harlington

Rolling stock used for the Heathrow Connect operation is owned by Heathrow Airport Holdings, and is supplied through the Heathrow Express company, operating as a joint venture between Great Western Railway and Heathrow Express.

In 2018, it is expected that these trains will be replaced by trains for London's Crossrail service, with this service likely to be integrated into the Crossrail network from December 2019.

Hull Trains

Depots and stabling points
Old Oak Common

Class 180   Alstom Adelante 4-car sets

180 109   180 110   180 111   180 113

Common lines of operation

Class 180   London King's Cross to Beverley and Hull

On order for delivery in 2019 are 5x Class 802 Hitachi AT300 5-car sets

Pictured here approaching Doncaster is Adelante set 180 109 in the First Hull Trains fleet, seen heading for London (photo courtesy of Kevin Cooper)

Transpennine Express

Depots and stabling points
Ardwick, Manchester   York

Class 185   Siemens Desiro 3-car sets

185 101	185 110	185 119	185 128	185 137
185 102	185 111	185 120	185 129	185 138
185 103	185 112	185 121	185 130	185 139
185 104	185 113	185 122	185 131	185 140
185 105	185 114	185 123	185 132	185 141
185 106	185 115	185 124	185 133	185 142
185 107	185 116	185 125	185 134	185 143
185 108	185 117	185 126	185 135	185 144
185 109	185 118	185 127	185 136	185 145

Seen here at Newcastle is 185 114 in the First TransPennine fleet, a 3-car diesel-powered Desiro set, pictured while heading for Manchester Airport

Class 350   Siemens Desiro 4-car sets

350 401	350 403	350 405	350 407	350 409
350 402	350 404	350 406	350 408	350 410

Pictured at Carlisle is 350 405 in the First TransPennine fleet, a 4-car electric-powered Desiro set, seen heading for Manchester

Class 397   CAF Civity 5-car sets (on order for 2018 delivery)

397 001	397 004	397 007	397 010
397 002	397 005	397 008	397 011
397 003	397 006	397 009	397 012

Class 802   Hitachi AT300 5-car sets (on order for 2019 delivery)

802 201	802 205	802 209	802 213	802 217
802 202	802 206	802 210	802 214	802 218
802 203	802 207	802 211	802 215	802 219
802 204	802 208	802 212	802 216	

Also on order for delivery in 2018 and 2019 are 66x Mark 5A carriages to form 13 5-coach sets for use on services between Liverpool and Newcastle, to be powered by Class 68 locomotives provided by Direct Rail Services

Common lines of operation

Class 185   Used on all TransPennine routes

Class 350   Manchester Airport to Edinburgh and Glasgow

UK Bus Registration Index

This section consists of an index of all of the buses with the UK operation of First bus, along with the operating company. All registrations are in age order, from old to new. The list of codes is as follows:

AB	Aberdeen	HD	Hampshire & Dorset	SW	South West
BE	Berkshire	LE	Leicester	SY	South Yorkshire
CU	Cymru	MA	Manchester	WE	West of England
EC	Eastern Counties	MW	Midland West	WY	West Yorkshire
EN	Essex	PM	Potteries		
GL	Glasgow	SE	Scotland East		

Reg		Reg		Reg		Reg		Reg		Reg		Reg	
260ERY	SW	OIG1795	SW	M967GDU	WY	R578SBA	SY	S793RWG	MA	T845MAK	MA	W703CWR	WY
481FPO	SW	OIG1796	SW	M506PNA	MA	R162TLM	WE	S797RWG	HD	T847MAK	WY	W705CWR	WY
620HOD	WE	OIG1797	SW	M516PNA	MW	R784WKW	SY	S806RWG	WE	T850MAK	WY	W707CWR	WY
530OHU	SW	OIG1798	SW	N345CJA	GL	R785WKW	SY	S807RWG	WE	T858MAK	SY	W709CWR	WY
552UKT	SW	OIG1799	SW	N528LHG	HD	R789WKW	SY	S809RWG	WY	T863MAK	SY	W711CWR	WY
3910WE	SY	OIG6939	BE	N763PAE	SW	R921WOE	WY	S812RWG	SY	T367NUA	SW	W712CWR	WE
CWG273	AB	OIG6941	BE	N121UHP	SW	R923WOE	WY	S814RWG	SY	T728REU	HD	W713CWR	WY
DRZ9713	LE	OIG6942	HD	N521WVR	PM	R929WOE	WY	S549SCV	SW	T730REU	WE	W714CWR	WY
FSU382	AB	OIG6943	HD	N522WVR	PM	R930WOE	WY	S652SNG	SW	T731REU	WE	W715CWR	WY
HIC1512	SW	OIG6944	HD	N527WVR	MA	R931WOE	WY	S658SNG	SW	T830RYC	SW	W718CWR	WY
HIG1519	SW	OIG6945	HD	N542WVR	HD	R411WPX	SW	S343SUX	SW	T824SFS	WY	W719CWR	WY
HIG1521	SW	OIG6946	HD	N545WVR	MW	R421WPX	SW	S374SUX	SW	T825SFS	WY	W721CWR	WE
HIG1523	SW	OIG6947	HD	P579EFL	HD	R422WPX	SW	S375SUX	SW	T919SSF	WY	W722CWR	WE
HIG1524	SW	OIG6948	HD	P106MFS	GL	R426WPX	SW	S377SUX	SW	T77TRU	HD	W723CWR	WY
HIG1527	SW	OIG6949	HD	P176NAK	HD	R617YCR	SW	S673SVU	SW	T20TVL	SW	W724CWR	WY
HIG1528	SW	OWB243	SW	P177NAK	HD	R571YNC	WY	S122UOT	HD	T472YTT	SW	W726CWR	WE
HIG1531	SW	PSU627	AB	P132NLW	SW	R932YOV	WY	S824WYD	WE	T473YTT	SW	W667CWT	WY
HIG1533	SW	PSU628	AB	P430ORL	SW	R933YOV	WY	S360XCR	WE	V129DND	MA	W308DWX	SW
HIG1538	SW	PSU629	AB	P920RYO	SW	R936YOV	WY	S362XCR	WE	V136DND	MA	W315DWX	SW
HIG1540	SW	PSU630	WE	P921RYO	SW	R940YOV	WY	S363XCR	WE	V360DVG	EN	W322DWX	SW
HIG8433	SW	RKZ4760	WE	P926RYO	SW	S672AAE	SW	T427GUG	GL	V832DYD	SW	W336DWX	SW
HIG8434	SW	TFO319	SW	P452SCV	SW	S673AAE	SW	T428GUG	WY	V833DYD	SW	W726DWX	SW
HIG8790	SW	TPR354	WE	P241UCW	SW	S682AAE	SW	T35JCV	SW	V835DYD	SW	W727DWX	SW
HVJ716	SW	UHW661	SW	P249UCW	SW	S683AAE	SW	T469JCV	SW	V133ESC	WY	W728DWX	SW
JDZ2339	SY	VJT738	SW	P252UCW	SW	S685AAE	SW	T470JCV	SW	V134ESC	WY	W729DWX	SW
JDZ2340	SY	WSU489	AB	P613WSU	WY	S689AAE	SW	T471JCV	SW	V135ESC	WY	W731DWX	SW
JDZ2391	SY	WSV409	SW	Q275LBA	AB	S691AAE	SW	T282JLD	WY	V136ESC	WY	W732DWX	SW
KDZ5104	SY	WYY752	WE	R703BAE	WE	S720AFB	SW	T283JLD	WY	V137ESC	WY	W733DWX	SW
KFX691	WE	XFF283	SW	R705BAE	WE	S721AFB	WE	T701JLD	MW	V138ESC	WY	W734DWX	SW
LSK570	AB	YIL8826	SW	R709BAE	WE	S724AFB	SW	T702JLD	MW	V139ESC	WY	W735DWX	SW
LSK571	AB	SRS56K	AB	R715BAE	CU	S10FTR	CU	T579JNG	SW	V140ESC	WY	W737DWX	SW
MIG3842	SW	D704GHY	SW	R904BOU	WE	S20FTR	CU	T864KLF	EN	V734FAE	WE	W738DWX	WY
MIG3844	SW	D705GHY	SW	R905BOU	WE	S30FTR	CU	T891KLF	SW	V701FFB	HD	W739DWX	SY
MIG3859	SW	D706GHY	SW	R908BOU	WE	S40FTR	CU	T801LLC	HD	V118FSF	GL	W741DWX	EC
MIG3863	SW	G102HNP	MW	R917BOU	WE	S50FTR	CU	T804LLC	HD	V855HBY	HD	W742DWX	EC
MIG3864	SW	G603NWA	SW	R918BOU	WE	S60FTR	CU	T808LLC	HD	V856HBY	EN	W743DWX	EC
MIG3865	SW	G605NWA	LE	R920COU	WE	S70FTR	CU	T809LLC	HD	V867HBY	MA	W745DWX	WY
MIG4760	SW	G609NWA	GL	R621CVR	MA	S80FTR	CU	T810LLC	HD	V869HBY	MA	W746DWX	WY
MIG4761	SW	G613NWA	GL	R680DPW	EN	S90FTR	CU	T819LLC	HD	V887HBY	HD	W748DWX	WY
MIG5685	SW	G622NWA	SW	R685DPW	EN	S100FTR	CU	T840LLC	GL	V899HLH	GL	W751DWX	WY
MIG9614	SW	G627NWA	WY	R688DPW	EN	S654FWY	WY	T846LLC	SW	V801KAF	SW	W752DWX	WY
MIG9615	SW	G72RND	PM	R290GHS	WE	S220KLM	CU	T847LLC	HD	V124LGC	SW	W756DWX	EC
MIG9616	SW	J461OVU	LE	R331GHS	WE	S723KNV	SW	T849LLC	HD	V760UVY	WY	W757DWX	EC
NDZ3164	SY	K1GRT	AB	R340GHS	MA	S214LLO	WY	T847LLC	HD	V765UVY	HD	W759DWX	WY
NER621	WE	K114PRV	WY	R813HWS	HD	S352NPO	HD	T819MAK	HD	V770UVY	WY	W761DWX	WY
NTL655	WE	L311PWR	SW	R616JUB	WY	S353NPO	HD	T820MAK	WY	V772UVY	WY	W762DWX	WY
OIG1788	SW	L637SEU	SW	R620JUB	WY	S354NPO	HD	T822MAK	MA	W179BVP	MA	W768DWX	WY
OIG1790	SW	L638SEU	SW	R625JUB	WY	S651RNA	HD	T833MAK	MA	W118CWR	WE	W769DWX	WY
OIG1791	SW	L650SEU	HD	R629JUB	WY	S658RNA	EC	T839MAK	WE	W119CWR	WE	W771DWX	WY
OIG1792	SW	L64UOU	WE	R346LGH	SW	S659RNA	EC	T840MAK	WY	W122CWR	WE	W772DWX	WY
OIG1794	SW	L304VSU	WY	R719RAD	SW	S665RNA	SW	T842MAK	MA	W702CWR	WY	W773DWX	WY

W774DWX EC	W813PAE WE	W361RJA MA	X788HLR MA	Y944CSF MA	Y774TNC SY	LK51UZA GL
W776DWX WY	W816PAE WE	W362RJA MA	X611HLT SW	Y945CSF SY	Y661UKU SY	LK51UZB GL
W778DWX WY	W818PAE WE	W363RJA MA	X612HLT GL	Y946CSF SY	Y344XBN SE	LK51UZE SW
W802DWX WY	W819PAE WE	W364RJA MA	X613HLT AB	Y947CSF SW	Y546XNW WY	LK51UZF GL
W803DWX WY	W821PAE WE	W365RJA MA	X614HLT GL	Y948CSF SY	Y547XNW WY	LK51UZG GL
W804DWX WY	W822PAE WE	W366RJA MA	X956HLT GL	Y949CSF SY	Y794XNW WY	LK51UZH GL
W805DWX WY	W824PAE WE	W682RNA SE	X957HLT SY	Y951CSF MA	Y795XNW SE	LK51UZJ GL
W806DWX WY	W602PAF SW	W594SNG AB	X958HLT AB	Y952CSF SY	Y796XNW WY	LK51UZL GL
W807DWX WY	W605PAF SW	W422SRP EC	X959HLT MA	Y953CSF SY	Y797XNW WY	LK51UZM GL
W808DWX WY	W606PAF SW	W425SRP EC	X962HLT AB	Y445CUB WY	Y798XNW WY	LK51UZN GL
W809DWX WY	W607PAF SW	W718ULL CU	X968HLT SE	Y446CUB WY	KP51VZO MW	LK51UZO HD
W811DWX WY	W609PAF SW	W719ULL CU	X969HLT GL	Y447CUB WY	KP51VZR MW	LK51UZP HD
W812DWX WY	W808PAF EN	W727ULL CU	X971HLT AB	Y449CUB WY	KP51VZS EN	LK51UZS EC
W813DWX WY	W809PAF SW	W931ULL WE	X972HLT MA	Y451CUB WY	KP51VZT WE	LK51UZT SW
W814DWX WY	W811PAF SW	W935ULL SW	X973HLT AB	Y1EDN SW	KP51VZW WE	LN51DUJ GL
W815DWX WY	W812PAF SW	W936ULL SW	X974HLT AB	Y2EDN SW	KP51VZX WY	LN51DUU GL
W816DWX WY	W813PAF SW	W937ULL WE	X975HLT AB	Y251HHL SE	KP51VZY WY	LN51DUV GL
W364EOW HD	W814PAF SW	W939ULL WE	X977HLT GL	Y252HHL SE	KP51VZZ WE	LN51DVG MW
W365EOW EN	W817PFB WE	W941ULL WE	X981HLT SE	Y253HHL SE	KP51WAJ SE	LN51DVH EN
W368EOW SY	W823PFB WE	W942ULL WE	X503JLO EN	Y254HHL WY	KP51WAO WE	LN51DVL GL
W371EOW WE	W829PFB SW	W946ULL WE	X104NSS SE	Y256HHL SW	KP51WAU WE	LN51DVM EN
W373EOW WE	W832PFB SW	W947ULL SW	X136NSS SE	Y901KND MA	KP51WBD WY	LN51DWA SE
W374EOW WE	W833PFB SW	W951ULL SE	X477NSS AB	Y904KND GL	KP51WBG WY	LN51DWD MW
W376EOW HD	W834PFB SW	W896VLN MA	X617NSS AB	Y905KND SW	KP51WBJ WE	LN51DWE GL
W379EOW EN	W702PHT HD	W905VLN EC	X618NSS EN	Y223NLF AB	KP51WBK WY	LN51DWF SY
W381EOW HD	W703PHT HD	W908VLN MA	X621NSS AB	Y224NLF GL	KP51WBL PM	LN51DWW MA
W801EOW HD	W704PHT HD	W912VLN MA	X622NSS AB	Y346NLF GL	KP51WBO WY	LN51DWY GL
W802EOW HD	W705PHT HD	W913VLN MA	X623NSS AB	Y932NLP GL	KP51WBT WE	LN51DWZ GL
W803EOW HD	W706PHT HD	W915VLN MA	X624NSS AB	Y933NLP GL	KP51WBU WE	LN51DXA GL
W804EOW HD	W707PHT HD	W916VLN MA	X797NWR WY	Y934NLP GL	KP51WBV WY	LN51DXD WE
W805EOW HD	W708PHT HD	W919VLN SE	X798NWR WY	Y984NLP GL	KP51WBY WY	LN51DXF GL
W806EOW HD	W416RCU SW	W921VLN SE	X474SCY SW	Y985NLP GL	KP51WBZ EN	LN51DXG WE
W807EOW CU	W586RFS WE	W924VLN SE	X475SCY SW	Y986NLP GL	KP51WCA WY	LN51GJJ GL
W808EOW HD	W588RFS AB	W926VLN MA	X476SCY SW	Y987NLP GL	KP51WCF WY	LN51GJK HD
W809EOW HD	W591RFS CU	W132VLO WE	X477SCY SW	Y988NLP GL	KP51WCG WE	LN51GJO SE
W811EOW CU	W592RFS SE	W840VLO WE	X425UMS GL	Y989NLP GL	KP51WCJ WE	LN51GJU EC
W812EOW CU	W596RFS CU	W213XBD SW	X426UMS GL	Y991NLP GL	KP51WCN WY	LN51GKA SY
W813EOW HD	W597RFS HD	W215XBD SW	X433UMS GL	Y992NLP GL	KP51WCO WE	LN51GKF SE
W814EOW CU	W598RFS HD	W216XBD PM	X448UMS GL	Y993NLP GL	KP51WCR WE	LN51GKJ SY
W815EOW HD	W601RFS HD	W217XBD PM	X856UOK WY	Y995NLP SE	KP51WCW WE	LN51GKK GL
W816EOW HD	W603RFS MA	W218XBD EC	X857UOK WY	Y996NLP GL	KP51WCX WE	LN51GKL GL
W311JND MA	W607RFS HD	W219XBD EC	X858UOK WY	Y997NLP GL	KP51WCY SW	LN51GKO EC
W313JND MA	W609RFS AB	W221XBD EC	X253USH AB	Y998NLP WE	KP51WDB WE	LN51GKP HD
W315JND MA	W713RHT SW	W223XBD EC	X256USH SE	Y626RSA AB	KP51WDD WE	LN51GKU CU
W319JND MA	W716RHT SW	W224XBD EC	X269USH WY	Y627RSA AB	KP51WDF WE	LN51GKV CU
W327JND MA	W331RJA MA	X684ADK MA	X272USH SE	Y628RSA AB	LK51JYO GL	LN51GKX CU
W329JND MA	W332RJA MA	X685ADK SW	X749VUA MA	Y629RSA AB	LK51UYD GL	LN51GKY CU
W331JND MA	W334RJA MA	X686ADK SW	X763VUA WY	Y631RSA AB	LK51UYF GL	LN51GKZ SY
W334JND MA	W335RJA MA	X689ADK EN	X764VUA WY	Y632RSA AB	LK51UYG GL	LN51GLF SW
W337JND MA	W336RJA MA	X692ADK EN	X766VUA WY	Y633RSA AB	LK51UYH GL	LN51GLJ SW
W339JND MA	W337RJA MA	X693ADK WE	X767VUA MA	Y634RSA AB	LK51UYJ GL	LN51GLK SW
W341JND MA	W338RJA MA	X694ADK WE	X779VUA WY	Y635RSA AB	LK51UYL SE	LN51GLV SY
W378JNE MA	W339RJA MA	X695ADK HD	X351VWT WY	Y636RSA SE	LK51UYM SE	LN51GLY SY
W379JNE MA	W342RJA MA	X699ADK MA	X353VWT WY	Y637RSA SY	LK51UYN SY	LN51GLZ SW
W771KBT WY	W346RJA MA	X401CSG MA	X356VWT MA	Y638RSA AB	LK51UYO SY	LN51GME SW
W772KBT WY	W347RJA MA	X735HLF EN	X357VWT MA	Y639RSA AB	LK51UYP GL	LN51GMG EN
W773KBT WY	W348RJA MA	X381HLR CU	X358VWT SY	Y701RSA AB	LK51UYR GL	LN51GMO EN
W774KBT WY	W349RJA MA	X383HLR SW	X359VWT SY	Y301RTD GL	LK51UYS GL	LN51GMU EN
W776KBT WY	W351RJA MA	X386HLR CU	Y181BGB GL	Y302RTD GL	LK51UYT GL	LN51GMV GL
W787KBT WY	W352RJA MA	X391HLR CU	Y182BGB GL	Y303RTD GL	LK51UYU GL	LN51GMX EN
W804PAE WE	W353RJA MA	X399HLR WE	Y937CSF SY	Y304RTD GL	LK51UYV GL	LN51GMY GL
W808PAE WE	W354RJA MA	X511HLR GL	Y939CSF SW	Y307RTD GL	LK51UYX GL	LN51GMZ GL
W809PAE WE	W356RJA MA	X512HLR GL	Y941CSF MA	Y633RTD WY	LK51UYY GL	LN51GNF EN
W811PAE WE	W357RJA MA	X513HLR MA	Y942CSF MA	Y634RTD WY	LK51UYZ GL	LN51GNJ EN
W812PAE WE	W358RJA MA	X779HLR GL	Y943CSF SY	Y949RTD GL	LK51UYZ GL	LN51GNP EN

LN51GNU	EN	SJ51DHL	GL	YJ51RFO	SY	EO02NEF	EN	LR02LXV	EC	LT02ZFC	CU	MV02VDD	SY
LN51GNV	SY	SJ51DHM	GL	YJ51RFX	SY	EO02NEJ	EN	LR02LXW	EC	LT02ZFJ	SE	MV02VDF	SY
LN51GNX	SY	SJ51DHN	GL	YJ51RFY	WY	EO02NCN	EN	LR02LXX	EC	LT02ZFK	GL	MV02VDG	SY
LN51GNY	GL	SJ51DHO	GL	YJ51RFZ	WY	EO02NEU	SW	LR02LXZ	EC	LT02ZFL	SE	MV02VDJ	SY
LN51GNZ	GL	SJ51DHP	GL	YJ51RGO	SW	EO02NEY	SW	LR02LYA	EC	ML02OFW	MA	MV02VDK	SY
LN51GOA	EN	SJ51DHV	GL	YJ51RGV	SW	EO02NFA	SW	LR02LYC	EC	ML02OFX	MA	MV02VDL	SY
LN51GOC	EN	SJ51DHX	GL	YJ51RGX	SW	EO02NFC	EC	LR02LYD	EC	ML02OFY	MA	MV02VDM	SY
LN51GOE	EN	SJ51DHZ	GL	YJ51RGY	SY	EO02NFD	PM	LR02LYF	EC	ML02OFZ	MA	MV02VDN	SY
LN51GOH	EN	SJ51DJD	GL	YJ51RGZ	SY	EO02NFE	PM	LR02LYG	EC	ML02OGA	MA	MV02VDO	SY
LN51NRJ	GL	SJ51DJE	GL	YJ51RHE	SY	EO02NFF	PM	LR02LYJ	EC	ML02OGB	MA	MV02VDP	SY
LN51NRK	GL	SJ51DJF	GL	YJ51RHF	SY	EO02NFG	EN	LR02LYK	EC	ML02OGC	MA	MV02VDR	SY
LN51NRL	EN	SJ51DJK	GL	YJ51RHK	SY	EO02NFH	EN	LR02LYO	SW	ML02OGD	MA	MV02VDT	SY
MA51AET	MA	SJ51DJO	GL	YJ51RHO	WY	EO02NFJ	EN	LR02LYS	SW	ML02OGE	MA	MV02VDX	SY
MA51AEW	MA	SJ51DJU	GL	YJ51RHU	WY	EO02NFK	EN	LR02LYT	SW	ML02OGF	MA	MV02VDY	SY
RD51FKV	BE	SJ51DJX	GL	YJ51RHV	WY	EO02NFL	EN	LR02LYU	SW	MV02VAA	SY	MV02VDZ	GL
RD51FKW	BE	SJ51DJY	GL	YJ51RHY	SW	EO02NFM	EN	LR02LYV	SW	MV02VAD	SY	MV02VEA	CU
RD51FKZ	BE	SJ51DJZ	GL	YJ51RHZ	SW	EO02NFN	EN	LR02LYW	SW	MV02VAE	SY	MV02VEB	CU
RD51FLA	BE	SJ51DKA	GL	YJ51RJO	SW	EO02NFP	EN	LR02LYX	EN	MV02VAF	SY	MV02VEF	WE
RG51FWZ	BE	SJ51DKD	GL	YJ51RJV	SW	EO02NFR	EN	LR02LYY	BE	MV02VAH	SY	MV02VEH	WE
RG51FXE	GL	SJ51DKE	GL	YJ51RKO	WY	EO02NFT	EN	LR02LYZ	HD	MV02VAJ	SY	MV02VEK	WE
RG51FXH	GL	SJ51DKF	GL	YJ51RKU	WY	EO02NFU	EN	LR02LZA	BE	MV02VAK	SY	MV02VEL	WE
SF51YAA	GL	SJ51DKK	SY	YJ51RKV	WY	EO02NFV	EN	LR02LZB	HD	MV02VAM	SY	MV02VEM	WE
SF51YAD	GL	SJ51DKL	GL	YJ51RPY	MA	EO02NFX	EN	LR02LZC	HD	MV02VAO	SY	PJ02PZP	SW
SF51YAE	GL	SJ51DKN	GL	YJ51RPZ	MA	KV02VVC	WE	LR02LZD	EN	MV02VAU	SY	PJ02PZY	SW
SF51YAG	GL	SN51MSU	SE	YJ51RRO	MA	KV02VVD	PM	LT02NTY	SE	MV02VAX	WE	SA02BZD	GL
SF51YAH	GL	SN51MSV	WY	YJ51RRU	MA	KV02VVE	PM	LT02NUA	SE	MV02VAY	WE	SA02BZE	GL
SF51YAJ	GL	SN51MSY	SE	YJ51RRV	MA	KV02VVF	PM	LT02NUE	SE	MV02VBA	WE	SA02BZF	GL
SF51YAK	GL	SN51UXX	EN	YJ51RRX	WY	KV02VVG	PM	LT02NUJ	SE	MV02VBB	WE	SA02BZG	GL
SF51YAO	GL	SN51UXY	EN	YJ51RRY	WY	KV02VVH	PM	LT02NUL	GL	MV02VBC	EC	SA02BZH	GL
SF51YAU	GL	SN51UXZ	EN	YJ51RRZ	WY	KV02VVJ	LE	LT02NVM	SY	MV02VBD	EC	SA02BZJ	GL
SF51YAV	GL	SN51UYA	EN	YJ51RSO	WY	KV02VVK	LE	LT02NVN	SY	MV02VBE	WE	SA02BZK	GL
SF51YAW	GL	SN51UYB	EN	YJ51RSU	WY	KV02VVL	LE	LT02NVO	EC	MV02VBF	SY	SA02BZL	WY
SF51YAX	GL	SN51UYC	EN	YJ51RSV	WY	KV02VVM	LE	LT02NVP	SY	MV02VBG	SY	SA02BZM	GL
SF51YAY	GL	SN51UYD	EN	YJ51RSX	WY	KV02VVN	LE	LT02NVR	SY	MV02VBJ	SY	SA02BZN	GL
SF51YBA	GL	SN51UYE	EN	YJ51RSY	WY	KV02VVO	LE	LT02NVU	GL	MV02VBK	SY	SK02ZYG	GL
SF51YBB	GL	SN51UYG	EN	YS51JVA	BE	KV02VVP	LE	LT02NVV	GL	MV02VBL	SY	SK02ZYH	GL
SF51YBC	GL	SN51UYH	EN	YS51JVD	AB	KV02VVR	LE	LT02NVW	GL	MV02VBM	SY	VU02PKX	SW
SF51YBD	GL	SN51UYJ	EN	YS51JVE	BE	KV02VVS	LE	LT02NVX	EC	MV02VBN	SY	VU02PKY	PM
SF51YBE	GL	SN51UYK	EN	YS51JVH	BE	KV02VVT	LE	LT02NVY	SE	MV02VBO	SY	WK02TYD	SW
SF51YBG	GL	SN51UYL	EN	YS51JVK	BE	KV02VVU	LE	LT02NVZ	GL	MV02VBP	SY	WK02TYH	SW
SF51YBH	GL	YJ51PZT	WY	YT51EZX	WY	KV02VVW	LE	LT02NWA	GL	MV02VBU	EC	WU02KVE	SY
SF51YBJ	GL	YJ51PZU	WY	AN02EDN	SW	KV02VVX	LE	LT02NWB	GL	MV02VBX	WE	WU02KVF	SY
SF51YBK	GL	YJ51PZV	WY	AO02RBX	EC	KV02VVY	LE	LT02NWC	GL	MV02VBY	EC	WU02KVH	SY
SF51YBL	GL	YJ51PZW	SY	AO02RBY	EC	KV02VVZ	LE	LT02NWD	GL	MV02VBZ	EC	WU02KVJ	SY
SF51YBM	GL	YJ51PZX	SY	AO02RBZ	SW	KV02VWA	LE	LT02ZBX	SE	MV02VCA	WE	WU02KVK	SY
SF51YBN	GL	YJ51PZY	SY	AO02RCU	SW	KV02VWB	LE	LT02ZBY	EN	MV02VCC	WE	WU02KVM	WY
SF51YBO	GL	YJ51RAU	MA	AO02RCV	AB	LR02LWW	HD	LT02ZBZ	EN	MV02VCD	SY	WU02KVW	WY
SF51YBP	GL	YJ51RAX	MA	AO02RCX	AB	LR02LWX	HD	LT02ZCA	EN	MV02VCE	SY	WU02KVO	WY
SF51YBR	GL	YJ51RCO	MA	AO02RCY	AB	LR02LWY	HD	LT02ZCE	SE	MV02VCF	SY	WU02KVP	WY
SF51YBS	GL	YJ51RCU	MA	AO02RCZ	GL	LR02LWZ	HD	LT02ZCF	SY	MV02VCG	SY	WU02KVR	WY
SF51YBT	GL	YJ51RCV	MA	AO02UDM	EN	LR02LXA	EC	LT02ZCJ	EC	MV02VCJ	SY	WU02KVS	SY
SH51MHY	GL	YJ51RCX	MA	AO02UDN	EN	LR02LXB	EC	LT02ZCK	EC	MV02VCK	SY	WU02KVT	WY
SH51MHZ	GL	YJ51RCZ	MA	BN02EDN	SW	LR02LXC	HD	LT02ZCL	SW	MV02VCL	SY	WU02KVV	WY
SH51MJE	GL	YJ51RDO	MA	BX02CMK	MA	LR02LXG	HD	LT02ZCN	SW	MV02VCM	WE	WU02KVW	WY
SH51MJF	GL	YJ51RDU	MA	CN02EDN	SW	LR02LXH	EC	LT02ZCO	SW	MV02VCO	WY	WV02EUP	EC
SH51MKF	SY	YJ51RDV	MA	EO02FKZ	SW	LR02LXJ	EC	LT02ZCU	EC	MV02VCO	WY	WV02EUR	EC
SH51MKG	GL	YJ51RDX	MA	EO02FLB	GL	LR02LXK	EC	LT02ZCV	EC	MV02VCP	EC	YG02DGY	WY
SH51MKJ	SY	YJ51RDY	MA	EO02FLC	GL	LR02LXL	EC	LT02ZCX	EC	MV02VCU	SY	YG02DGZ	WY
SH51MKK	GL	YJ51RDZ	SY	EO02FLG	SY	LR02LXM	HD	LT02ZCY	SY	MV02VCW	EC	YG02DHA	WY
SH51MKL	GL	YJ51REU	SY	EO02FLH	SW	LR02LXN	EC	LT02ZDH	SY	MV02VCX	EC	YG02DHC	WY
SJ51DHD	SY	YJ51RFE	WY	EO02FLJ	SW	LR02LXO	EC	LT02ZDJ	SY	MV02VCZ	WE	YG02DHD	WY
SJ51DHE	GL	YJ51RFF	WY	EO02FLK	SW	LR02LXR	EC	LT02ZDK	SY	MV02VDA	WY	YG02DHE	WY
SJ51DHF	SY	YJ51RFK	WY	EO02NDX	EN	LR02LXS	EC	LT02ZDL	EC	MV02VCZ	WE	YG02DHF	WY
SJ51DHG	SY	YJ51RFL	SY	EO02NDY	EN	LR02LXT	EC	LT02ZFA	CU	MV02VDA	WY	YG02DHJ	SY
SJ51DHK	GL	YJ51RFN	SY	EO02NDZ	EN	LR02LXU	EC	LT02ZFB	SW	MV02VDC	EC	YG02DHK	SY

164

YG02DHL WY	LT52WUG WY	YM52UVK WY	LK03LME PM	VU03YKE MW	CU53ASO CU	LK53FEJ EN
YG02DHM WY	LT52WUH WY	YM52UVL WY	LK03LMF PM	WR03YZL WE	CU53AUO CU	LK53LYH WE
YG02DHN WY	LT52WUJ WY	YM52UVN WY	LK03LNF BE	WR03YZM WE	CU53AUP CU	LK53LYJ WE
YG02DHO WY	LT52WUK SE	YM52UVO GL	LK03LNU PM	WR03YZN WE	CU53AUT CU	LK53LYO WE
YG02DHP SW	LT52WUL SE	YM52UVP GL	LK03LNV PM	WR03YZP WE	CU53AUV CU	LK53LYP WE
YG02DHU WY	LT52WUV EC	YM52UVR WY	LK03LNW PM	WR03YZR WE	CU53AUW CU	LK53LYR WE
YG02DHV WY	LT52WUW EC	YM52UVS SE	LK03LNX PM	WR03YZT WE	CU53AUX CU	LK53LYT WE
YG02DHY SW	LT52WUX EC	YM52UVU SE	LK03NGE PM	WR03YZU WE	CU53AUY CU	LK53LYU WE
YG02DKO WE	LT52WUY EC	YM52UVW GL	LK03NGF EN	WR03YZV WE	CU53AVB CU	LK53LYV WE
YG02DKU EC	LT52WVA EC	YM52UVZ GL	LK03NGG PM	WR03YZW WE	CU53AVJ CU	LK53LYW WE
YG02DKV WY	LT52WVB EN	YM52UWA SE	LK03NGJ SE	WR03YZX WE	CU53AVK CU	LK53LYX WE
YG02DLD WY	LT52WVD EN	YM52UWB WY	LK03NGN SE	WR03YZY WE	CU53AVL CU	LK53LYY WE
YG02DLJ WY	LT52WVE EN	YM52UWD WY	LK03NGU SE	WR03YZZ WE	CU53AVM CU	LK53LYZ WE
YG02DLK SW	LT52WVF EC	YM52UWF GL	LK03NGV SE	WR03ZBC WE	CU53AVN CU	LK53LZA WE
YG02DLN WY	LT52WVG EC	YM52UWG SE	LK03NGX SE	WR03ZBD WE	CU53AVO CU	LK53LZB WE
YG02DLO WE	LT52WVH EC	YM52UWH SE	LK03NGY SE	YN03ZVW HD	CU53AVP CU	LK53LZC WE
YG02DLU WY	LT52WVJ EC	YM52UWJ GL	LK03NGZ GL	YN03ZVX WY	CU53AVR CU	LK53LZD WE
YG02DLV SW	LT52WVL SW	YM52UWK GL	LK03NHA GL	YS03ZKB EN	CU53AVT CU	LK53LZE WE
YG02DLX WY	LT52WVM WY	YM52UWN SE	LK03NHB GL	YS03ZKC EN	CU53AVV CU	LK53LZF WE
YG02DLY WY	LT52WVN WY	YR52VEH EC	LK03NHC GL	YS03ZKD EN	CU53AVW CU	LK53LZG WE
YG02DLZ EC	LT52WVO WE	YR52VEK EN	LK03NHD GL	YS03ZKF EN		LK53LZH WE
YP02ABN EN	LT52WVP WE	YR52VEL EN	LK03NHE GL	YS03ZKG EN	LK53EXT GL	LK53LZL EC
EG52FFJ SW	LT52WVY WE	YR52VEP EN	LK03NHH SY	YS03ZKG GL	LK53EXU GL	LK53LZM WE
EG52FFK SW	LT52WVZ GL	YR52VEU EN	LK03NHJ SY	YS03ZKH EN	LK53EXV GL	LK53LZN WE
EG52FFL SW	LT52WWA WE	YR52VEY EN	LK03NHL SY	YS03ZKJ EN	LK53EXW GL	LK53LZO WE
EG52FFT SW	LT52WWB WE	YR52VFO EN	LK03NHM SY	YS03ZKK EN	LK53EXZ GL	LK53LZP WE
EG52FFU SW	LT52WWC WE	YU52VXH SY	LK03NHN SY	YS03ZKL EN	LK53EYA GL	LK53LZR WE
EG52FFV SW	LT52WWD WE	YU52VXJ SY	LK03NKN EN	YS03ZKM EN	LK53EYB GL	LK53LZT WE
EG52FFY SW	LT52WWE WE	YU52VXK SY	LK03NLD PM	YV03UBA SW	LK53EYC GL	LK53LZU WE
EG52FFZ WY	LT52WWF WY	YU52VXL SY	LK03NLN PM	YV03UBB SW	LK53EYD GL	LK53LZV WE
EG52FGA WY	LT52WWG WY	YU52VXM SY	LK03UEX PM	YV03UBC SW	LK53EYF GL	LK53LZW WE
EG52FGC SW	LT52WWH WY	YU52VXN SY	LK03UEY PM	YV03UBD SW	LK53EYG GL	LK53LZX WE
EG52FGD SW	LT52WWJ SY	YU52VXO SY	LK03UEZ PM	YV03UBE SW	LK53EYH GL	LK53MBF WE
EG52FGE SW	LT52WWK SY	YU52VXP SY	LK03UFA EN	YV03UOV WY	LK53EYJ GL	LK53MBX SW
EG52FGF SW	LT52WWL SY	YU52VXR SY	LK03UFB EN	YV03UOW WY	LK53EYL GL	LK53MDE SW
EG52FGJ SW	LT52WWM WY	YU52VXS SY	LK03UFC EN	YV03UOY WY	LK53EYM GL	LK53MDF SW
EG52FGK SW	LT52WWN SY	YU52VXT SY	SJ03DNY GL	AU53HJJ EN	LK53EYO GL	LK53MDJ SW
EG52FGU SW	LT52WWO SY	YU52VXV SY	SJ03DOA GL	AU53HJK EN	LK53EYP GL	LK53PNO SW
EG52FGV SW	LT52WWP SY	YU52VXW SY	SJ03DOH SE	AU53HJN EN	LK53EYR EN	SN53ESU CU
EG52FGX SW	LT52WWR SY	YU52VXX SY	SJ03DPE GL	AU53HJO EN	LK53EYT GL	SN53ESV CU
EG52FHC SW	LT52WWS SY	YU52VXY SY	SJ03DPN GL	AU53HJV EC	LK53EYU GL	SN53ESY CU
EG52FHD SW	LT52WWU SY	YU52VYE SY	SJ03DPU GL	AU53HJX EN	LK53EYV EN	SN53ETD CU
KU52RXJ SW	LT52WWV EC	YU52VYF SY	SJ03DPV GL	AU53HJY EN	LK53EZC EN	SN53ETE CU
LT52WTE SW	LT52WWX EC	YU52VYG SY	SJ03DPX SW	AU53HJZ EN	LK53EZD EN	SN53ETF CU
LT52WTF EC	LT52WWY SW	YU52VYH SY	SJ03DPY SW	AU53HKA EN	LK53EZE EN	SN53KHH GL
LT52WTG SW	LT52WWZ EC	YU52VYJ SY	SJ03DPZ SE	AU53HKB EN	LK53EZF GL	SN53KHJ SE
LT52WTJ EC	LT52WXC SY	YU52VYK SY	SN03CLX GL	AU53HKC EN	LK53EZV GL	SN53KHK SE
LT52WTK EC	LT52WXD SY	YU52VYL SY	SN03CLY GL	AU53HKD EC	LK53EZW GL	SN53KHL GL
LT52WTL EC	LT52WXF SY	YU52VYM WE	SN03LGG CU	AU53HKE EC	LK53EZX GL	SN53KHM GL
LT52WTM EC	LT52WXG EN	YU52VYN WY	SN03LGJ CU	AU53HKF EC	LK53EZZ GL	SN53KHO SE
LT52WTN SW	LT52WXH SY	YU52VYO WY	SN03LGK CU	AU53HKG EC	LK53FCG GL	SN53KHP SE
LT52WTO SW	LT52WXK EN	YU52VYP WY	SN03WLD EN	AU53HKH EC	LK53FCH GL	SN53KJX EN
LT52WTP SW	LT52XAA EN	YU52VYR WY	SN03WLK EN	AU53HKJ EC	LK53FCJ GL	SN53KJY EN
LT52WTR EC	LT52XAB EN	YU52VYS WY	SN03WLW EN	AU53HKK EC	LK53FCL GL	SN53KJZ SW
LT52WTU SW	LT52XAC EN	YU52VYT SY	SN03WME EN	AU53HKL EC	LK53FCX GL	SN53KKA SW
LT52WTV EC	LT52XAE EN	YU52VYV SE	SN03WMM EN	AU53HKM EC	LK53FCY GL	SN53KKB SW
LT52WTW EC	LT52XAF EN	YU52VYW SY	SN03WMX EN		LK53FCZ GL	SN53KKC SW
LT52WTX EC	LT52XAL SE	YU52VYX SY	TT03TRU SW	CU53APO CU	LK53FDA GL	SN53KKD SW
LT52WTY SY	LT52XAM SE	YU52VYY SE	VU03YJW MW	CU53APV CU	LK53FDD EN	SN53KKE SW
LT52WTZ SY		YU52VYZ SE	VU03YJX SW	CU53APX CU	LK53FDX EN	
LT52WUA SY	SK52OJF SW	YU52VZA SY	VU03YJY SW	CU53APY CU	LK53FDY EN	VX53OEN CU
LT52WUB SY	SK52OKD SW	CU03BHV CU	VU03YJZ SW	CU53APZ CU	LK53FDZ PM	VX53OEO CU
LT52WUC SY	SK52OKF SW	CU03BHW CU	VU03YKB MW	CU53ARO CU	LK53FEF EN	VX53OER PM
LT52WUD SY	WK52SYE SW	LK03LLX PM	VU03YKC MW	CU53ARX CU	LK53FEG GL	VX53OET CU
LT52WUE SE	WV52HSX	LK03LLZ PM	VU03YKD MW	CU53ARZ CU	LK53FEH EN	VX53OEU MW

VX53OEV	CU	YJ04FYG	WY	CU54HYR	CU	SF54OSL	GL	SF54TKX	GL	WU54EHO	WE	YJ54XVC	WY
VX53VJV	PM	YJ04FYH	WY	CU54HYT	CU	SF54OSM	GL	SF54TKY	GL	WX54XCM	WE	YJ54XVD	WY
VX53VJZ	PM	YJ04FYK	WY	CU54HYV	CU	SF54OSN	CL	SF54TKZ	GL	WX54XCN	WE	YJ54XVM	WY
VX53VKA	PM	YJ04FYL	WY	CU54HYW	CU	SF54OSO	GL	SF54TLJ	GL	WX54XCO	WE	YJ54XVN	WY
VX53VKB	PM	YJ04FYM	WY	CU54HYX	CU	SF54OSP	GL	SF54TLK	GL	WX54XCP	WE	YJ54XVO	WY
YK53GXR	WY	YJ04FYN	WY	CU54HYY	CU	SF54OSR	GL	SF54TLN	GL	WX54XCR	WE	YJ54XVP	WY
YK53GXT	WY	YJ04FYP	WY	CU54HYZ	CU	SF54OSU	GL	SF54TLO	GL	WX54XCT	SY	YJ54XVR	WY
YK53GXU	WY	YJ04FYR	WY	CU54HZA	CU	SF54OSV	GL	SF54TLU	GL	WX54XCU	SY	YJ54XVT	WY
YK53GXV	WY	YJ04FYS	WY	CU54HZB	CU	SF54OSW	GL	SF54TLX	GL	WX54XCV	WE	YJ54XVU	WY
YN53EFE	GL	YJ04FYT	WY	EU54BNJ	EN	SF54OSX	GL	SF54TLY	GL	WX54XCW	GL	YJ54XVW	SW
YN53EFF	GL	YJ04FYU	WY	EU54BNK	EN	SF54OSY	GL	SF54TLZ	GL	WX54XCY	GL	YJ54XVX	WY
YN53EFG	GL	YJ04FYV	WY	EY54BPX	SW	SF54OSZ	GL	SF54TMO	GL	WX54XCZ	GL	YJ54XVY	WY
YN53EFH	WY	YJ04FYW	WY	EY54BPZ	AB	SF54OTA	GL	SF54TMU	GL	WX54XDA	CU	YJ54XVZ	WY
YN53EFJ	WY	YJ04FYX	WY	EY54BRF	AB	SF54OTB	GL	SF54TMV	GL	WX54XDB	CU	YJ54XWA	WY
YN53EFK	SE	YJ04FYY	WY	EY54BRV	AB	SF54OTC	GL	SN54KDF	SE	WX54XDC	WY	YJ54YCO	WY
YN53EFL	GL	YJ04FYZ	WY	EY54BRX	AB	SF54OTD	GL	SN54KDJ	SE	WX54XDD	CU	YJ54YCP	WY
YN53EFM	GL	YJ04FZH	WY	EY54BRZ	AB	SF54OTE	GL	SN54KDK	SE	WX54XDE	WE	YK54ENL	WY
YN53EFO	GL	YJ04FZK	WY	KP54AZA	PM	SF54OTG	GL	SN54KDO	SE	WX54XDF	WE	YK54ENM	WY
YN53EFP	GL	YJ04FZL	WY	KP54AZB	EN	SF54OTH	GL	SN54KDU	SE	WX54XDG	WE	YK54ENN	WY
YN53EFR	GL	YJ04FZM	WY	KP54AZC	EN	SF54OTJ	GL	SN54KDV	SE	WX54XDH	WE	YK54ENO	WY
YN53EFT	GL	YJ04FZN	WY	KP54AZD	EN	SF54OTK	GL	SN54KDX	SE	WX54XDJ	WE	YK54ENP	WY
YN53EFU	GL	YJ04FZP	WY	KP54AZF	LE	SF54OTL	GL	SN54KDZ	SE	WX54XDK	WE	YN54APF	AB
YN53EFV	GL	YJ04FZR	WY	KP54AZG	LE	SF54OTM	GL	SN54KEJ	SE	WX54XDL	WE	YN54APK	EN
YN53EFW	GL	YJ04FZS	WY	KP54AZJ	LE	SF54OTN	GL	SN54KEK	SE	WX54ZHM	AB	YN54APX	EN
YN53EFX	GL	YJ04FZT	WY	KP54AZL	LE	SF54OTP	GL	SN54KEU	SE	WX54ZHN	AB	YN54NXZ	AB
YN53EFZ	GL	YJ04FZU	WY	KP54AZN	PM	SF54OTR	GL	SN54KFA	GL	WX54ZHO	SE	YN54NYV	AB
YN53EGC	GL	YJ04FZV	WY	KP54AZU	EN	SF54OTT	GL	SN54KFC	GL	YA54WBK	WY	YN54NZA	HD
YN53ELJ	WY	YJ04FZX	WY	KP54AZV	SW	SF54OTU	GL	SN54KFD	SE	YA54WBL	WY	YN54NZC	HD
YN53ELO	WE	YJ04FZY	WY	KP54KAO	PM	SF54OTV	GL	SN54KFE	SE	YA54WBN	WY	YN54NZD	HD
YN53EOA	WY	YJ04FZZ	WY	KP54KAU	EN	SF54OTW	GL	SN54KFF	SE	YA54WBO	WY	YN54NZE	HD
YN53EOB	WY	YK04EZG	WY	KP54KAX	EC	SF54OTX	GL	SV54CFV	AB	YJ54BSV	GL	YN54NZF	HD
YN53EOC	WY	YK04EZH	WY	KP54KBE	PM	SF54OTY	GL	SV54CFY	AB	YJ54BVA	WY	YN54NZG	HD
YN53EOD	WY	YK04EZJ	WY	KP54KBF	EN	SF54OTZ	GL	TL54TVL	SW	YJ54BVB	WY	YN54NZH	HD
YN53EOE	WY	YK04EZL	WY	KP54KBJ	PM	SF54OUA	GL	TO54TRU	SY	YJ54BVC	WY	YN54NZJ	HD
YN53EOF	SY	YK04EZM	WY	KP54KBK	PM	SF54OUB	GL	TT54TVL	SW	YJ54XTO	WY	YN54NZK	HD
YN53EOG	SY	YN04AJU	SW	KP54KBN	PM	SF54OUC	GL	VX54MOV	PM	YJ54XTP	WY	YN54NZM	HD
YN53EOH	SY	YN04AJV	BE	KP54KBO	PM	SF54OUD	GL	VX54MPE	PM	YJ54XTR	WY	YN54NZO	HD
YN53EOJ	SY	YN04GLV	HD	KP54LAE	PM	SF54OUE	GL	VX54MPF	PM	YJ54XTT	WY	YN54NZP	HD
YN53EOK	SY	YN04GME	PM	KP54LAO	PM	SF54OUG	GL	VX54MPO	PM	YJ54XTU	WY	YN54NZR	HD
YN53EOL	GL	YN04GMF	PM	KX54AHP	MW	SF54OUH	GL	VX54MPU	PM	YJ54XTV	WY	YN54NZT	HD
YN53VBT	SW	YN04GNV	HD	KX54AHU	EN	SF54OUJ	GL	VX54MPV	PM	YJ54XTW	WY	YN54NZU	HD
YN53VBU	SW	YN04GNX	HD	KX54AHY	EN	SF54OUK	GL	VX54MPY	PM	YJ54XTX	WY	YN54NZV	HD
YN53VBV	SW	YN04GNY	HD	KX54ANR	EN	SF54OUL	GL	VX54MPZ	PM	YJ54XTZ	WY	YN54NZW	HD
BU04EZF	BE	YN04GNZ	HD	LK54FNC	EN	SF54OUM	GL	VX54MRO	PM	YJ54XUA	WY	YN54NZX	HD
BU04EZG	BE	YN04KWR	SW	LK54FNE	EN	SF54OUN	GL	VX54MRU	PM	YJ54XUB	WY	YN54NZY	HD
CU04AYP	hd	YN04YJC	PM	LK54FNF	HD	SF54THV	GL	VX54MRV	PM	YJ54XUC	WY	YN54NZZ	HD
CU04AYS	HD	YN04YJD	PM	LK54FNH	HD	SF54THX	GL	VX54MRY	PM	YJ54XUD	WY	YN54OCK	PM
LK04HYP	WE	YN04YJE	PM	LK54FNJ	HD	SF54THZ	GL	VX54MSO	PM	YJ54XUE	WY		
RA04YGX	WE	YN04YJF	PM	LK54FNL	SW	SF54TJO	GL	VX54MTF	MW	YJ54XUF	WY	AU05DMF	EC
SF04HXW	GL	YN04YJG	PM	MX54GZA	MA	SF54TJU	GL	VX54MTJ	MW	YJ54XUG	WY	AU05DMO	EC
SF04HXX	GL	VW04VAU	WY	MX54GZB	MA	SF54TJV	GL	VX54MTK	MW	YJ54XUH	WY	AU05DMV	EC
SF04ZPE	GL	BX54UDE	SW	MX54GZC	MA	SF54TJX	GL	VX54MTO	MW	YJ54XUK	WY	AU05DMX	EC
SF04ZPG	GL	BX54UDU	SW	MX54GZD	MA	SF54TJY	GL	VX54MTU	GL	YJ54XUM	WY	AU05DMY	EC
SN04CKX	SE	BX54VUN	SW	MX54GZE	MA	SF54TJZ	GL	VX54MTV	MW	YJ54XUN	WY	AU05DMZ	EC
SN04CKY	GL	CU54CYX	SE	MX54GZF	MA	SF54TKA	GL	VX54MTY	WY	YJ54XUO	WY	AU05MUO	EN
SN04CLF	SE	CU54CYY	SW	MX54GZG	MA	SF54TKC	GL	VX54MTZ	GL	YJ54XUP	WY	AU05MUP	EN
SN04CNK	GL	CU54CYZ	CU	MX54GZH	MA	SF54TKD	GL	VX54MUA	MW	YJ54XUR	WY	AU05MUV	EN
TT04TRU	SW	CU54DCE	SW	RX54AOV	HD	SF54TKE	GL	VX54MUB	MW	YJ54XUT	WY	AU05MUW	EN
TU04TRU	GL	CU54DCF	SE	RX54AOY	HD	SF54TKJ	GL	VX54MUM	PM	YJ54XUU	WY	AU05MUY	EC
WM04NZU	SW	CU54HYK	CU	RX54OGZ	BE	SF54TKK	GL	VX54MUV	MW	YJ54XUV	WY	AU05MVA	EC
YJ04FYB	WY	CU54HYL	CU	SF54OSD	GL	SF54TKN	GL	WA54OLN	SW	YJ54XUW	WY	CU05LGJ	SE
YJ04FYC	WY	CU54HYM	CU	SF54OSE	GL	SF54TKO	GL	WA54OLO	SW	YJ54XUX	WY	CU05LGK	SE
YJ04FYD	WY	CU54HYN	CU	SF54OSG	GL	SF54TKT	GL	WA54OLP	SW	YJ54XUY	WY	EU05AUK	EN
YJ04FYE	WY	CU54HYO	CU	SF54OSJ	GL	SF54TKU	GL	WA54OLR	SW	YJ54XVA	WY	EU05AUL	EC
YJ04FYF	WY	CU54HYP	CU	SF54OSK	GL	SF54TKV	GL	WA54OLT	SW	YJ54XVB	WY	EU05AUM	EC

EU05AUN	EC	MX05CDY	EN	SF05KUH	AB	SV05DXJ	AB	WX05RVT	WE	YK05FLB	WY	LK55ACJ	WE
EU05AUO	EN	MX05CDZ	EN	SF05KUJ	GL	SV05DXK	AB	WX05RVU	WE	YK05FLC	WY	LK55ACO	GL
EU05AUP	EN	MX05CEA	EN	SF05KUK	GL	SV05DXL	AB	WX05RVV	EC	YK05FOP	WY	MX55FFD	MA
EU05DXR	EN	MX05CEF	EN	SF05KWY	CU	SV05DXM	AB	WX05RVW	CU	YK05FOT	WY	MX55FFE	MA
EU05DXS	EN	MX05CEJ	LE	SF05KWZ	CU	SV05DXO	AB	WX05RVY	CU	YK05FOU	WY	MX55FFG	MA
EU05DXT	SW	MX05CEK	EN	SF05KXA	CU	SV05DXP	AB	WX05RVZ	EC	YK05FOV	WY	MX55FFH	MA
EY05FYP	SW	MX05CEO	EN	SF05KXB	CU	SV05DXR	AB	WX05RWE	WE	YK05FPA	WY	MX55FFJ	MA
HX05BUJ	HD	MX05CEU	EN	SF05KXC	CU	SV05DXS	AB	WX05RWF	WE	YN05GXF	SW	MX55FFK	MA
HX05BUO	HD	MX05CEV	EN	SF05KXD	CU	SV05DXT	AB	WX05SVD	EC	YN05GXM	SW	MX55FFL	MA
KX05AOC	LE	MX05CEY	EN	SF05KXE	CU	SV05DXU	AB	WX05SVE	WE	YN05GXO	SW	MX55FFM	MA
KX05AOD	LE	MX05CFA	EN	SF05KXH	CU	SV05DXW	AB	WX05UAF	WE	YN05GXR	SW	MX55FFO	MA
KX05AOE	LE	MX05CFD	EN	SF05KXJ	GL	SV05DXX	AB	WX05UAG	WE	YN05GYA	MA	MX55FFP	MA
KX05MGV	PM	MX05CFE	EN	SF05KXK	GL	SV05DXY	AB	WX05UAJ	PM	YN05GYB	MA	MX55FFR	MA
KX05MGY	LE	MX05CFG	LE	SF05KXL	GL	TT05TRU	SW	WX05UAK	PM	YN05GYC	MA	MX55FFS	MA
KX05MGZ	EC	MX05CFJ	EN	SF05KXM	GL	VX05JWW	PM	WX05UAL	PM	YN05GYD	MA	MX55FFT	MA
KX05MHA	EC	MX05CFK	MA	SN05DZO	EN	VX05LVS	MW	WX05UAM	EN	YN05GYE	MA	MX55FFU	MA
KX05MHE	EC	MX05CFL	MA	SN05DZP	EN	VX05LVT	MW	WX05UAN	EN	YN05GYF	MA	MX55FFV	MA
KX05MHF	EC	MX05CFM	MA	SN05DZR	EN	VX05LVU	MW	WX05UAO	EN	YN05GYG	MA	MX55FFW	MA
KX05MHJ	EC	MX05CFN	EN	SN05DZS	EN	VX05LVV	MW	YA05SOJ	WY	YN05GYH	MA	MX55FFY	MA
KX05MHK	EC	MX05CFO	MA	SN05DZT	EN	VX05LVW	MW	YA05SOU	WY	YN05GYJ	MA	MX55FFZ	MA
KX05MHL	EC	MX05CFP	MA	SN05DZU	SW	VX05LVY	MW	YJ05KNV	WY	YN05GYK	MA	MX55FGA	MA
KX05MHM	EC	MX05CFU	EN	SN05DZV	SW	VX05LVZ	MW	YJ05KNW	WY	YN05GYO	MA	MX55FGC	MA
KX05MHN	EC	MX05CFV	LE	SN05DZW	SW	VX05LWC	MW	YJ05KNX	WY	YN05GYP	MA	MX55FGE	MA
KX05MHO	EC	MX05CFY	LE	SN05DZX	EN	VX05LWD	MW	YJ05KNY	WY	YN05GYR	MA	MX55FGF	MA
KX05MHU	EC	MX05CGE	LE	SN05DZY	SW	VX05LWE	MW	YJ05KNZ	WY	YN05GYS	MA	MX55FGG	MA
KX05MHV	EC	MX05CGF	LE	SN05DZZ	SW	VX05LWF	MW	YJ05KOB	WY	YN05GYT	MA	MX55FGJ	MA
KX05MHY	PM	MX05CGG	LE	SN05EAA	SW	VX05LWG	MW	YJ05KOD	WY	YN05GYU	MA	MX55FGK	MA
KX05MHZ	PM	MX05CGK	PM	SN05EAC	WE	VX05LWH	MW	YJ05KOE	WY	YN05GYV	MA	MX55FGM	MA
KX05MJE	PM	MX05CGO	MA	SN05EAE	EC	WA05UNE	SE	YJ05KOH	WY	YN05GYW	MA	MX55FGN	MA
KX05MJF	LE	MX05CGU	PM	SN05EAF	EN	WA05UNF	AB	YJ05VUW	WY	YN05HCL	PM	MX55FGP	MA
KX05MJJ	LE	MX05CGV	MA	SN05EAG	EN	WA05UNG	SE	YJ05VUX	WY	YN05HCO	PM	MX55FGU	MA
KX05MJK	LE	MX05CGY	LE	SN05EAJ	EC	WX05OZF	SE	YJ05VUY	WY	YN05HCP	PM	MX55FHC	MA
KX05MJO	LE	MX05CGZ	MA	SN05EAM	EN	WX05RRV	CU	YJ05VVA	WY	YN05HCU	PM	MX55FHD	MA
KX05MJU	LE	MX05CHC	PM	SN05EAO	EN	WX05RRY	SW	YJ05VVB	WY	YN05HCV	PM	MX55FHE	MA
KX05MJV	LE	MX05CHD	EC	SN05EAP	EN	WX05RRZ	CU	YJ05VVC	WY	YN05HCX	PM	MX55FHF	MA
KX05MJY	LE	MX05CHF	PM	SN05HEJ	WE	WX05RSO	SW	YJ05VVD	WY	YN05HCY	PM	MX55FHH	MA
LK05DXP	SE	MX05CHG	PM	SN05HWD	SE	WX05RSU	WE	YJ05VVE	WY	YN05HCZ	PM	MX55HHL	WE
LK05DXR	SY	MX05CHH	MA	SN05HWE	SE	WX05RSV	SY	YJ05VVF	WY	YN05HGA	HD	MX55HHO	WE
LK05DXS	SW	MX05CHJ	MA	SN05HWF	SE	WX05RSY	SY	YJ05VVG	WY	BX55NZV	HD	MX55HHP	WE
LK05DXT	SE	MX05CHK	MA	SN05HWG	SE	WX05RSZ	WE	YJ05VVH	WY	CV55ABK	SW	MX55HHR	WE
LK05DXU	SE	MX05CHL	MA	SN05HWH	SE	WX05RTO	SY	YJ05VVK	WY	CV55ACO	SW	MX55LDJ	MA
LK05DYO	SW	MX05CHN	MA	SN05HWJ	SE	WX05RTU	WY	YJ05VVL	WY	CV55ACX	SE	MX55LDK	MA
LK05FCE	HD	MX05CHO	MA	SN05HWK	SE	WX05RTV	WE	YJ05VVM	WY	CV55ACY	SE	MX55NWC	SE
MX05CBF	EN	MX05CHV	MA	SN05HWL	WE	WX05RTZ	WE	YJ05VVN	GL	CV55ACZ	SW	MX55NWD	HD
MX05CBU	EN	MX05CHY	MA	SN05HWM	SE	WX05RUA	WE	YJ05VVO	GL	CV55AFA	SE	MX55NWE	MA
MX05CBV	EN	MX05CHZ	MA	SN05HWO	SE	WX05RUC	WE	YJ05VVP	WY	CV55AFE	SE	MX55NWH	MA
MX05CBY	EN	MX05CJE	MA	SN05HWP	SE	WX05RUJ	WE	YJ05VVR	WY	CV55AFF	SE	MX55UAA	MA
MX05CCA	EN	MX05CJF	MA	SN05HWR	SE	WX05RUO	WE	YJ05VVS	WY	CV55AGX	AB	SF55TXA	HD
MX05CCD	EN	MX05CJJ	MA	SN05HWS	SE	WX05RUR	WE	YJ05VVT	WY	CV55AGY	SE	SF55TXB	HD
MX05CCF	EN	MX05CJO	MA	SN05HWT	SE	WX05RUU	WE	YJ05VVU	WY	CV55AGZ	SE	SF55TXC	SE
MX05CCJ	EN	MX05CJU	MA	SN05HWU	SE	WX05RUV	WE	YJ05VVW	WY	CV55AHA	SE	SF55UAD	SW
MX05CCK	EN	MX05CJV	MA	SN05HWV	SE	WX05RUW	WE	YJ05VVX	WY	CV55AMU	SE	SF55UAE	SW
MX05CCN	EN	MX05CJY	MA	SN05HWW	SE	WX05RUY	WE	YJ05VVY	WY	CV55AMX	SE	SF55UAG	GL
MX05CCO	EN	MX05CJZ	MA	SN05HWX	SE	WX05RVA	WE	YJ05VVZ	WY	CV55ANF	AB	SF55UAH	GL
MX05CCU	LE	MX05CKA	MA	SN05HWY	SE	WX05RVC	WE	YJ05VWA	WY	CV55ANP	AB	SF55UAJ	GL
MX05CCV	EN	MX05CKC	MA	SN05HWZ	SE	WX05RVE	WE	YJ05VWE	WY	CV55AOO	AB	SF55UAK	SW
MX05CCY	EN	MX05CKD	EN	SN05HXA	SE	WX05RVF	WE	YJ05VWF	WY	EU55NWS	SW	SF55UAL	SW
MX05CCZ	EN	MX05CKE	MA	SN05HXB	SE	WX05RVJ	WE	YJ05VWG	WY	HX55AOH	HD	SF55UAM	GL
MX05CDE	EN	MX05CKF	MA	SV05DXA	AB	WX05RVK	WE	YJ05VWH	WY	HX55AOJ	SE	SF55UAN	SY
MX05CDF	EN	MX05CKJ	MA	SV05DXC	AB	WX05RVL	WE	YJ05XOP	HD	HX55AOK	HD	SF55UAO	GL
MX05CDK	EN	MX05CKO	MA	SV05DXD	AB	WX05RVM	WE	YK05CDN	SW	LK55ABU	SE	SF55UAP	SY
MX05CDN	EN	MX05CKP	WE	SV05DXE	AB	WX05RVN	WE	YK05CDO	SW	LK55ABV	MW	SF55UAR	SY
MX05CDO	EN	MX05CLF	WE	SV05DXF	AB	WX05RVO	WE	YK05FJE	WY	LK55ABX	SE	SF55UAS	SY
MX05CDU	EN	PL05UBR	EN	SV05DXG	AB	WX05RVP	WE	YK05FJF	WY	LK55ABZ	WY	SF55UAT	SY
MX05CDV	EN	PL05UBS	EN	SV05DXH	AB	WX05RVR	EC	YK05FJJ	WY	LK55ACF	WE	SF55UAU	SY

SF55UAV	GL	WJ55CSV	HD	YK55AUP	WY	MX06VPM	SY	SF06GZE	GL	YJ06XKO	WY	YN06CGU	CU
SF55UAW	SY	WJ55CTE	HD	YK55AUU	WY	MX06VPN	SY	SF06GZG	GL	YJ06XKP	WY	YN06CGX	CU
SF55UAX	SY	WJ55CTF	HD	YK55AVF	WY	MX06VPO	MA	SF06GZII	GL	YJ06XKS	WY	YN06NXP	SW
SF55UAY	SY	WX55HVZ	WE	YK55AVG	WY	MX06VPP	MA	SF06GZJ	GL	YJ06XKT	WY	YN06NXW	SW
SF55UAZ	SY	WX55HWA	WE	YK55AVJ	WY	MX06VPR	MA	SF06GZK	GL	YJ06XKU	WY	YN06TDO	EN
SF55UBA	SY	WX55HWB	WE	YK55AVM	WY	MX06VPT	MA	SF06GZL	GL	YJ06XKV	WY	YN06TDU	EN
SF55UBB	GL	WX55HWC	WE	YK55JCN	WY	MX06VPU	MA	SF06GZM	GL	YJ06XKW	WY	YN06TDV	EN
SF55UBC	SY	WX55HWD	WE	YN55PXK	CU	MX06VPV	MA	SF06GZN	GL	YJ06XKX	WY	YN06TDX	EN
SF55UBD	SY	WX55HWE	WE	YN55PXL	CU	MX06VPW	MA	SF06GZO	GL	YJ06XKY	WY	YN06TDZ	EN
SF55UBE	SY	WX55TVZ	WE	BX06NZT	HD	MX06VPY	MA	SF06GZP	GL	YJ06XKZ	WY	YN06UPZ	PM
SF55UBG	SY	WX55TZA	WE	CN06BXF	PM	MX06VPZ	MA	SF06GZR	GL	YJ06XLA	WY	YN06URA	GL
SF55UBH	SY	WX55TZB	WE	CN06BXH	PM	MX06VRC	MA	SF06GZS	GL	YJ06XLB	WY	YN06URB	GL
SF55UBJ	SY	WX55TZC	WE	DC06FNG	WE	MX06YXJ	MA	SF06GZT	GL	YJ06XLC	WY	YN06URC	GL
SF55UBK	SY	WX55TZD	WE	DC06FNH	WE	MX06YXK	MA	SF06GZV	GL	YJ06XLD	WY	YN06URD	GL
SF55UBL	SY	WX55TZE	WE	EU06KDK	PM	MX06YXL	MA	SF06GZX	GL	YJ06XLE	WY	YN06URE	GL
SF55UBM	SY	WX55TZF	CU	MH06ZSP	WY	MX06YXM	MA	SF06GZY	GL	YJ06XLF	WY	YN06URF	GL
SF55UBN	SY	WX55TZG	CU	MH06ZSW	WY	MX06YXN	GL	SF06GZZ	GL	YJ06XLG	WY	YN06URG	GL
SF55UBO	SY	WX55TZH	GL	MV06CXB	MA	MX06YXO	GL	SF06HAA	GL	YJ06XLH	WY	YN06URH	GL
SF55UBP	SY	WX55TZJ	GL	MV06CZG	MA	MX06YXP	GL	SF06HAE	GL	YJ06XLK	WY	YN06URJ	GL
SF55UBR	SY	WX55TZK	GL	MV06CZJ	MA	MX06YXR	GL	SF06HAO	GL	YJ06XLL	WY	YN06WME	PM
SF55UBS	SY	WX55TZL	GL	MV06CZS	MA	MX06YXS	SY	SF06HAU	GL	YJ06XLM	WY	YN06WMF	PM
SF55UBT	SY	WX55TZM	EC	MV06CZT	MA	MX06YXT	SY	SF06HAX	GL	YJ06XLN	WY	YN06WMG	PM
SF55UBU	GL	WX55TZN	GL	MV06DWZ	MA	SF06GKX	GL	SF06HBA	GL	YJ06XLO	WY	YN06WMJ	PM
SF55UBV	GL	WX55TZO	GL	MV06DYU	SW	SF06GXG	GL	SF06HBB	GL	YJ06XLP	WY	YN06WMK	PM
SF55UBW	GL	WX55TZP	CU	MX06AEB	SW	SF06GXH	GL	SF06HBC	GL	YJ06XLR	WY	YN06WML	PM
SF55UBX	GL	WX55TZR	GL	MX06VMW	MA	SF06GXJ	GL	SN06AHK	SE	YJ06XLS	WY	YN06WMM	PM
SN55CXE	EN	WX55TZS	GL	MX06VMZ	MA	SF06GXL	GL	SV06GRF	AB	YJ06XLT	WY	YN06WMO	PM
SN55CXF	EN	WX55TZT	WE	MX06VNB	MA	SF06GXM	GL	SV06GRK	AB	YJ06XLU	WY	YN06WMP	PM
SN55CXH	EN	WX55TZU	EC	MX06VNC	MA	SF06GXN	GL	SV06GRU	AB	YJ06XLW	WY	YN06WMT	PM
SN55CXJ	EN	WX55TZV	CU	MX06VND	MA	SF06GXO	GL	SV06GRX	AB	YJ06XLX	WY	MX56ACV	MA
SN55HDZ	SE	WX55TZW	EC	MX06VNE	MA	SF06GXP	GL	WK06AEE	CU	YJ06XLY	WY	MX56ACY	MA
SN55HEJ	SE	WX55TZY	CU	MX06VNF	MA	SF06GXR	GL	WK06AEF	CU	YJ06XLZ	WY	MX56ACZ	GL
SN55HEU	SE	WX55TZZ	CU	MX06VNK	MA	SF06GXS	GL	WK06AFU	CU	YJ06XMA	WY	MX56ADO	GL
SN55HEV	SE	WX55UAA	WE	MX06VNL	MA	SF06GXT	GL	WK06AFV	CU	YJ06XMB	WY	MX56ADU	GL
SN55HFA	SE	WX55UAB	WE	MX06VNM	MA	SF06GXU	GL	WX06OMF	SW	YJ06XMC	WY	MX56ADV	GL
SN55HFB	SE	WX55UAC	WE	MX06VNN	MA	SF06GXV	GL	WX06OMG	SW	YJ06XMD	WY	MX56ADZ	GL
SN55HFC	SE	WX55UAD	WE	MX06VNO	MA	SF06GXW	GL	WX06OMH	SW	YJ06XME	WY	MX56AEA	GL
SN55HFD	SE	WX55VHK	WE	MX06VNP	MA	SF06GXX	GL	WX06OMJ	SW	YJ06XMF	WY	MX56AEB	GL
SN55HFE	SE	WX55VHL	WE	MX06VNR	MA	SF06GXY	GL	WX06OMK	HD	YJ06XMH	WY	MX56AEC	GL
SN55HFF	SE	WX55VHM	WE	MX06VNS	MA	SF06GXZ	GL	WX06OML	SW	YJ06XMK	WY	MX56AED	SY
SN55HFG	SE	WX55VHN	WE	MX06VNT	MA	SF06GYA	GL	WX06OMM	WE	YJ06XML	WY	MX56AEE	SY
SN55HFH	SE	WX55VHO	WE	MX06VNU	MA	SF06GYB	GL	WX06OMO	WE	YJ06XMM	WY	MX56AEF	SY
SN55HFJ	SE	WX55VHP	WE	MX06VNV	MA	SF06GYC	GL	WX06OMP	WE	YJ06XMO	WY	MX56AEG	SW
SN55HFK	SE	WX55VHR	WE	MX06VNW	MA	SF06GYD	GL	WX06OMR	WE	YJ06XMP	WY	MX56AEJ	SW
SN55HFL	SE	WX55VHT	WE	MX06VNY	MA	SF06GYE	GL	WX06OMS	WE	YJ06XMO	WY	MX56AEK	SW
SN55JVA	SE	WX55VHU	WE	MX06VNZ	MA	SF06GYG	GL	WX06OMT	WE	YJ06XMP	WY	MX56AEL	SW
SN55JVC	SE	WX55VHV	WE	MX06VOA	MA	SF06GYH	GL	WX06OMU	WE	YJ06YSK	SW	MX56AEM	SW
SN55JVD	SE	WX55VHW	WE	MX06VOB	MA	SF06GYJ	GL	WX06OMV	WE	YK06AOU	WY	MX56AEN	SW
SN55JVE	SE	WX55VHY	WE	MX06VOC	MA	SF06GYK	GL	WX06OMW	WE	YK06ATO	WY	MX56AEO	SW
SN55JVG	SE	WX55VHZ	WE	MX06VOD	MA	SF06GYN	GL	WX06OMY	WE	YK06ATU	WY	MX56AEP	SW
SN55JVH	SE	WX55VJA	WE	MX06VOF	MA	SF06GYO	GL	WX06OMZ	WE	YK06ATV	WY	MX56AET	SW
SN55JVJ	SE	WX55VJC	WE	MX06VOG	MA	SF06GYP	GL	WX06ONA	WE	YK06ATX	WY	MX56AEU	SW
SN55JVK	SE	WX55VJD	WE	MX06VOH	MA	SF06GYR	GL	WX06ONB	WE	YK06ATY	WY	MX56AEV	SW
SN55JVL	SE	WX55VJE	WE	MX06VOP	MA	SF06GYS	GL	WX06ONC	WE	YK06ATZ	WY	MX56AEW	SW
SN55JVM	SE	WX55VJF	WE	MX06VOU	MA	SF06GYT	GL	YJ06WTV	WY	YK06AUC	WY	MX56AEY	SW
SN55JVO	SE	WX55VJG	WE	MX06VOV	MA	SF06GYU	GL	YJ06WTX	WY	YK06AUL	WY	MX56AEZ	CU
SN55JVP	SE	WX55VJJ	WE	MX06VOY	MA	SF06GYV	GL	YJ06WTZ	WY	YK06CZZ	WY	MX56AFA	CU
SN55KKE	SE	YJ55CAO	WY	MX06VPA	MA	SF06GYW	GL	YJ06WUA	WY	YK06DAA	WY	MX56AFE	CU
SN55KKF	SE	YJ55CAU	WY	MX06VPC	MA	SF06GYX	GL	YJ06XEK	WY	YK06DNN	WY	MX56AFF	CU
TT55TRU	SW	YJ55CAV	WY	MX06VPD	MA	SF06GYY	GL	YJ06XEL	WY	YK06DTZ	WY	MX56AFJ	CU
WJ55CRX	SW	YK55AAJ	WY	MX06VPE	MA	SF06GYZ	GL	YJ06XFR	WY	YK06DYJ	WY	MX56AFK	CU
WJ55CRZ	SW	YK55AAN	WY	MX06VPG	SW	SF06GZA	GL	YJ06XKK	WY	YK06EFR	WY	MX56AFN	CU
WJ55CSF	HD	YK55AUE	WY	MX06VPJ	SW	SF06GZB	GL	YJ06XKL	WY	YK06EFS	WY	MX56AFO	CU
WJ55CSO	HD	YK55AUF	WY	MX06VPK	SW	SF06GZC	GL	YJ06XKM	WY	YK06EHE	WY	MX56AFU	CU
WJ55CSU	HD	YK55AUH	WY	MX06VPL	SY	SF06GZD	GL	YJ06XKN	WY			MX56AFV	CU

MX56AFY CU	YJ56WGA WY	SF07FCL GL	YJ07WFM HD	YN07WFY WY	SN57HDG SE	WX57HLN WE
MX56AFZ CU	YJ56ZMU WY	SF07FCM GL	YJ07WFN HD	YN07WFZ WY	SN57HDH SE	WX57HLO WE
MX56AGO CU	YJ56ZTM WY	SF07FCO GL	YJ07WFO HD	YN07WGA WY	SN57HDJ SE	WX57HLP WE
MX56AGU CU	AU07DXS PM	SF07FCP GL	YJ07WFP HD	BG57ZGJ SW	SN57HZX SE	WX57HLR WE
MX56HXZ MA	AU07DXT PM	SF07FCV GL	YJ07WFR CU	BV57MSO SW	SN57HZY SE	WX57HLU WE
MX56HYO PM	AU07DXV PM	SF07FCX GL	YJ07WFS CU	BV57MSU CU	SN57HZZ SE	WX57HLV WE
MX56HYP PM	AU07DXW PM	SF07FCY GL	YJ07WFT CU	BV57MSX SW	SN57JAO SE	WX57HLW WE
MX56NLJ PM	AU07DXX PM	SF07FCZ GL	YJ07WFU CU	BV57MSY SW	SN57JAU SE	WX57HLY WE
MX56NLK PM	CN07HVG MW	SF07FDA GL	YJ07WFV WE	CN57EFB MW	SN57JBE SE	WX57HLZ WY
SF56GYP GL	CN07HVH MW	SF07FDC GL	YJ07XMB WY	CN57EFE MW	SN57JBO SE	YJ57NFF WY
SF56GYR GL	CN07HVJ MW	SF07FDD GL	YJ07XND WY	CN57EFF MW	SN57JBU SE	YJ57VTV WY
SF56GYS GL	CN07HVK MW	SF07FDE GL	YJ07XWF WY	DK57SPZ MW	SN57JBV SE	YJ57VVA WY
SF56GYT GL	CN07HVL MW	SF07FDG GL	YJ07XWG WY	DK57SXF EC	SN57JBX SE	YJ57VYX WY
WA56FTK WE	CN07HVM MW	SF07FDJ GL	YK07AYA SY	DK57SXG EC	SN57JBZ SE	YJ57VYY WY
WA56FTN WE	CN07KZK PM	SF07FDK GL	YK07AYB SY	KX57BWF EN	SN57JCJ SE	YJ57WKB WY
WA56FTO WE	CN07KZL PM	SF07FDL GL	YK07AYC SY	LK57EJD EN	SN57JCO SE	YJ57WKC WY
WA56FTP WE	CN07KZM PM	SF07FDM GL	YK07AYD SY	LK57EJE EN	SN57JCU SE	YJ57YSK WY
WA56FTT WE	HY07FSU HD	SF07FDN GL	YK07AYE SY	LK57EJF EN	SN57JCV SE	YJ57YSL WY
WA56FTU WE	HY07FSV HD	SF07FDO GL	YK07AYF SY	LK57EJG EN	SN57JCX SE	YJ57YSM WY
WA56FTV SW	HY07FSX HD	SF07FDP GL	YK07AYG SY	LK57EJJ EN	SN57JCY SE	YJ57YSN WY
WA56FTX WE	HY07FSZ HD	SF07FDU GL	YK07AYH SY	LK57EJL EN	SN57JCZ SE	YJ57YSO WY
WA56FTY WE	HY07FTA HD	SF07FDV GL	YK07AYJ SY	MX57HDZ MA	SN57JDF SE	YJ57YSP WY
WA56FTZ WE	LK07CCA BE	SF07FDX GL	YK07AYL SY	MX57HEJ WY	SN57JDJ SE	YJ57YSR WY
WA56FUB WE	LK07CCD BE	SF07FDY GL	YK07AYM SY	SF57MKA GL	SN57JDK SE	YK57CJF WY
WA56FUD WE	LK07CCE BE	SF07FDZ GL	YK07AYN SY	SF57MKC GL	SN57MSU SE	YK57CJJ WY
WA56FUE WE	LK07CCF BE	SF07FEG GL	YK07AYO SY	SF57MKD GL	SV57EYH AB	YK57CJO WY
WA56OAO MA	LK07CCJ BE	SF07FEH GL	YK07AYP SY	SF57MKG GL	SV57EYJ AB	YK57CJU WY
WA56OAP SW	LK07CCN BE	SF07FEJ GL	YK07AYS SY	SF57MKJ GL	SV57EYK AB	YK57CJV WY
WA56OAS EC	LK07CCO BE	SF07FEK GL	YK07AYT SY	SF57MKK GL	VX57CYO PM	YK57CJX WY
WA56OAU MA	LK07CCU BE	SF07FEM GL	YK07AYU SY	SF57MKL GL	WX57HJO WE	YK57CJY WY
WA56OAV MA	LK07CCV BE	SF07FEO GL	YK07AYV SY	SF57MKM GL	WX57HJU WE	YK57CJZ WY
WK56ABZ CU	LK07CCX BE	SF07FEP GL	YK07AYW SY	SF57MKN GL	WX57HJV WE	YK57EZS WY
WX56HJZ WY	LK07CDE BE	SF07FET GL	YK07AYX SY	SF57MKO GL	WX57HJY WE	YK57EZT WY
WX56HKA WY	LK07CDF BE	SF07FEU GL	YK07AYY WY	SF57MKP GL	WX57HJZ WE	YK57EZU WY
WX56HKB WE	LK07CDN BE	SK07JVN SE	YK07AYZ WY	SF57MKU GL	WX57HKA WE	YK57EZV WY
WX56HKC WE	MX07BPY MA	SK07JVO SE	YK07BJX WY	SF57MKV GL	WX57HKB WE	YK57EZW WY
WX56HKD WE	MX07BPZ MA	SK07JVP SE	YK07BJY WY	SF57MKX GL	WX57HKC WE	YK57EZX WY
WX56HKE WE	MX07BRF MA	SV07EHB AB	YK07BJZ WY	SF57MKZ GL	WX57HKD WE	YK57EZZ WY
WX56HKF WE	MX07BRV MA	SV07EHC AB	YK07FTP WY	SF57MLE GL	WX57HKE WE	YK57FAA WY
WX56HKG WE	MX07BRZ MA	SV07EHD AB	YK07FTT WY	SF57MLJ GL	WX57HKF WE	YK57FCL WY
YJ56AOT SW	MX07BSO MA	SV07EHE AB	YK07FTU WY	SF57MLK GL	WX57HKG WE	YN57BVU SE
YJ56AOU SW	MX07BSU MA	SV07EHF AB	YK07FTX WY	SF57MLL GL	WX57HKH WE	YN57BVV SE
YJ56EAA WY	MX07BSV MA	SV07EHG AB	YK07FUA WY	SF57MLN GL	WX57HKJ WE	YN57BVW CU
YJ56EAC WY	MX07BSY MA	SV07EHH AB	YK07FUD WY	SF57MLO GL	WX57HKK WE	YN57BVX CU
YJ56EAE WY	MX07BSZ MA	SV07EHJ AB	YN07MKD WY	SF57MLU GL	WX57HKL WE	YN57BVY CU
YJ56EAF WY	MX07BTE MA	SV07EHK AB	YN07MKE WY	SF57MLV GL	WX57HKM WE	YN57BVZ SE
YJ56EAG WY	MX07BTF MA	SV07EHL AB	YN07MKF WY	SK57ADO SE	WX57HKN WE	YN57BWU SE
YJ56LJE WY	MX07BTO WY	TT07TRU SW	YN07MKG WY	SK57ADU SE	WX57HKO WE	YN57RJU SY
YJ56LJF WY	MX07BTU WY	YJ07FLP WY	YN07MKJ WY	SK57ADV SE	WX57HKP WE	YN57RJZ SY
YJ56LJK WY	MX07BTV WY	YJ07LVL WY	YN07MKK WY	SK57ADX SE	WX57HKT WE	YN57RKA SY
YJ56LJL WY	MX07BTY WY	YJ07LVM WY	YN07MKL WY	SK57ADZ SE	WX57HKU WE	YN57RKJ SY
YJ56LJN WY	MX07BTZ WY	YJ07LVN WY	YN07MKM WY	SK57AEA GL	WX57HKV WE	AY08EKT EN
YJ56LJY WY	MX07BUA WY	YJ07LVO WY	YN07MKO WY	SK57AEB SE	WX57HKW WE	CU08ACY CU
YJ56LKC WY	MX07BUE MA	YJ07LVR WY	YN07MKP WY	SK57AEC SE	WX57HKY WE	CU08ACZ CU
YJ56LKD WY	MX07BUF WY	YJ07LVS WY	YN07MKV WY	SN57HCP SE	WX57HKZ WE	CU08ADO CU
YJ56LKE WY	MX07BUH WY	YJ07LVT WY	YN07MKX SY	SN57HCU SE	WX57HLA WE	CU08ADV CU
YJ56LLG WY	MX07BUJ WY	YJ07LVU WY	YN07MKZ WY	SN57HCV SE	WX57HLC WE	CU08ADX CU
YJ56LLK WY	MX07BUU MA	YJ07LVV WY	YN07MLE SY	SN57HCX SE	WX57HLD WE	CU08ADZ CU
YJ56LLN WY	MX07BUV MA	YJ07LVW WY	YN07MLJ SY	SN57HCY SE	WX57HLE WE	CU08AHN CU
YJ56LLO WY	MX07OZD MW	YJ07LWC WY	YN07MLK SY	SN57HCZ SE	WX57HLF WE	CU08AHO CU
YJ56LMX WY	SF07FCC GL	YJ07LWD WY	YN07MLL WY	SN57HDA SE	WX57HLG WE	CU08AHP CU
YJ56LNA WY	SF07FCD GL	YJ07LWE WY	YN07MLO SY	SN57HDC SE	WX57HLH WE	CU08AHV CU
YJ56LRL WY	SF07FCE GL	YJ07LWF WY	YN07MLU SY	SN57HDD SE	WX57HLJ WE	CU08AHX CU
YJ56LRN WY	SF07FCG GL	YJ07WBK WY	YN07WFW WY	SN57HDE SE	WX57HLK WE	EU08FHB EC
YJ56LRU WY	SF07FCJ GL	YJ07WBL WY	YN07WFX WY	SN57HDF SE	WX57HLM WE	FJ08FYN EC

FN08AZZ	MW	YJ08CDZ	WY	YJ08XYP	WY	AU58ECC	EC	MX58DWJ	MA	MX58DZS	MA	WX58JWV	WE
HX08DHE	HD	YJ08CEA	WY	YJ08XYR	WY	AU58ECD	EC	MX58DWK	MA	MX58DZT	MA	WX58JWW	WE
HX08DHF	HD	YJ08CEF	WY	YJ08XYS	WY	AU58ECE	EC	MX50DWL	MA	MX58DZU	MA	WX58JWY	WE
HX08DHG	HD	YJ08CEK	WY	YJ08XYT	WY	AU58ECF	EC	MX58DWM	MA	MX58DZV	MA	WX58JWZ	WE
HX08DHJ	HD	YJ08CCN	WY	YJ08ZGI	WY	AU58ECJ	EC	MX58DWN	MA	MX58DZW	MA	WX58JXA	WE
HX08DHK	HD	YJ08CEO	WY	YJ08ZGM	WY	AU58ECN	EC	MX58DWO	MA	MX58DZY	MA	WX58JXB	WE
HX08DHL	HD	YJ08CEU	WY	YJ08ZGN	WY	AU58ECT	EC	MX58DWP	MA	MX58DZZ	MA	WX58JXC	WE
HX08DHY	HD	YJ08CEV	WY	YJ08ZGO	WY	AU58ECV	EC	MX58DWU	MA	MX58EAA	MA	WX58JXD	WE
LK08FKY	WE	YJ08CEX	WY	YJ08ZGP	WY	AU58ECW	EC	MX58DWV	MA	MX58EAC	MA	WX58JXE	WE
LK08FKZ	EN	YJ08CEY	WY	YN08LCK	SY	AU58ECX	EC	MX58DWW	MA	MX58EAF	MA	WX58JXF	WE
LK08FLA	WE	YJ08CFA	WY	YN08LCL	SY	AU58ECY	EC	MX58DWY	MA	MX58EAG	MA	WX58JXG	WE
LK08FLX	EN	YJ08CFD	WY	YN08LCM	SY	AU58ECZ	EC	MX58DWZ	MA	MX58EAJ	MA	WX58JXH	WE
LK08FMC	BE	YJ08CFE	WY	YN08LCO	SY	AU58EDC	EC	MX58DXA	MA	MX58EAK	MA	WX58JXJ	WE
LK08FMD	BE	YJ08GVE	WY	YN08LCP	SY	AU58EDF	EC	MX58DXB	MA	MX58EAM	MA	WX58JXK	WE
LK08FME	BE	YJ08GVF	WY	YN08LCT	GL	AU58EDJ	EC	MX58DXC	MA	MX58EAO	MA	WX58JXL	WE
LK08FMF	BE	YJ08GVG	WY	YN08LCU	GL	AU58EDK	EC	MX58DXD	MA	MX58EAP	MA	WX58JXM	WE
LK08FMG	BE	YJ08GVK	WY	YN08LCV	GL	AU58FFH	EN	MX58DXE	MA	MX58EAY	MA	WX58JXN	WE
LK08FMJ	BE	YJ08GVL	WY	YN08LCW	GL	AU58FFJ	EC	MX58DXF	MA	MX58EBA	MA	WX58JXO	WE
LK08FNL	BE	YJ08GVM	WY	YN08LCY	GL	AU58FFK	EC	MX58DXG	MA	MX58EBC	MA	WX58JXP	WE
SF08SMU	GL	YJ08GVN	WY	YN08LCZ	GL	AU58FFL	EC	MX58DXH	MA	MX58EBD	MA	WX58JXR	WE
SF08SMV	GL	YJ08GVO	WY	YN08LDA	GL	AU58FFM	EC	MX58DXJ	MA	MX58EBF	MA	WX58JXS	WE
SF08SMX	GL	YJ08GVP	WY	YN08LDC	GL	AU58FFN	EC	MX58DXK	MA	MX58EBG	MA	WX58JXT	WE
SF08SNJ	GL	YJ08GVR	WY	YN08LDD	GL	AU58FFO	EC	MX58DXL	MA	MX58EBK	MA	WX58JXU	WE
SF08SNK	GL	YJ08GVT	WY	YN08NLL	SY	AU58FFP	EC	MX58DXM	MA	MX58EBL	MA	WX58JXV	WE
SF08SNN	GL	YJ08GVU	WY	YN08NLM	SY	AU58FFR	EN	MX58DXO	MA	MX58EBM	MA	WX58JXW	WE
SF08SNU	GL	YJ08GVV	WY	YN08NLO	SY	AU58FFS	SY	MX58DXP	MA	MX58EBN	MA	WX58JXY	WE
SF08SNV	GL	YJ08GVW	WY	YN08NLP	SY	AU58FFT	EN	MX58DXR	MA	MX58KZA	CU	WX58JXZ	WE
SF08SNX	GL	YJ08GVX	WY	YN08NLR	SY	AU58FFV	EN	MX58DXS	MA	MX58KZB	CU	WX58JYA	WE
SF08SNY	GL	YJ08GVY	WY	YN08NLT	SY	AU58FFW	EN	MX58DXT	MA	SF58ATY	GL	WX58JYB	WE
SF08SNZ	GL	YJ08GVZ	WY	YN08NLU	SY	BG58OLR	WY	MX58DXU	MA	SF58ATZ	GL	WX58JYC	WE
SV08FHA	AB	YJ08GWA	WY	YN08NLV	SY	BG58OLT	WY	MX58DXV	MA	SF58AUA	GL	WX58JYD	WE
SV08FHB	AB	YJ08GWC	WY	YN08NLX	SY	BG58OLU	WY	MX58DXW	MA	SF58AUC	GL	WX58JYE	WE
SV08FHC	AB	YJ08GWD	WY	YN08NLY	SY	BG58OLV	WY	MX58DXZ	MA	SN58CFK	EN	WX58JYF	WE
SV08FHD	AB	YJ08GWE	WY	YN08NLZ	SY	BG58OLX	WY	MX58DYA	MA	SN58CFL	EN	WX58JYG	WE
SV08FHE	AB	YJ08GWF	WY	YN08NMA	SY	BG58OMA	WY	MX58DYC	MA	SN58CFM	EN	WX58JYH	WE
SV08FHF	AB	YJ08GWG	WY	YN08NME	SY	BG58OMB	WY	MX58DYD	MA	SN58CFO	WE	WX58JYJ	WE
SV08FHG	AB	YJ08GWK	WY	YN08NMF	SY	BG58OMC	WY	MX58DYF	MA	SN58CFP	EN	WX58JYK	WE
SV08FXP	AB	YJ08GWL	WY	YN08NMJ	SY	BG58OMD	WY	MX58DYG	MA	SN58CFU	EN	WX58JYL	WE
SV08FXR	AB	YJ08GWM	WY	YN08NMK	SY	BG58OME	WY	MX58DYH	MA	SN58CFV	WE	WX58JYN	WE
SV08FXS	AB	YJ08GWN	WY	YN08NMM	SY	BG58OMF	WY	MX58DYJ	MA	SN58CFX	EN	WX58JYO	WE
SV08FXT	AB	YJ08GWO	WY	YN08NMU	SY	BG58OMH	WY	MX58DYM	MA	SN58CFY	EN	WX58JYP	WE
SV08FXU	AB	YJ08GWP	WY	YN08NMV	SY	BG58OMJ	WY	MX58DYN	MA	SN58CFZ	EN	WX58JYR	WE
SV08FXW	AB	YJ08GWU	WY	YN08NMX	SY	BG58OMK	WY	MX58DYO	MA	SN58CGE	WE	WX58JYS	WE
SV08FXX	AB	YJ08GWV	WY	YN08NMY	SY	BG58OML	WY	MX58DYP	MA	SN58CGF	EN	WX58JYT	WE
SV08FXY	AB	YJ08GWW	WY	YN08OWO	SW	EU58JWZ	EN	MX58DYS	MA	SN58CGG	WE	WX58JYU	WE
SV08FXZ	AB	YJ08GWX	WY	YN08OWP	SW	FJ58YSL	EN	MX58DYT	MA	SN58CGK	EN	YJ58CEV	HD
SV08FYA	AB	YJ08GWY	WY	YN08OWR	SW	LK58ECV	WY	MX58DYU	MA	SN58CGO	EN	YJ58GMO	WY
SV08FYB	AB	YJ08XCN	WY	YN08OWU	SW	LK58ECW	WY	MX58DYV	MA	SN58CGU	WE	YJ58GMU	WY
SV08FYC	AB	YJ08XCO	WY	YN08OWV	SW	LK58ECX	WY	MX58DYW	MA	SN58CGV	WE	YJ58GNP	WY
WA08MVE	SW	YJ08XCP	WY	YN08PLF	SY	LK58ECY	WY	MX58DYY	MA	SN58CGX	EN	YJ58GNU	WY
WA08MVF	SW	YJ08XCR	WY	YN08PLO	SY	LK58ECZ	WY	MX58DZA	MA	SN58CGY	EN	YJ58GNV	WY
WA08MVG	SW	YJ08XCS	WY	YN08PLU	SY	LK58EDF	EC	MX58DZB	MA	SN58CGZ	EN	YJ58GNW	WY
WK08ESV	SW	YJ08XXW	WY	YN08PLX	SY	LK58EDJ	EC	MX58DZC	MA	SN58CHC	WE	YJ58GNX	WY
WX08LNN	WE	YJ08XYB	WY	YN08PLY	SY	LK58EDL	BE	MX58DZD	MA	SN58CHD	WE	YJ58RNN	WY
WX08LNO	WE	YJ08XYC	WY	YN08PMO	WY	MX58DVU	MA	MX58DZE	MA	SN58CHF	WE	YJ58RNO	WY
WX08LNP	WE	YJ08XYD	WY	YN08PMU	WY	MX58DVV	MA	MX58DZF	MA	SN58CHG	EN	YJ58RNU	WY
YJ08CDE	WY	YJ08XYE	WY	YN08PMV	WY	MX58DVW	MA	MX58DZG	MA	SN58CHH	EN	YJ58RNV	WY
YJ08CDF	WY	YJ08XYF	WY	YN08PMX	WY	MX58DVY	MA	MX58DZH	MA	SN58CHJ	WE	YJ58RNX	WY
YJ08CDK	WY	YJ08XYG	WY	YN08PMY	WY	MX58DVZ	MA	MX58DZJ	MA	SN58CHK	EN	YJ58RNY	WY
YJ08CDN	WY	YJ08XYH	WY	YN08PNE	WY	MX58DWA	MA	MX58DZK	MA	SN58CHL	WE	YJ58RNZ	WY
YJ08CDO	WY	YJ08XYK	WY	YN08PNF	WY	MX58DWC	MA	MX58DZL	MA	SN58CHO	EN	YJ58ROH	WY
YJ08CDU	WY	YJ08XYL	WY	YN08PNJ	WY	MX58DWD	MA	MX58DZN	MA	SN58ENR	EN	YJ58ROU	WY
YJ08CDV	WY	YJ08XYM	WY	YN08PNK	WY	MX58DWE	MA	MX58DZO	MA	SN58ENT	EN	YJ58RPO	WY
YJ08CDX	WY	YJ08XYN	WY	YX08HJF	EN	MX58DWF	MA	MX58DZP	MA	ST58JPT	EC	YJ58RPU	WY
YJ08CDY	WY	YJ08XYO	WY	AU58ECA	EC	MX58DWG	MA	MX58DZR	MA	WX58JWU	WE	YJ58RPV	WY

YJ58RPX WY	HY09AOU CU	SN09CCF AB	YJ09FWY MA	YJ09OBS WY	WX59BZF LE	BD11CEU MA
YJ58RPY WY	HY09AUO HD	SN09CCJ AB	YJ09FWZ WY	YJ09OBT WY	WX59BZG LE	BD11CEV MA
YJ58RPZ WY	HY09AUV HD	SN09CCK AB	YJ09FXA WY	YJ09OBU WY	WX59BZH LE	BD11CEX EC
YJ58RRO WY	HY09AUW HD	SN09CCO AB	YJ09FXB WY	YJ09OBV WY	WX59BZJ LE	BD11CEY MA
YJ58RRU WY	HY09AUX HD	SN09CCU AB	YJ09FXC WY	YJ09OBW WY	WX59BZK LE	BD11CFA MA
YJ58RRV WY	HY09AZA CU	SN09CCV AB	YJ09FXD WY	YJ09OBX WY	WX59BZL WE	BD11CFE MA
YJ58RRX WY	HY09AZB HD	SN09CCX AB	YJ09FXE WY	YJ09OBY WY	WX59BZM WE	BD11CFF MA
YJ58RRY WY	HY09AZC HD	SN09CCY AB	YJ09FXF WY	YJ09OBZ WY	WX59BZN LE	BD11CFG MA
YJ58RRZ WY	HY09AZD HD	SN09CCZ AB	YJ09FXG WY	YJ09OCA WY	WX59BZO LE	BD11CFJ MA
YJ58RSO WY	HY09AZF HD	SN09CDE AB	YJ09FXH MA	YJ09OCB WY	YJ59KSO WY	BD11CFK EC
YJ58RSU WY	HY09AZG HD	SN09CDF AB	YJ09NYA WY	YJ09OCC WY	YJ59KSU WY	BD11CFM EC
YJ58RSV WY	HY09AZJ HD	SN09CDK AB	YJ09NYB WY	YJ09OCD WY	YJ59KSV WY	BD11CFN EC
YJ58RSX WY	HY09AZL HD	SN09CDO AB	YJ09NYC WY	YJ09OCE WY	YJ59KSY WY	BD11CFO EC
YJ58RSY WY	HY09AZN HD	SN09EZW SE	YJ09NYD WY	YJ09OCF WY	YJ59KSZ WY	BD11CFP EC
YJ58RSZ WY	HY09AZO HD	SN09EZX SE	YJ09NYF WY	YJ09OCG WY	BJ10VGA WE	BD11CFU EC
YJ58RTO WY	MX09GXY MA	SN09FAU SE	YJ09NYG WY	YJ09OUS GL	BJ10VGC WE	BD11CFV EC
YJ58RTU WY	MX09GXZ MA	SN09FBA SE	YJ09NYH WY	YN09HFH SY	BJ10VGD WE	BD11CFX EC
YJ58RTV WY	MX09GYA MA	SN09FBB SE	YJ09NYK WY	YN09HFJ SY	BJ10VGE WE	BD11CFY EC
YJ58RTX WY	MX09GYB MA	SN09FBC SE	YJ09NYM WY	YN09HFK SY	BJ10VGF WE	BD11CFZ EC
YJ58RVA WY	MX09GYC MA	SN09FBD SE	YJ09NYN WY	YN09HFL SY	BJ10VGG WE	BD11CGE EC
YN58ERX SY	MX09GYD MA	SN09FBE SE	YJ09NYO WY	YN09HFM SY	MX10DXU MW	BD11CGF EC
YN58ERY SY	MX09GYE MA	SN09FBF SE	YJ09NYP WY	YX09ACV EC	WK10AZU SW	BJ11EBU WE
YN58ERZ SY	MX09GYF MA	ST09JPT EC	YJ09NYR WY	YX09ACY EC	YX10AXP GL	BJ11EBV WE
YN58ESF SY	MX09GYG MA	VT09JPT EC	YJ09NYS WY	YX09ACZ EC	YX10AYL GL	BJ11EBY WE
YN58ESG SY	MX09GYH MA	WX09KBK WE	YJ09NYT WY	YX09ADO EC	BJ60BZA WY	BJ11EBZ WE
YN58ESO SY	MX09GYJ MA	WX09KBN WE	YJ09NYU WY	YX09ADU HD	BJ60BZB WY	BJ11ECA EN
YN58ESU SY	MX09GYK MA	WX09KBO WE	YJ09NYV WY	YX09ADV SW	BJ60BZC WY	BJ11ECC EN
YN58ESV SY	MX09HUK MA	WX09KBP WE	YJ09NYW WY	YX09ADZ SW	BJ60BZD WY	BJ11ECD EN
YN58ESY SY	MX09HUO MA	WX09KBU WE	YJ09NYX WY	YX09AFN WE	BJ60BZE WY	BJ11ECE EN
YN58ETA SY	MX09HUP MA	WX09KBV WE	YJ09NYY WY	YX09AFO WE	BJ60BZF WY	BJ11ECF EN
YN58ETD SY	MX09HUU MA	WX09KBY WE	YJ09NZY WY	YX09AFU WE	EU60LFS EN	BJ11ECN EN
YN58ETE SY	MX09LMF MA	WX09KBZ WE	YJ09OAA WY	YX09AFV WE	SN60CAA EC	BJ11ECT EN
YN58ETF SY	MX09LMJ MA	WX09KCA WE	YJ09OAB WY	YX09AFY WE	SN60EAA SW	BJ11ECV EN
YN58ETJ SY	MX09LMK MA	WX09KCC WE	YJ09OAC WY	YX09AFZ WE	SN60EAC SW	BJ11ECW EN
YN58ETK SY	MX09LML MA	WX09KCE WE	YJ09OAD WY	YX09AGO WE	SN60EAE SW	BJ11ECX BE
YN58ETL SY	PT09JPT MW	WX09KCF WE	YJ09OAE WY	YX09AGU WE	SN60EAF SW	BJ11ECY BE
YN58ETO SY	RT09JPT EC	WX09KCG WE	YJ09OAG WY	YX09AGV WE	SN60EAG SW	BJ11XGY BE
YN58ETR SY	SF09LDD GL	WX09KCJ WE	YJ09OAH WY	YX09AGZ WE	SN60EAJ SW	BJ11XHY WE
YN58ETT WY	SF09LDE GL	WX09KCK WE	YJ09OAL WY	YX09AHA WE	SN60EAM SW	BJ11XHZ WE
YN58ETU SY	SF09LDJ GL	WX09KCN WE	YJ09OAM WY	YX09AHC HD	SN60EAO SW	BP11JWA WY
YN58ETV SY	SF09LDK GL	YJ09FVE WY	YJ09OAN WY	YX09AHD HD	SN60EAP SW	BP11JWC WY
YN58ETX SY	SF09LDL GL	YJ09FVF WY	YJ09OAO WY	YX09AHE HD	SN60EAW SW	BP11JWD WY
YN58ETY SY	SF09LDN GL	YJ09FVG WY	YJ09OAP WY	YX09AHF HD	YJ60KCA MA	BP11JWE WY
YX58FRJ SW	SF09LDO GL	YJ09FVH WY	YJ09OAS WY	YX09AHG HD	YJ60KCC MA	BP11JWF WY
YX58FRK SW	SF09LDU GL	YJ09FVK WY	YJ09OAU WY	YX09AHK SW	YJ60KCE MA	BP11JWG WY
YX58FRL SW	SF09LDV GL	YJ09FVL WY	YJ09OAV WY	MX59AVP SW	YJ60KCF MA	BP11JWJ WY
YX58FRN SW	SF09LDX GL	YJ09FVM WY	YJ09OAW WY	SN59AWV EN	YJ60KCG MA	BP11JWK WY
YX58FRP SW	SF09LDY GL	YJ09FVN WY	YJ09OAX WY	VT59JPT EN	YJ60KCK MA	BP11JWL WY
YX58HVF EN	SF09LDZ GL	YJ09FVO WY	YJ09OAY WY	WX59BYM LE	YJ60KCN MA	BP11JWM WY
YX58HVG EN	SF09LEJ GL	YJ09FVP WY	YJ09OAZ WY	WX59BYN LE	YJ60KCO MA	BP11JWN WY
YX58HVH EN	SF09LEU GL	YJ09FWA WY	YJ09OBA WY	WX59BYO WE	YJ60KCU MA	BP11JWO WY
YX58HVJ EN	SF09LFA GL	YJ09FWB WY	YJ09OBB WY	WX59BYP WE	YJ60KCV MA	BP11JWU WY
YX58HVK EN	SF09LFB GL	YJ09FWC WY	YJ09OBC WY	WX59BYR WE	YJ60KDF MA	BP11JWV WY
YX58HVL EN	SN09CAU AB	YJ09FWL WY	YJ09OBD WY	WX59BYS WE	YJ60KDK MA	BP11JWW WY
YX58HWF HD	SN09CAV AB	YJ09FWM WY	YJ09OBE WY	WX59BYT WE	YJ60KDN MA	BP11JWX WY
YX58HWG HD	SN09CAX AB	YJ09FWN WY	YJ09OBF WY	WX59BYU WE	YJ60KDO MA	SN11FOJ GL
YX58HWH HD	SN09CBF AB	YJ09FWO WY	YJ09OBG WY	WX59BYV WE	YJ60KDU MA	SN11FOK GL
YX58HWJ HD	SN09CBO AB	YJ09FWP WY	YJ09OBH WY	WX59BYW HD	YJ60KDV MA	SN11FOM GL
HY09AJV WY	SN09CBU AB	YJ09FWR WY	YJ09OBK WY	WX59BYY HD	YJ60KDX MA	SN11FOT GL
HY09AJX CU	SN09CBV AB	YJ09FWS WY	YJ09OBL WY	WX59BYZ WY	YJ60LRN CU	SN11FOU GL
HY09AKF CU	SN09CBX AB	YJ09FWT WY	YJ09OBM WY	WX59BZA WE	BD11CDX EC	SN11FOV GL
HY09AKG CU	SN09CBY AB	YJ09FWU WY	YJ09OBN WY	WX59BZB WE	BD11CDY EC	SN11FPA GL
HY09AOR HD	SN09CCA AB	YJ09FWV WY	YJ09OBO WY	WX59BZC LE	BD11CDZ EC	SN11FPC GL
HY09AOS HD	SN09CCD AB	YJ09FWW MA	YJ09OBP WY	WX59BZD LE	BD11CEN MA	SN11FPD GL
HY09AOT HD	SN09CCE AB	YJ09FWX MA	YJ09OBR WY	WX59BZE LE	BD11CEO MA	

YX11HNW	SW	BD12TDV	WY	BN12JYL	EC	SN12AFZ	MA	SN12AOP	WE	SN62AMV	GL	BD13NFR	WY
YX11HNY	SW	BF12KWC	HD	BN12JYO	EC	SN12AGO	MA	SN12AOR	MA	SN62ANR	SE	BD13NFV	WY
YX11HNZ	SW	BF12KWD	HD	BN12JYP	EC	SN12AGU	MA	YJ12GXV	MA	SN62ANIJ	SE	BD13OHK	WY
YX11HPO	BE	BF12KWE	HD	BN12JYR	EC	SN12AGV	MA	YJ12GXZ	MA	SN62AOA	SE	BD13OHL	WY
YX11HPP	BE	BF12KWG	HD	BN12JYS	EC	SN12AGX	MA	YJ12MYF	MA	SN62AOC	SE	BD13OHN	WY
BN61MWE	MA	BF12KWH	HD	BN12JYT	EC	SN12AGY	MA	YJ12MYG	MA	SN62AOF	GL	BD13OHO	WY
BN61MWF	MA	BF12KWJ	HD	BN12JYU	EC	SN12AGZ	MA	YJ12MYK	MA	SN62AOG	GL	BD13OHP	WY
BN61MWG	MA	BF12KWK	HD	BN12JYV	EC	SN12AHA	MA	YJ12MYL	MA	SN62AOZ	MA	BD13OHR	WY
BN61MWJ	MA	BF12KWL	HD	BN12JYW	EC	SN12AHC	MA	YJ12MYO	MA	SN62APF	SE	BD13OHS	WY
BN61MWK	MA	BF12KWM	HD	BN12WNX	EC	SN12AHD	MA	YJ12MYP	MA	SN62APO	SE	BG13VUC	WY
BN61MWL	MA	BF12KWN	HD	BN12WNY	EC	SN12AHE	MA	YJ12MYR	MA	SN62APZ	SE	BG13VUD	WY
BN61MWM	MA	BF12KWO	HD	BN12WNZ	EC	SN12AHF	MA	YJ12MYS	MA	SN62ASO	SE	BG13VUE	WY
BN61MWO	MA	BF12KWP	HD	BN12WOA	EC	SN12AHG	MA	YJ12MYT	MA	SN62ASU	SE	BT13YVV	WY
BN61MWP	MA	BF12KWR	HD	BN12WOB	EC	SN12AHJ	MA	YJ12MYV	MA	SN62ASX	SE	BT13YVW	WY
BN61MWU	MA	BF12KWS	HD	BN12WOC	EC	SN12AHK	MA	YJ12MZD	MA	SN62ASZ	SE	BT13YVX	WY
BN61MWV	MA	BF12KWU	WY	BN12WOD	WY	SN12AHL	MA	YJ12MZF	MA	SN62ATZ	SE	BT13YVY	WY
BN61MWW	MA	BF12KXU	EC	BN12WOH	WY	SN12AHO	MA	YX12CHK	GL	SN62AUC	SE	BT13YVZ	WY
BN61MWX	MA	BF12KXV	EC	BN12WOJ	WY	SN12AHP	MA	YX12CHL	GL	SN62AUH	SE	BT13YWA	WY
BN61MWY	MA	BG12UKM	WY	BN12WOM	WY	SN12AHU	MA	YX12CHU	GL	SN62AUJ	SE	BT13YWB	WY
MX61BAV	SW	BG12YJF	WY	BN12WOR	WY	SN12AHV	MA	YX12CJF	GL	SN62AUK	SE	BT13YWC	WY
MX61BBZ	SW	BG12YJH	WY	BN12WOU	WY	SN12AHX	MA	YX12CJJ	GL	SN62AUU	SE	BT13YWD	WY
MX61BCF	SW	BG12YJJ	WY	BN12WOV	WY	SN12AHY	MA	YX12CJO	GL	SN62AUW	SE	BT13YWD	WY
SN61DDU	GL	BG12YJK	WY	BN12WOX	WY	SN12AHZ	MA	YX12CJU	GL	SN62AWA	WE	BV13ZZZ	WY
SN61BDV	GL	BG12YJL	WY	BN12WOY	WY	SN12AJO	MA	LK62FUJ	SY	SN62AWF	WE	BV13ZBC	EN
SN61BDX	GL	BG12YJM	WY	BN12WPA	WY	SN12AJU	MA	LK62HJD	SY	SN62AWG	WE	BV13ZBD	EN
SN61BDY	GL	BG12YJN	WY	BN12WPD	WY	SN12AJV	MA	LK62HJX	SY	SN62AWO	WE	BV13ZBE	EN
SN61BDZ	GL	BG12YJO	WY	BN12WPE	WY	SN12AJX	MA	LK62HKG	SY	SN62AWR	WE	BV13ZBF	EN
SN61BEJ	GL	BG12YJP	WY	BN12WPF	WY	SN12AJY	MA	MX62ANR	LE	SN62AWY	WE	BV13ZBG	EN
SN61BEO	GL	BG12YJR	WY	BN12WPJ	WY	SN12AKF	MA	MX62ARU	SW	SN62AXB	WE	BV13ZBJ	EN
SN61BEU	GL	BG12YJS	WY	MX12DYM	SW	SN12AKG	MA	MX62AVV	SW	SN62AXC	WE	BV13ZBL	EN
SN61BEY	GL	BG12YJT	WY	MX12DZA	SW	SN12AKJ	MA	MX62AXH	LE	SN62AXH	SE	BV13ZBN	EN
SN61BFA	GL	BG12YJU	WY	MX12JXV	SW	SN12AKK	MA	MX62AXN	SW	SN62AXK	SE	BV13ZBO	EN
SN61BFE	GL	BG12YJV	WY	SN12ADU	MA	SN12AKO	MA	SN62ABU	GL	SN62AXO	SE	BV13ZBP	EN
SN61BFF	GL	BG12YJW	WY	SN12ADV	MA	SN12AKP	MA	SN62ABV	GL	SN62AXU	SE	BV13ZBR	EN
SN61BFJ	GL	BG12YJX	WY	SN12ADX	WE	SN12AKU	MA	SN62ABX	GL	SN62AXW	SE	BV13ZBT	EN
SN61BFK	GL	BG12YJY	WY	SN12ADZ	WE	SN12AKV	MA	SN62ABZ	GL	SN62AXY	SE	BV13ZBU	EN
SN61BFL	GL	BG12YJZ	WY	SN12AEA	WE	SN12AKX	MA	SN62ACX	GL	SN62AXZ	SE	BV13ZBW	EN
SN61BFM	GL	BG12YKA	WY	SN12AEB	WE	SN12AKY	MA	SN62ACZ	GL	SN62AYA	SE	BV13ZBX	EN
SN61BFO	GL	BG12YKB	WY	SN12AEC	WE	SN12AKZ	MA	SN62ADU	GL	SN62AYB	SE	BV13ZBY	EN
SN61BFP	GL	BG12YKC	WY	SN12AEE	MA	SN12ALO	MA	SN62ADV	GL	SN62AYJ	SE	BV13ZBZ	EN
SN61BFU	GL	BG12YKD	WY	SN12AEF	MA	SN12ALU	MA	SN62AEA	GL	SN62AYV	BE	BV13ZCA	EN
SN61BFV	GL	BG12YKE	WY	SN12AEG	WE	SN12AMK	MA	SN62AEF	GL	SN62AYZ	BE	BV13ZCE	EN
SN61BFX	GL	BG12YKF	WY	SN12AEJ	WE	SN12AMO	MA	SN62AEK	GL	SN62AZA	BE	BV13ZCF	BE
SN61BFY	GL	BJ12VNR	WY	SN12AEK	WE	SN12AMU	MA	SN62AET	GL	SN62AZB	BE	BV13ZCJ	BE
SN61BFZ	GL	BJ12VNS	WY	SN12AEL	MA	SN12AMV	MA	SN62AEU	GL	SN62AZW	BE	BV13ZCK	BE
BD12SZY	WY	BJ12VWO	WY	SN12AEM	MA	SN12AMX	MA	SN62AEY	GL	SN62DBO	BE	BV13ZCL	BE
BD12SZZ	WY	BJ12VWP	WY	SN12AEO	MA	SN12ANF	MA	SN62AFE	GL	SN62DBV	BE	BV13ZCN	BE
BD12TAU	WY	BJ12VWR	WY	SN12AEP	MA	SN12ANP	MA	SN62AFJ	GL	SN62DCX	SW	BV13ZCO	BE
BD12TAV	WY	BJ12VWS	WY	SN12AET	MA	SN12ANR	MA	SN62AFK	GL	SN62DCY	SW	BV13ZCT	BE
BD12TBO	WY	BJ12VWT	WY	SN12AEU	MA	SN12ANU	MA	SN62AFU	GL	SN62DCZ	SW	BV13ZCU	BE
BD12TBU	WY	BJ12VWU	WY	SN12AEV	MA	SN12ANV	MA	SN62AFY	GL	YN62GXS	BE	BV13ZCX	BE
BD12TBV	WY	BJ12VWV	WY	SN12AEW	MA	SN12ANX	MA	SN62AFZ	GL	YN62GYR	BE	BV13ZCY	BE
BD12TBX	WY	BJ12VWW	WY	SN12AEX	MA	SN12AOA	MA	SN62AGV	GL	YX62DVM	WE	BV13ZDH	WY
BD12TBY	WY	BJ12VWX	WY	SN12AEY	MA	SN12AOB	MA	SN62AGY	GL	YX62DWG	WE	BV13ZDJ	WY
BD12TBZ	WY	BJ12VWY	WY	SN12AEZ	MA	SN12AOC	MA	SN62AHD	GL	YX62DWM	WE	MX13BAV	SW
BD12TCJ	MA	BJ12VXA	WY	SN12AFA	MA	SN12AOD	MA	SN62AHF	GL	YX62DWO	WE	MX13BBF	SW
BD12TCK	WY	BJ12VXB	WY	SN12AFE	MA	SN12AOE	MA	SN62AHL	GL	YX62DXC	WE	MX13BBJ	SW
BD12TCO	WY	BJ12VXC	WY	SN12AFF	MA	SN12AOF	MA	SN62AHV	GL	YX62DXF	WE	MX13BCU	SW
BD12TCU	WY	BJ12VXD	WY	SN12AFJ	MA	SN12AOG	MA	SN62AHX	GL	YX62DXH	WE	MX13NBA	WE
BD12TCV	WY	BJ12VXE	WY	SN12AFK	MA	SN12AOH	MA	SN62AJU	GL	BD13NFK	WY	SM13NBB	WE
BD12TCX	WY	BN12JYF	EC	SN12AFO	MA	SN12AOJ	MA	SN62AJV	GL	BD13NFL	WY	SM13NBC	WE
BD12TCY	WY	BN12JYG	EC	SN12AFU	WE	SN12AOK	WE	SN62AKG	GL	BD13NFM	WY	SM13NBD	WE
BD12TCZ	WY	BN12JYH	EC	SN12AFV	WE	SN12AOL	MA	SN62AKJ	GL	BD13NFN	WY	SM13NBE	WE
BD12TDO	WY	BN12JYJ	EC	SN12AFX	MA	SN12AOM	MA	SN62AKO	GL	BD13NFO	WY	SM13NBF	WE
BD12TDU	MA	BN12JYK	EC	SN12AFY	MA	SN12AOO	MA	SN62AKP	GL	BD13NFP	WY	SM13NBG	WE

SM13NBJ	WE	SN13CLJ	MA	SN13EDO	GL	YX13AKF	EN	SK63KHE	SY	SK63KME	HD	YX63LJF	EC
SM13NBK	WE	SN13CLO	MA	SN13EDP	GL	YX13AKG	EN	SK63KHF	SY	SK63KMF	HD	YX63LJJ	EC
SM13NBL	WE	SN13CLU	MA	SN13EDR	GL	YX13AKJ	EN	SK63KHG	SY	SK63KMG	HD	YX63LJK	EC
SM13NBN	PM	SN13CLV	MA	SN13EDU	GL	YX13AKK	EN	SK63KHJ	SY	SK63KMJ	HD	YX63LJL	EC
SM13NBO	PM	SN13CLX	MA	SN13EDV	GL	YX13AKN	EN	SK63KHL	SY	SK63KMM	HD	YX63LJN	EC
SM13NBX	PM	SN13CLY	MA	SN13EDX	GL	YX13AKO	EN	SK63KHM	SY	SK63KMO	HD	YX63LJO	EC
SM13NBY	PM	SN13CLZ	MA	SN13EEF	GL	YX13AKP	EN	SK63KHO	SY	SK63KMU	HD	YX63LJU	EC
SM13NBZ	PM	SN13CME	MA	SN13EEG	GL	YX13AKU	CU	SK63KHP	SY	SK63KMV	HD	YX63LJV	EC
SM13NCA	PM	SN13CMF	MA	SN13EEH	GL	YX13AKV	CU	SK63KHR	SY	SK63KMX	HD	YX63LJY	EC
SM13NCC	LE	SN13CMK	MA	SN13EEJ	GL	YX13AKY	CU	SK63KHT	HD	SK63KMY	HD	YX63LJZ	EC
SM13NCD	LE	SN13CMO	AB	SN13EEM	GL	YX13BNA	CU	SK63KHU	HD	SK63KMZ	HD	YX63LKA	EC
SM13NCE	LE	SN13CMU	AB	SN13EEO	GL	YX13BNB	CU	SK63KHV	HD	SK63KNA	HD	YX63LKC	EC
SM13NCF	LE	SN13CMV	AB	SN13EEP	GL	YX13BND	CU	SK63KHW	HD	SK63KNB	HD	YX63LKD	EC
SM13NCJ	MA	SN13CMX	AB	SN13EES	GL	YX13BNE	CU	SK63KHX	HD	SK63KNC	HD	YX63LKE	EC
SM13NCN	MA	SN13CMY	AB	SN13EET	GL	YX13BNF	CU	SK63KHY	HD	SK63KND	HD	YX63LKF	EC
SM13NCO	MA	SN13CMZ	AB	SN13EEU	GL	YX13BNJ	CU	SK63KHZ	HD	SK63KNE	HD	YX63LKG	EC
SM13NCU	HD	SN13CNA	AB	SN13EEV	GL	YX13BNK	CU	SK63KJA	HD	SK63KNF	HD	YX63LKJ	EC
SM13NCV	HD	SN13CNC	AB	SN13EEW	GL	YX13BNL	CU	SK63KJE	HD	SK63KNG	WE	YX63LKK	EC
SM13NDJ	SY	SN13CNE	AB	SN13EEX	GL	YX13BNN	CU	SK63KJF	HD	SK63KNH	WE	YX63LKL	EC
SM13NDK	SY	SN13CNF	AB	SN13EEY	GL	BF63HDC	SW	SK63KJJ	HD	SK63KNJ	WE	YX63LKM	EC
SM13NDL	SY	SN13CNJ	AB	SN13EEZ	GL	BF63HDN	HD	SK63KJN	HD	SK63KNL	WE	YX63LKN	EC
SM13NDN	SY	SN13CNK	AB	SN13EFA	GL	BF63HDO	HD	SK63KJO	HD	SK63KNM	WE	YX63LKO	EC
SM13NDO	SY	SN13CNO	AB	SN13EFB	GL	BF63HDU	HD	SK63KJU	HD	SK63KNN	WE	YX63LKU	CU
SM13NDU	SY	SN13CNU	AB	SN13EFC	GL	BF63HDV	BE	SK63KJV	HD	SK63KNO	WE	YX63LKV	BE
SM13NDV	SY	SN13CNV	AB	SN13EFD	GL	BF63HDX	BE	SK63KJX	HD	SK63KNP	WE	YX63LKY	BE
SM13NDX	SY	SN13CNX	AB	SN13EFE	GL	BF63HDY	BE	SK63KJY	HD	SK63KNR	WE	YX63LKZ	BE
SM13NDY	SY	SN13CNY	AB	SN13EFF	GL	BJ63UHZ	BE	SK63KJZ	HD	SK63KNS	WE	YX63LLC	BE
SM13NDZ	SY	SN13CNZ	AB	SN13EFG	GL	BJ63UJV	BE	SK63KKA	HD	SK63KNU	WE	YX63LLD	BE
SM13NEF	SY	SN13COA	AB	SN13EFH	GL	BJ63UJW	BE	SK63KKB	HD	SK63KNV	WE	YX63LLE	BE
SM13NEJ	SY	SN13COH	AB	SN13EFJ	GL	BJ63UJX	BE	SK63KKC	HD	SK63KNX	WE	YX63LLF	BE
SM13NEN	SY	SN13COJ	AB	SN13EFK	GL	BJ63UJZ	BE	SK63KKD	HD	SK63KNY	WE	YX63LLG	BE
SM13NEO	SY	SN13COU	AB	SN13EFL	GL	MX63XAM	SW	SK63KKE	HD	SL63GBF	CU	YX63LLJ	CU
SM13NEU	SY	SN13CPE	AB	SN13NAE	WE	MX63XAN	SW	SK63KKF	HD	SL63GBO	CU	YX63ZUD	CU
SM13NEY	SY	SN13EAY	GL	SN13NAO	WE	MX63XAP	SW	SK63KKG	HD	SL63GBU	CU	YX63ZVA	CU
SN13CGF	GL	SN13EBA	GL	YJ13HLR	CU	SK63ATY	GL	SK63KKH	HD	SL63GBV	CU	YX63ZVB	CU
SN13CGG	GL	SN13EBC	GL	YJ13HLU	CU	SK63ATZ	GL	SK63KKJ	WE	SL63GBX	CU	YX63ZVC	CU
SN13CGK	GL	SN13EBD	GL	YJ13HLV	CU	SK63AUA	GL	SK63KKL	WE	SL63GBY	CU	YX63ZVD	CU
SN13CGO	GL	SN13EBF	GL	YJ13HLW	CU	SK63AUC	GL	SK63KKM	WE	SL63GBZ	CU	YX63ZVE	CU
SN13CGU	GL	SN13EBG	GL	YJ13HLX	CU	SK63AUE	GL	SK63KKN	WE	SL63GCF	CU	YX63ZVF	CU
SN13CGV	GL	SN13EBJ	GL	YJ13HLY	CU	SK63AUF	GL	SK63KKO	WE	SL63GCK	CU	YX63ZVG	CU
SN13CGX	GL	SN13EBK	GL	YJ13HLZ	CU	SK63AUH	GL	SK63KKP	WE	SN63KHH	SY	YX63ZVH	CU
SN13CHO	EN	SN13EBL	GL	YJ13HMA	CU	SK63AUJ	GL	SK63KKR	WE	SN63MYH	WE	YY63WBT	BE
SN13CHV	EN	SN13EBM	GL	YJ13HMC	CU	SK63AUL	GL	SK63KKS	WE	SN63MYJ	WE	YY63WBU	BE
SN13CHX	EN	SN13EBO	GL	YJ13HMD	CU	SK63AUM	GL	SK63KKU	WE	SN63MYK	WE	MX14FUT	SW
SN13CHY	EN	SN13EBP	GL	YJ13HME	CU	SK63AUN	GL	SK63KKV	WE	SN63MYL	WE	SL14DBO	WY
SN13CJV	MA	SN13EBU	GL	YJ13HMF	CU	SK63KFY	MA	SK63KKW	WE	SN63MYM	WE	SL14DBU	WY
SN13CJX	MA	SN13EBV	GL	YJ13HMG	CU	SK63KFZ	MA	SK63KKX	WE	SN63MYO	WE	SL14DBV	WY
SN13CJY	MA	SN13EBX	GL	YJ13HMH	CU	SK63KGA	MA	SK63KKY	WE	SN63MYP	GL	SL14DFD	SY
SN13CJZ	MA	SN13EBZ	GL	YJ13HMK	CU	SK63KGE	MA	SK63KKZ	WE	SN63MYR	GL	SL14DFE	SY
SN13CKA	MA	SN13ECA	GL	YJ13HMU	CU	SK63KGF	MA	SK63KLA	WE	SN63MYS	GL	SL14DFF	SY
SN13CKC	MA	SN13ECC	GL	YJ13HMV	CU	SK63KGG	MA	SK63KLC	WE	SN63MYT	GL	SL14DFG	SY
SN13CKD	MA	SN13ECD	GL	YJ13HMX	CU	SK63KGJ	MA	SK63KLD	WE	SN63MYU	GL	SL14DFK	SY
SN13CKE	MA	SN13ECF	GL	YX13AEF	EN	SK63KGN	MA	SK63KLE	BE	SN63MYV	GL	SL14LMF	SY
SN13CKF	MA	SN13ECJ	GL	YX13AEV	CU	SK63KGO	SY	SK63KLF	BE	SN63MYW	GL	SL14LMJ	SY
SN13CKG	MA	SN13ECT	GL	YX13AEW	CU	SK63KGP	SY	SK63KLJ	BE	SN63MYX	GL	SL14LMK	SY
SN13CKJ	MA	SN13ECV	GL	YX13AEY	CU	SK63KGU	SY	SK63KLL	BE	SN63MYY	GL	SL14LMM	SY
SN13CKK	MA	SN13ECW	GL	YX13AEZ	CU	SK63KGV	SY	SK63KLM	HD	SN63MYZ	GL	SL14LMO	SY
SN13CKL	MA	SN13ECX	GL	YX13AFA	CU	SK63KGX	SY	SK63KLO	HD	SN63MZD	GL	SL14LMU	SY
SN13CKO	MA	SN13ECY	GL	YX13AFE	CU	SK63KGY	SY	SK63KLP	HD	SN63MZE	GL	SL14LMV	SY
SN13CKP	MA	SN13ECZ	GL	YX13AHN	EN	SK63KGZ	SY	SK63KLS	HD	SN63MZF	GL	SL14LMY	SY
SN13CKU	MA	SN13EDC	GL	YX13AHO	EN	SK63KGX	SW	SK63KLU	HD	SN63MZG	GL	SL14LNA	SY
SN13CKV	MA	SN13EDF	GL	YX13AHP	EN	SK63KHA	SW	SK63KLV	HD	YX63LHK	CU	SL14LNC	SY
SN13CKX	MA	SN13EDJ	GL	YX13AHU	EN	SK63KHB	SW	SK63KLX	HD	YX63LHL	CU	SN14CTV	MA
SN13CKY	MA	SN13EDK	GL	YX13AHV	EN	SK63KHC	SW	SK63KLZ	HD	YX63LHM	CU	SN14CTX	MA
SN13CLF	MA	SN13EDL	GL	YX13AHZ	EN	SK63KHD	SY	SK63KMA	HD	YX63LHR	BE	SN14CTY	MA

SN14DTX	CU	SN14DXX	SE	SN14ECE	HD	SN14FGK	WE	YJ14BKO	HD	SN64CHH	WY	SN64COU	SE
SN14DTY	CU	SN14DXY	SE	SN14ECF	HD	SN14FGM	WE	YJ14BPF	MA	SN64CHJ	WY	SN64CPE	SE
SN14DTZ	CU	SN14DXZ	SE	SN14ECJ	HD	SN14TPZ	HD	YJ14BPK	MA	SN64CHK	WY	SN64CPF	SE
SN14DUA	CU	SN14DYA	SE	SN14ECT	HD	SN14TRV	HD	YJ14BPO	MA	SN64CHL	WY	SN64CPK	SE
SN14DUH	CU	SN14DYB	GL	SN14ECV	HD	SN14TRX	HD	YJ14BVA	HD	SN64CHO	WY	SN64CPO	SE
SN14DUJ	CU	SN14DYC	GL	SN14ECW	HD	SN14TRZ	MA	YJ14BVB	HD	SN64CHV	WY	SN64CPU	EC
SN14DUU	CU	SN14DYD	GL	SN14ECX	HD	SN14TSO	MA	YJ14BVC	HD	SN64CHX	EN	SN64CPV	EC
SN14DUV	CU	SN14DYF	GL	SN14ECY	HD	SN14TSU	MA	YJ14BVD	HD	SN64CHY	EN	SN64CPX	EC
SN14DUY	CU	SN14DYG	GL	SN14ECZ	AB	SN14TSV	MA	YJ14BVE	HD	SN64CHZ	EN	SN64CPY	EC
SN14DVB	CU	SN14DYH	GL	SN14EDC	AB	SN14TSX	MA	YJ14BVF	HD	SN64CJE	EN	SN64CPZ	EC
SN14DVC	CU	SN14DYJ	GL	SN14EDF	AB	SN14TSY	MA	YW14FHU	SW	SN64CJF	EN	SN64CRF	EC
SN14DVF	CU	SN14DYM	GL	SN14EDJ	AB	SN14TSZ	MA	YX14RUC	CU	SN64CJJ	EN	SN64CRJ	EC
SN14DVG	CU	SN14DYO	GL	SN14EDK	AB	SN14TTE	MA	YX14RUH	CU	SN64CJO	EN	SN64CRK	EC
SN14DVH	CU	SN14DYP	GL	SN14EDL	AB	SN14TTF	MA	YX14RUJ	CU	SN64CJU	EN	SN64CRU	EC
SN14DVJ	CU	SN14DYS	GL	SN14EDO	AB	SN14TTJ	MA	YX14RUO	CU	SN64CJV	EN	SN64CRV	EC
SN14DVK	CU	SN14DYT	GL	SN14EDP	AB	SN14TTK	MA	YX14RUR	CU	SN64CJX	EN	SN64CRX	EC
SN14DVL	CU	SN14DYU	GL	SN14EDR	AB	SN14TTO	MA	YX14RUU	CU	SN64CJY	SE	SN64CRZ	EC
SN14DVM	SY	SN14DYV	GL	SN14EDU	AB	SN14TTU	MA	YX14RUV	CU	SN64CJZ	SE	SN64CSF	SY
SN14DVO	SY	SN14DYW	GL	SN14EDV	AB	SN14TTV	MA	YX14RUW	CU	SN64CKA	SE	SN64CSO	SY
SN14DVP	SY	SN14DYX	GL	SN14FDP	AB	SN14TTX	MA	YX14RUY	CU	SN64CKC	SE	YJ64DYX	MA
SN14DVR	SY	SN14DYY	GL	SN14FDU	AB	SN14TTY	MA	YX14RVA	CU	SN64CKD	SE	YX64VPJ	CU
SN14DVT	SY	SN14DZA	GL	SN14FDV	AB	SN14TTZ	MA	YX14RVC	CU	SN64CKE	SE	YX64VPK	CU
SN14DVU	SY	SN14DZB	GL	SN14FDX	AB	SN14TUA	MA	YX14RVE	CU	SN64CKF	SE	YX64VPL	CU
SN14DVV	SY	SN14DZC	GL	SN14FDY	AB	SN14TUH	MA	YX14RVF	CU	SN64CKG	SE	YX64VPM	CU
SN14DVW	SY	SN14DZD	GL	SN14FDZ	AB	SN14TUJ	MA	YX14RVJ	CU	SN64CKJ	SE	SL15RVO	CU
SN14DVX	SY	SN14DZE	GL	SN14FEF	AB	SN14TUO	MA	YX14RVK	CU	SN64CKK	SE	SL15RVP	CU
SN14DVY	SY	SN14DZF	GL	SN14FEG	AB	SN14TUP	MA	YX14RVL	CU	SN64CKL	SE	SL15RVR	CU
SN14DVZ	SY	SN14DZG	GL	SN14FEH	AB	SN14TUV	MA	YX14RVM	CU	SN64CKO	SE	SL15RVT	CU
SN14DWC	SY	SN14DZH	GL	SN14FEJ	AB	SN14TUW	MA	YX14RVN	CU	SN64CKP	SE	SL15RVU	CU
SN14DWD	SY	SN14DZJ	GL	SN14FEK	AB	SN14TUY	WY	YX14RVO	CU	SN64CKU	SE	SL15RVV	CU
SN14DWE	SY	SN14DZK	GL	SN14FEM	AB	SN14TVA	WY	YX14RVP	CU	SN64CKV	SE	SL15RVW	CU
SN14DWF	SY	SN14DZL	GL	SN14FEO	AB	SN14TVC	WY	YX14RVR	CU	SN64CKX	SE	SL15RVX	CU
SN14DWG	SY	SN14DZM	MA	SN14FEP	AB	SN14TVD	WY	YX14RVT	CU	SN64CKY	SE	SL15RVY	CU
SN14DWJ	SY	SN14DZO	MA	SN14FET	AB	SN14TVE	WY	YX14RVU	CU	SN64CLF	WE	SL15RVZ	HD
SN14DWK	SY	SN14DZP	MA	SN14FEU	HD	SN14TVF	WY	YX14RVV	CU	SN64CLJ	WE	SL15RWE	HD
SN14DWL	SY	SN14EAA	MA	SN14FEV	HD	SN14TVJ	WY	YX14RVW	CU	SN64CLO	WE	SL15RWF	HD
SN14DWM	SY	SN14EAC	MA	SN14FEX	HD	SN14TVK	WY	YX14RVY	CU	SN64CLU	WE	SL15RWJ	HD
SN14DWO	SY	SN14EAE	MA	SN14FFA	HD	SN14TVL	WY	YX14RVZ	CU	SN64CLV	WE	SL15RWK	HD
SN14DWP	SY	SN14EAF	MA	SN14FFC	HD	SN14TVM	WY	YX14RWE	CU	SN64CLX	WE	SL15RWN	HD
SN14DWU	SY	SN14EAG	MA	SN14FFD	HD	SN14TVO	WY	YX14RWF	CU	SN64CLY	WE	SL15RWO	HD
SN14DWV	SY	SN14EAJ	MA	SN14FFE	HD	SN14TVP	WY	YX14RWJ	CU	SN64CLZ	WE	SL15RWU	HD
SN14DWW	SY	SN14EAM	MA	SN14FFG	HD	SN14TVT	WY	YX14RWK	CU	SN64CME	WE	SL15RWV	HD
SN14DWX	SY	SN14EAO	MA	SN14FFH	HD	SN14TVU	WY	YX14RWN	CU	SN64CMF	WE	SL15RWW	HD
SN14DWY	SY	SN14EAP	MA	SN14FFJ	HD	SN14TVV	WY	YX14RWO	CU	SN64CMK	WE	SL15RWX	CU
SN14DWZ	HD	SN14EAW	MA	SN14FFK	HD	SV14FYR	AB	SN64CFM	MW	SN64CMO	WE	SL15XWY	CU
SN14DXA	HD	SN14EAX	MA	SN14FFL	HD	SV14FYS	AB	SN64CFO	MW	SN64CMU	WE	SL15XWZ	CU
SN14DXB	HD	SN14EAY	MA	SN14FFM	HD	SV14FZC	AB	SN64CFP	MW	SN64CMV	EN	SL15XXA	CU
SN14DXC	HD	SN14EBA	MA	SN14FFO	HD	SV14FZD	AB	SN64CFU	MW	SN64CMX	EN	SL15ZFH	WY
SN14DXD	HD	SN14EBC	HD	SN14FFP	HD	YJ14BHA	WY	SN64CFV	MW	SN64CMY	EN	SL15ZFJ	WY
SN14DXE	HD	SN14EBD	HD	SN14FFR	HD	YJ14BHD	WY	SN64CFX	MW	SN64CMZ	EN	SL15ZFK	WY
SN14DXF	HD	SN14EBF	HD	SN14FFS	HD	YJ14BHE	WY	SN64CFY	MW	SN64CNA	EN	SL15ZFM	WY
SN14DXG	HD	SN14EBG	HD	SN14FFT	HD	YJ14BHF	WY	SN64CFZ	MW	SN64CNC	EN	SL15ZFN	WY
SN14DXH	HD	SN14EBJ	HD	SN14FFU	WE	YJ14BHK	WY	SN64CGE	PM	SN64CNE	EN	SL15ZFO	WY
SN14DXJ	MA	SN14EBK	HD	SN14FFV	WE	YJ14BHL	WY	SN64CGF	PM	SN64CNF	EN	SL15ZFP	WY
SN14DXK	MA	SN14EBL	HD	SN14FFW	WE	YJ14BJX	MA	SN64CGG	PM	SN64CNJ	EN	SL15ZFR	WY
SN14DXL	MA	SN14EBM	HD	SN14FFX	WE	YJ14BJY	MA	SN64CGK	PM	SN64CNK	EN	SL15ZFS	WY
SN14DXM	MA	SN14EBO	HD	SN14FFY	WE	YJ14BJZ	MA	SN64CGO	PM	SN64CNO	SY	SL15ZFT	WY
SN14DXO	MA	SN14EBP	HD	SN14FFZ	WE	YJ14BKA	HD	SN64CGU	PM	SN64CNU	SY	SL15ZFV	WY
SN14DXP	MA	SN14EBU	HD	SN14FGA	WE	YJ14BKD	HD	SN64CGV	PM	SN64CNV	SY	SL15ZFW	WY
SN14DXR	MA	SN14EBV	HD	SN14FGC	WE	YJ14BKE	HD	SN64CGX	PM	SN64CNX	SY	SL15ZFX	WY
SN14DXS	MA	SN14EBX	HD	SN14FGD	WE	YJ14BKF	HD	SN64CGY	PM	SN64CNY	SY	SL15ZFY	WY
SN14DXT	MA	SN14EBZ	HD	SN14FGE	WE	YJ14BKG	HD	SN64CHC	WY	SN64CNZ	SY	SL15ZFZ	WY
SN14DXU	MA	SN14ECA	HD	SN14FGF	WE	YJ14BKK	HD	SN64CHD	WY	SN64COA	SY	SL15ZGA	WY
SN14DXV	MA	SN14ECC	HD	SN14FGG	WE	YJ14BKL	HD	SN64CHF	WY	SN64COH	SY	SL15ZGB	WY
SN14DXW	SE	SN14ECD	HD	SN14FGJ	WE	YJ14BKN	HD	SN64CHG	WY	SN64COJ	SY	SM15WCR	WE

SM15WCT	WE	YJ15AOX	GL	SM65EFB	EN	SN65OGC	GL	SN65OKV	SE	SN65ZDY	GL	SK16GVU	EC
SN15ABF	LE	YJ15AOY	GL	SM65EFC	EN	SN65OGD	GL	SN65OKW	HD	SN65ZDZ	GL	SK16GVV	EC
SN15ABK	CU	YJ15AOZ	GL	SM65EFD	SY	SN65OGE	GL	SN65OKX	HD	SN65ZFA	GL	SK16GVW	EC
SN15ABO	CU	YJ15AYK	WY	SM65EFE	SY	SN65OGF	GL	SN65OKZ	HD	SN65ZFB	GL	SK16GVX	EC
SN15ABU	CU	YJ15AYL	WY	SM65EFF	SY	SN65OGG	GL	SN65OLA	HD	SN65ZFC	GL	SK16GVY	EC
SN15ABV	CU	YJ15AYM	WY	SM65EFG	SY	SN65OGH	GL	SN65OLB	HD	SN65ZFD	GL	SK16GVZ	EC
SN15ACF	BE	YJ15AYN	WY	SM65EFH	SY	SN65OGJ	GL	SN65OLC	HD	SN65ZFE	GL	SK16GWA	EC
SN15ACJ	BE	YJ15AYO	WY	SM65EFJ	SY	SN65OGK	GL	SN65OLE	HD	SN65ZFF	GL	SL16PZZ	WY
SN15ACK	BE	YJ15AYP	WY	SM65EFK	SY	SN65OGL	GL	SN65OLG	HD	SN65ZFG	GL	SL16RAU	SY
SN15ACU	BE	BF65HVN	AB	SM65EFL	SY	SN65OGM	GL	SN65OLH	HD	SN65ZFH	GL	SL16RAX	SY
SN15ACV	BE	BF65HVO	AB	SM65EFN	SY	SN65OGO	GL	SN65OLJ	HD	SN65ZFJ	GL	SL16RBF	SY
SN15ACX	HD	BL65OXT	MA	SM65GFV	SY	SN65OGP	GL	SN65OLK	HD	SN65ZFK	GL	SL16RBO	SY
SN15ACY	HD	BL65OXU	MA	SM65GFX	SY	SN65OGR	GL	SN65OLM	HD	SN65ZFL	GL	SL16RBU	SY
SN15ACZ	HD	BL65OXV	MA	SM65GFY	SY	SN65OGT	GL	SN65OLO	HD	SN65ZFM	GL	SL16RBV	SY
SN15ADO	CU	BL65OYZ	MA	SM65GFZ	SY	SN65OGU	GL	SN65OLP	HD	SN65ZFO	GL	SL16RBX	SY
SN15ADU	CU	BL65YZD	MA	SM65GGA	SY	SN65OGV	GL	SN65OLR	HD	SN65ZFP	GL	SL16RBY	SY
SN15ADV	CU	BL65YZE	MA	SM65GGE	SY	SN65OGW	GL	SN65OLT	HD	SN65ZFR	GL	SL16RBZ	SY
SN15ADX	CU	BL65YZF	MA	SM65GGF	SY	SN65OGX	GL	SN65OLU	HD	SN65ZFS	GL	SL16RCF	SY
SN15ADZ	CU	BL65YZG	MA	SM65LMV	SY	SN65OGY	GL	SN65OLX	WY	SN65ZFT	GL	SL16RCO	SY
SN15AEA	CU	BL65YZH	MA	SM65LMX	SY	SN65OGZ	GL	SN65OMF	WE	SN65ZFU	GL	SL16RCU	SY
SN15AEB	CU	BL65YZJ	MA	SM65LMY	SY	SN65OHA	GL	SN65OMH	WE	SN65ZFV	GL	SL16RCV	SY
SN15AEC	CU	BL65YZK	MA	SM65LNA	SY	SN65OHR	GL	SN65OMJ	WE	SN65ZFW	GL	SL16RCX	SY
SN15AED	CU	BW65DBX	MA	SM65LNC	SY	SN65OHS	GL	SN65OMK	WE	SN65ZFX	GL	SL16RCY	SY
SN15AEE	CU	BW65DBY	MA	SM65LND	SY	SN65OHT	GL	SN65OML	WE	SN65ZFY	GL	SL16RCZ	SY
SN15AEF	CU	BW65DBZ	MA	SM65LNH	BE	SN65OHU	GL	SN65OMM	WE	SN65ZFZ	AB	SL16RDO	SY
SN15AEG	CU	BW65DCE	MA	SM65LNJ	BE	SN65OHV	GL	SN65OMO	WE	SN65ZGA	AB	SL16RDU	SY
SN15AEJ	CU	BW65DCF	MA	SM65LNK	BE	SN65OHW	GL	SN65OMP	WE	SN65ZGB	AB	SL16RDV	SY
SN15AEK	CU	BW65DCO	MA	SM65LNN	BE	SN65OHX	GL	SN65OMR	WE	SN65ZGC	AB	SL16RDX	SY
SN15AEL	EN	BW65DCU	MA	SM65LNO	LE	SN65OHY	GL	SN65OMS	WE	SN65ZGE	AB	SL16RDY	WY
SN15AEM	EN	BW65DCV	MA	SM65LNP	LE	SN65OJE	SE	SN65OMT	WE	SN65ZGG	AB	SL16RDZ	WY
SN15AEO	EN	BW65DCX	MA	SM65LNR	MW	SN65OJF	SE	SN65OMU	WE	SN65ZGH	AB	SL16REU	WY
SN15AEP	EN	SK65PVY	WE	SM65WMC	MW	SN65OJG	SE	SN65ZBZ	WE	SN65ZGS	WE	SL16RFE	WY
SN15AET	EN	SK65PVZ	WE	SM65WMD	MW	SN65OJJ	SE	SN65ZCA	WE	SN65ZGT	WE	SL16RFF	WY
SN15AEU	EN	SK65PWE	WE	SM65WME	MW	SN65OJK	SE	SN65ZCE	WE	YX65RHY	CU	SL16RFJ	WY
SN15AEV	EN	SK65PWF	WE	SM65WMF	MW	SN65OJL	SE	SN65ZCF	WE	YX65RHZ	CU	SL16RFK	WY
SN15AEW	EN	SK65PWJ	WE	SM65WMG	MW	SN65OJM	SE	SN65ZCJ	WE	YX65RJJ	CU	SL16RFN	WY
SN15AEX	EN	SK65PWL	WE	SM65WMJ	MW	SN65OJO	SE	SN65ZCK	WE	YX65RJO	CU	SL16RFO	WY
SN15AEY	EN	SK65PWN	WE	SM65WMK	MW	SN65OJP	SE	SN65ZCL	WE	YX65RJU	CU	SL16RFX	WY
SN15AEZ	EN	SK65PWO	WE	SM65WML	MW	SN65OJR	SE	SN65ZCO	WE	SK16GTZ	LE	SL16RFY	WY
SN15AFA	EN	SK65PWX	EC	SM65WMO	LE	SN65OJS	SE	SN65ZCT	WE	SK16GUA	LE	SL16RFZ	WY
SN15AFE	EN	SK65PWY	EC	SM65WMP	LE	SN65OJT	SE	SN65ZCU	WE	SK16GUC	LE	SL16RGO	WY
SN15AFF	EN	SK65PWZ	EC	SM65WMT	LE	SN65OJU	SE	SN65ZCV	WE	SK16GUD	LE	SL16RGU	WY
SN15AFJ	EN	SK65PXA	EC	SM65WMU	LE	SN65OJV	SE	SN65ZCX	WE	SK16GUE	LE	SL16RGV	WY
SN15AFK	EN	SK65PXB	EC	SM65WMV	LE	SN65OJW	SE	SN65ZCY	WE	SK16GUF	LE	SL16RGX	WY
SN15ELC	SE	SK65PXC	EC	SM65WMW	LE	SN65OJX	SE	SN65ZCZ	WE	SK16GUG	LE	SL16RGY	WY
SO15CUA	WE	SK65PXD	EC	SM65WMX	LE	SN65OJY	SE	SN65ZDA	WE	SK16GUH	LE	SL16RGZ	WY
SO15CUC	WE	SK65PXE	EC	SM65WMY	LE	SN65OJZ	SE	SN65ZDC	WE	SK16GUJ	LE	SL16RHA	WY
SO15CUG	WE	SK65PXF	EC	SM65WMZ	LE	SN65OKA	SE	SN65ZDD	WE	SK16GUO	LE	SL16RHE	WY
SO15CUH	WE	SK65PXG	EC	SM65WNA	LE	SN65OKB	SE	SN65ZDE	WE	SK16GUU	LE	SL16RHF	WY
SO15CUJ	WE	SK65PXH	EC	SM65WNB	LE	SN65OKC	LE	SN65ZDF	WE	SK16GUW	LE	SL16RHJ	WY
SO15CUK	WE	SK65PXJ	EN	SN65CVJ	SE	SN65OKD	LE	SN65ZDG	WE	SK16GUX	LE	SL16YOH	WY
SO15CUU	WE	SK65PXL	EN	SN65CVK	SE	SN65OKE	LE	SN65ZDH	WE	SK16GVA	LE	SL16YOJ	WY
SO15CUV	WE	SK65PXM	EN	SN65CVL	SE	SN65OKF	LE	SN65ZDJ	WE	SK16GVC	LE	SL16YOK	WY
SO15CUW	WE	SK65PXN	EN	SN65CVM	SE	SN65OKG	LE	SN65ZDK	WE	SK16GVD	LE	SL16YOM	WY
SO15CUX	WE	SK65PXO	EN	SN65OFR	GL	SN65OKH	MW	SN65ZDL	WE	SK16GVE	LE	SL16YON	WY
SO15CUY	WE	SK65PXP	EN	SN65OFS	GL	SN65OKJ	MW	SN65ZDM	GL	SK16GVF	LE	SL16YOO	WY
SO15CVA	WE	SK65PXR	EN	SN65OFT	GL	SN65OKK	MW	SN65ZDO	GL	SK16GVG	LE	SL16YOP	WY
WK15DLZ	SW	SK65PXS	EN	SN65OFU	GL	SN65OKL	MW	SN65ZDP	GL	SK16GVJ	LE	SL16YOR	WY
WK15DME	SW	SM65EEU	EN	SN65OFV	GL	SN65OKN	MW	SN65ZDR	GL	SK16GVL	LE	SL16YOT	WY
WK15DMF	SW	SM65EEV	EN	SN65OFW	GL	SN65OKO	CU	SN65ZDS	GL	SK16GVM	LE	SL16YOV	WY
WK15DMO	SW	SM65EEW	EN	SN65OFX	GL	SN65OKP	CU	SN65ZDT	GL	SK16GVN	LE	SL16YOW	WY
WK15DMU	SW	SM65EEX	EN	SN65OFY	GL	SN65OKR	SE	SN65ZDU	GL	SK16GVO	LE	SL16YOY	WY
WK15DMV	SW	SM65EEY	EN	SN65OFZ	GL	SN65OKS	SE	SN65ZDV	GL	SK16GVR	EC	SL16YPA	WY
WK15DMX	SW	SM65EEZ	EN	SN65OGA	GL	SN65OKT	SE	SN65ZDW	GL	SK16GVT	EC	SL16YPC	WY
YJ15AOW	GL	SM65EFA	EN	SN65OGB	GL	SN65OKU	SE	SN65ZDX	GL			SL16YVP	WY

SN16OSC	GL	SN66WGC	SE	SN66WKU	EN	WK66CDO	SW	YX66WCG	HD	YX66WFO	PM	YX66WKZ	WE
SN16OSD	GL	SN66WGD	SE	WK66BYU	SW	WK66CDU	SW	YX66WDT	WE	YX66WFP	PM	YX66WLA	WE
SN16OSE	GL	SN66WGE	SE	WK66BYV	SW	WK66CDV	SW	YX66WDU	WE	YX66WFR	PM	YX66WLB	WE
SN16OSF	GL	SN66WGF	SE	WK66BYW	SW	WK66CDX	SW	YX66WDV	WE	YX66WGO	WE	YX66WLC	WE
SN16OSG	GL	SN66WGG	SE	WK66BYX	SW	WK66CDY	SW	YX66WDW	WE	YX66WGP	WE	YX66WLD	WE
SN16OSJ	GL	SN66WGJ	SE	WK66BYY	SW	YJ66AOB	GL	YX66WDY	WE	YX66WGU	WE	YX66WLE	WE
SN16OSK	GL	SN66WGK	SE	WK66BYZ	SW	YX66WBD	EN	YX66WDZ	WE	YX66WJG	WY	YX66WLF	WE
SN16OSL	GL	SN66WGM	SE	WK66BZA	SW	YX66WBE	EN	YX66WEA	WE	YX66WKC	WY	YX66WLG	WE
SN16OSM	GL	SN66WGO	SE	WK66BZB	SW	YX66WBF	EN	YX66WEC	WE	YX66WKD	WY	YY66OZV	EN
SN16OSO	GL	SN66WGP	SE	WK66BZC	SW	YX66WBG	EN	YX66WEF	WE	YX66WKE	WY	YY66OZW	EN
YY16YLN	SY	SN66WGU	SE	WK66BZD	SW	YX66WBJ	HD	YX66WEH	WE	YX66WKH	WY	YY66OZX	EN
YY16YLO	SY	SN66WGV	SE	WK66CCA	SW	YX66WBL	HD	YX66WEJ	WE	YX66WKJ	WY	YY66PAO	EN
YY16YLP	SY	SN66WGW	SE	WK66CCD	SW	YX66WBM	HD	YX66WEK	WE	YX66WKK	WY	YY66PBF	EN
YY16YLR	SY	SN66WGX	SE	WK66CCE	SW	YX66WBO	HD	YX66WEO	WE	YX66WKL	WY	YY66PBO	EN
YY16YLS	SY	SN66WGY	SE	WK66CCF	SW	YX66WBP	HD	YX66WEP	WE	YX66WKM	WE	YY66PBU	EN
YY16YLT	SY	SN66WGZ	SE	WK66CCJ	SW	YX66WBT	HD	YX66WEU	WE	YX66WKN	WE	YY66PBV	EN
YY16YLU	SY	SN66WHA	SE	WK66CCN	SW	YX66WBU	HD	YX66WEV	WE	YX66WKO	WE	YY66PBX	EN
YY16YLV	SY	SN66WHB	SE	WK66CCO	SW	YX66WBV	HD	YX66WEW	WE	YX66WKP	WE	YY66PBZ	EN
YY16YLW	SY	SN66WKK	EN	WK66CCU	SW	YX66WBW	HD	YX66WFA	WE	YX66WKR	WE	YY66PCF	EN
YY16YLX	SY	SN66WKL	EN	WK66CCV	SW	YX66WBY	HD	YX66WFB	WE	YX66WKS	WE	YY66PCO	EN
BT66MRO	MA	SN66WKM	EN	WK66CCX	SW	YX66WBZ	HD	YX66WFC	WE	YX66WKU	WE		
BT66MRU	MA	SN66WKO	EN	WK66CCY	SW	YX66WCA	HD	YX66WFJ	PM	YX66WKV	WF		
BT66MRV	MA	SN66WKP	EN	WK66CCZ	SW	YX66WCC	HD	YX66WFK	PM	YX66WKW	WE		
BT66MRX	MA	SN66WKR	EN	WK66CDE	SW	YX66WCD	HD	YX66WFL	PM	YX66WKY	WE		
BT66MRY	MA	SN66WKS	EN	WK66CDF	SW	YX66WCE	HD	YX66WFM	PM				
SN66WGA	SE	SN66WKT	EN	WK66CDN	SW			YX66WFN	PM				